EDUCATIONAL ADMINISTRATION
A Management Approach

RONALD W. REBORE

University of Missouri-St. Louis

PRENTICE-HALL, INC., Englewood Cliffs, New Jersey 07632

Library of Congress Cataloging in Publication Data

Rebore, Ronald W.
  Educational administration.

  Includes bibliographies and index.
  1. School management and organization. 2. Educational
law and legislation–United States. 3. School management
and organization–United States. I. Title.
LB2805.R393   1985   371.2   84-8416
ISBN 0-13-235664-3

Editorial supervision
  and interior design: Serena Hoffman
Cover design: Wanda Lubelska/Filip Pagowski
Manufacturing buyer: Barbara Kelly Kittle

PRINTED IN THE UNITED STATES OF AMERICA

10 9 8 7 6 5 4 3 2 1

ISBN 0-13-235664-3 01

PRENTICE-HALL INTERNATIONAL, INC., *London*
PRENTICE-HALL OF AUSTRALIA PTY. LIMITED, *Sydney*
EDITORA PRENTICE-HALL DO BRASIL, LTDA., *Rio de Janeiro*
PRENTICE-HALL CANADA INC., *Toronto*
PRENTICE-HALL OF INDIA PRIVATE LIMITED, *New Delhi*
PRENTICE-HALL OF JAPAN, INC., *Tokyo*
PRENTICE-HALL OF SOUTHEAST ASIA PTE. LTD., *Singapore*
WHITEHALL BOOKS LIMITED, *Wellington, New Zealand*

In Memoriam
William T. Rebore, Sr.

Managing the educational enterprise is a privilege and a critically important function because of its impact on the learning-instructional process, which, in turn, will influence the destiny of the local community, the nation, and, indeed, the world.

Contents

PART II: MANAGING
THE EDUCATIONAL ENTERPRISE

**5   THE ROLE AND FUNCTION
OF THE SUPERINTENDENT OF SCHOOLS 73**

**6   THE ROLE AND FUNCTION
OF THE COMMUNITY-RELATIONS ADMINISTRATOR 99**

11   THE ROLE AND FUNCTION OF THE CURRICULUM AND PUPIL-PERSONNEL ADMINISTRATORS   232

12 THE ROLE AND FUNCTION OF THE BUILDING PRINCIPAL 250

Preface

The proper and effective management of school districts is one of the most important issues facing public education in the United States. In fact, during the last two decades, administration has occupied a central position because the decisions of superintendents, principals, and other administrators have had a pervasive impact upon the educational experiences of children.

Books about educational administration have been written from many different perspectives; some are concerned with selected topics and issues, such as personnel management and the financing of public education; others address the entire educational administrative function. Most of the latter treat the subject on a theoretical basis and leave much to be desired in terms of putting theory into practice.

Four major trends in public education have surfaced over the last ten years that will occupy the attention of school administrators for decades to come. These trends demand an updated approach to the entire field of educational administration.

First, the general state of the economy and the taxpayers' revolt have resulted in the failure of tax-levy elections and in decreased state aid to school districts. Because revenues are not keeping pace with inflation, administrators have been faced with reevaluating the scope and content of the programs that constitute a free public education.

Second, the development of new technologies has forced school administrators to incorporate these advances into the curriculum so that students can be properly prepared to make use of calculators, microcomputers, videotape recorders, and so on. In addition, these same technological advances have altered management techniques and required administrators to use such equipment as microcomputers in their daily operations.

Third, personnel issues continue to occupy a central place in school-district administration. Declining enrollments have caused some administrators to take a closer look at the performance evaluation of teachers, in addition to reduction in force and early-retirement incentive programs. Other administrators are vitally concerned with collective bargaining and affirmative action.

Fourth, social issues remain a constant concern of many school administrators. Desegregation, pupil discipline, one-parent families, drug and alcohol abuse, among many others, have caused administrators to address the effects of these problems upon the instructional program.

Thus, a fresh approach has been mandated by circumstances on how educational administration is treated in textbooks used in degree programs for potential administrators. This book is intended to meet the needs of professors who teach introductory courses in educational administration. It should also be of interest to superintendents of schools, building-level principals, and other central-office administrators, teachers, and staff members who wish to update their knowledge of educational administration.

Chapters 1 through 4 are concerned with the fundamentals of managing the educational enterprise, while chapters 5 through 12 concentrate on the management of various administrative functions. Each chapter is written from a technical perspective and identifies those processes, procedures, and techniques (a management approach) necessary to effectively administer contemporary school districts. Many chapters also contain extensive exhibits and appendices that highlight the concepts presented in the chapter. This is a practical and comprehensive treatment of educational administration that bridges the gap between theory and practice.

What makes this presentation unique, however, is not only its technical orientation, but also the vehicle by which the material is elucidated in Part II (Managing the Educational Enterprise). Chapters 5 through 12 are concerned with the role and function of major school administrators. Therefore, educational administration is viewed in terms of specific positions, making it of significant value not only to graduate students, but also to the old hands.

Ronald W. Rebore

1

Public schools have the mission to transmit the culture of our American society to the children and youth of our country for the purpose of preserving our free, democratic way of life.

Introduction to the Structural Framework of Public Education

THE GOVERNANCE FRAMEWORK

America's system of universal free elementary and secondary education is one of its distinguishing characteristics. It is generally considered the best way to safeguard our freedom and the strongest guarantee of economic and social welfare for our citizens.

The school as an institution receives its mandate from the society it serves. It is, however, only one of many institutions. The government, home, church, and other forces also play a role in our society.

These institutions have complementary purposes. In various ways, each provides for the advancement of society in general and the individual citizen in particular. The educational programs of the school would be ineffective without the support of government, the family, and the churches. At the same time, however, a hallmark of modern-day society and these institutions is change, as dramatically pointed out by the National School Public Relations Association.

> Calculators, cable television, microcomputers, video discs, satellites, teleconferencing—the list of new technologies arriving on the scene almost daily is growing and becoming more important to our lives. Only a decade ago, the idea of computers being as common in the home as the television was looked upon as an idea as far-fetched as man walking on the moon was in the middle of this century.
>
> No one will deny that the . . . [present] is the age of technology, an age as dramatic as the industrial revolution in its capacity to change the way we live. Students today will have their future, and much of their present, dominated by electronic wizardry. And unless they have an understanding of and the ability to use the new technology, they will be as illiterate as persons who cannot read or write."[1]

This statement focuses on communicative and technological advancement, but in any given society, many kinds of change occur simultaneously. The family, church, school, and government, with all their components, are all evolving entities.

Change is simultaneously continual and accelerative, and is further complicated by the fact that it occurs unevenly. Technology may be advancing faster than educational programs can be changed to reflect these advances, often leaving the individual years behind.

Our perception of reality and how this relates to societal and individual needs determines the content of our educational programs. Although fundamental principles such as individual freedom, individual responsibility, and democratic government must be continually taught in our schools, the accelerating rate of change also demands that our schools be flexible enough to adjust to new developments and conditions.

At various times in our history, educators and professional organizations have formally stated the objectives of American education. Three of the most often-repeated statements are listed in Table 1-1; all have a great deal in common. While these statements could hardly be improved upon and should be studied by all concerned with education, the objectives must be understood within the context of continual evolution.

Responsibilities of Federal and State Government

Carrying out the objectives cited in Table 1-1 is the responsibility of the individual states. The United States Constitution is conspicuous in its ommission of any provision for or specific reference to education. The Tenth Amendment to the Constitution, ratified in 1791, states that "the powers not delegated to the United States by the Constitution, nor prohibited by it to the States, are reserved to the States respectively, or to the people." Thus, education has consistently been considered a state function.

However, the federal government has been involved in education. Through the legislative branch, Congress provides funds to local school districts for special services and programs. Through the United States Office of Education, the executive branch of the government exercises authority over educational matters. The

TABLE 1-1 Objectives of American Education

1952 TEN IMPERATIVE NEEDS[a]	1960 FOUR DIMENSIONS OF THE TASK OF THE SCHOOL[b]	1966 IMPERATIVES IN EDUCATION[c]
1. Family life	D. Productive dimensions 15. Home and family	2. To make urban life satisfying
2. Health	C. Personal dimensions 9. Physical: bodily health and development 10. Emotional: mental 11. Ethical: moral integrity 12. Esthetics: cultural and leisure pursuits	3. To strengthen the moral fabric of society 4. To deal constructively with psychological tensions
3. Ability to think and communicate clearly 4. Arts (esthetics) 5. Science	A. Intellectual dimensions 1. Possession of knowledge: concepts 2. Communication of knowledge: skills 3. Creation of knowledge: habits 4. Desire for knowledge: values	1. To discover and nurture creative talent
6. Use of leisure		6. To make best use of leisure time
7. Occupational skill 8. Ability to consume wisely	D. Productive dimensions 13. Vocation: selective 14. Vocation: preparative 16. Consumer: personal buying, selling, investment	7. To prepare people for the world of work 8. To keep democracy
9. Civic understanding	B. Social dimensions 6. Man to state: civic rights and duties 7. Man to country	5. To make intelligent use of resources
10. Human relations	B. Social dimensions 5. Man to man: cooperation in day-to-day relations 8. Man to world: relationships of peoples	9. To work with other peoples of the world for human betterment

[a] Educational Policies Commission, National Education Association, *Education for all American Youth: A Further Look* (Washington, D.C.: The Association, 1954).

[b] L. M. Downey, *The Task of Public Education* (Chicago: Midwest Administration Center, The University of Chicago, 1960).

[c] American Association of School Administrators, *Imperatives in Education, Report of the AASA Commission on Imperatives in Education* (Arlington, Virginia: The Association, 1966).

many Supreme Court decisions affecting education testify to the influence of the federal judiciary on our schools.

The American Association of School Administrators in 1965 issued a document entitled, *The Federal Government and Public Schools.* It listed five reasons for the interest in education on the national level.

1. When the nation fights poverty and unemployment, the public schools are one of its principal weapons.
2. When the nation promotes economic growth, its investment in education brings unique dividends.
3. When the nation provides for the common defense, it calls on the schools to play a crucial role.
4. When the nation builds unity out of diversity by delicately blending the cultures of people from many lands, it looks first and foremost to the schools.
5. When the nation refers its complex problems to the people for final decision, it needs more than ever an informed electorate.[2]

In an ever-shrinking world, the objectives of American education are of grave concern to both the federal and state governments. The federal government, however, should not supplant state jurisdiction, but rather should complement and enrich the latter's efforts. Note the accommodating relationship between the objectives outlined in Table 1-1 and the position of the American Association of School Administrators on federal involvement in education.

The authority to create and govern public schools is embodied in state constitutions and exercised by their legislatures, all of which have delegated certain aspects of this authority to local units, boards of education. To insure some control over local units, state legislatures have established minimum educational-program and teacher-certification requirements and provided funds to help finance education.

The administrative arm of the state legislature is the State Department of Education, which is usually governed by a board and administered by a commissioner or state superintendent. Figure 1-1 depicts the relationship between the state and local educational agencies.

FIGURE 1-1: JURISDICTIONAL FLOW-CHART

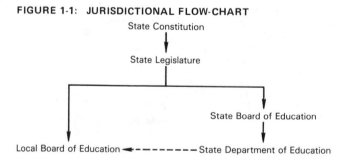

The National Council of Chief State School Officers has properly emphasized the state's educational responsibility and its relationship to local and federal agencies as follows:

> Our system of constitutional government makes the states responsible for the organization and administration of public education and for general supervision of nonpublic schools. Each state has in practice delegated authority to organize and operate schools to various types of local administrative units of its own creation (Boards of Education). Within its general unity, our system of education leaves room for diversified programs among states and local administrative units.
>
> Local, state and federal governments all have a vital interest in education. Each can contribute most effectively only if there is appropriate allocation of responsibility among them and only if relations among them are properly defined. Initiative and responsibility must be encouraged in the local units which operate most of the schools. The states must insure organization, financial support and effective administration of education programs of suitable quality and make certain these programs are available to every child. The federal government has an obligation to provide supplementary assistance to the states in accord with the national interest in universal education.
>
> Local school boards and other state education authorities represent the public in the administration of education. Working with their professional staffs, these authorities are responsible for carefully planned programs of education and for obtaining the participation of the people in planning the kinds of schools and education they need and want.[3]

Responsibilities of the Board of Education

School districts are perhaps the most democratically controlled of any government agency. The citizens of a local community elect school-board members, who are charged with formulating policies for the organization and administration of the schools. State departments of education exercise some regulatory authority, assuring that a minimum educational program is provided in every school district, but the citizens of the local district maintain control of the schools through locally elected boards.

It is essential to keep in mind that education is a *state* function, a principle consistently upheld by the courts. By virtue of the authority delegated to them by the state legislature, school boards represent the state, even though their members are locally elected. Board members, as individuals, exercise no authority outside a legally constituted meeting. Policies can be agreed upon only in an official meeting, and individual members cannot commit the board to any definite action except as authorized by the board at a legal meeting.

In exercising its authority to govern schools, the board of education should carefully formulate and adopt policy statements. This very difficult task cannot be accomplished successfully without guidance from the professional educational staff and, at times, an attorney. There are many more factors affecting board decisions today than there were as recently as five years ago.

Many styles can be used to construct a policy. Chapter 2 will address the specifics of policy construction and establish its importance in terms of school-board operations.

After the board of education establishes its policies, the superintendent of schools and his or her staff decides upon administrative processes to implement them.

THE ADMINISTRATIVE FRAMEWORK

Theoretical Foundations

Administration is indispensable for all institutions in organized society. Yet it is often taken for granted and has become the scapegoat for many social problems.

The need for administration is evident wherever there is a task to be performed by two or more people. Many ancient records of significant events describe administrative activities. Building the pyramids in Egypt, supervising medieval feudal domains, or governing colonies in distant hemispheres demanded some skill in and an appreciation of the administrative process.

Our understanding of the nature of administration has evolved. The earliest concepts involved the *action model*. Administrators were those who took charge of an activity and accomplished a task. The formal study of administration is a recent phenomenon whose strongest adherents are found in the business world, where much study is devoted to effective managerial leadership. Drucker considers managers to be the basic and scarcest resource in an enterprise.[4]

The need for the formal study of administration in public education grew out of the increased complexity of urban school districts. The illusion that anyone with a good general education could become an effective administrator was quickly shattered in the period following World War II.

Knezevich defines administration as "a social process concerned with identifying, maintaining, stimulating, controlling, and unifying formally and informally organized human and material energies within an integrated system designed to accomplish predetermined objectives."[5] The school administrator fulfills these requisites by developing and establishing administrative processes, procedures, and techniques that harness human and material energies. Administrative leadership has the potential to use these energies to fulfill educational objectives.

Knezevich's definition also views administration as an executive activity, distinct from policy making. Administration is primarily concerned with the implementation, not the making, of policy. More specifically, the administration of a district is responsible for carrying out the policies of the board of education.

The systems approach to administration has gained steadily in popularity since President Johnson mandated its implementation in federal agencies, and the outcry for accountability in the public section has advanced its use. In the systems approach, the school is viewed as a network of interrelated subsystems. Emphasis is given to formulating short- and long-range objectives that can be translated into operational activities that can be implemented and evaluated.

Although this text has adopted the concept underlying the systems approach, it does not use the precise language and style of the advocates for this approach. Rather, administration is viewed as a process composed of various functions. Three of the most critical functions in a school system are personnel administration, instructional programs administration, and support services administration. Support services here include transportation, food service, and financial management. Each of these functions has goals that are implemented through administrative processes, procedures, and techniques.

Functions are performed by administrators within a given organizational framework. The remaining portion of this section delineates and clarifies the role of the superintendent of schools and major central-office administrators.

Organization of the Central Office

Historically and, in most states, by statutory mandate, school boards have delegated the responsibility for implementing policies to a chief executive officer, the superintendent of schools. The superintendent assumes full control for all operations. As school districts grow in complexity, it becomes necessary to develop specialized functions, and the central-office staff comes into being. However, all employees, professional and other, ultimately report to the superintendent and are subordinate to him or her. The superintendent is the only employee who regularly and directly deals with the board of education.

The two latest trends in school administration, and particularly in the superintendency, emphasize (1) management techniques rather than instructional leadership, and (2) the administrative team approach to the central-office and building-level management. In most districts, the administrative team is a cluster of similarly educated administrators who amplify the efforts of the superintendent.[6] They usually hold the title of deputy, associate, or assistant superintendent. In most school districts, those called director or coordinator are not members of the administrative team, but support personnel.

One is formally designated a member of the administrative team by being appointed to the superintendent's cabinet, a strategy-planning and decision-making body. The heads of personnel administration, instructional programs administration, and support service administration (the three major functions) are typically included in the cabinet.

This formal organization is not meant to imply that the superintendent confines the "team" effort to only the highest levels of school district administration. Rather, it is an attempt to share the administrative policy-making process with key administrators. The issues facing school systems today are so varied that the superintendent must have continual counsel in order to make effective decisions.

Because there is a need in all school districts to identify various echelons in the administrative organization, it is recommended that the title of director or

FIGURE 1-2: DISTRICT ORGANIZATION

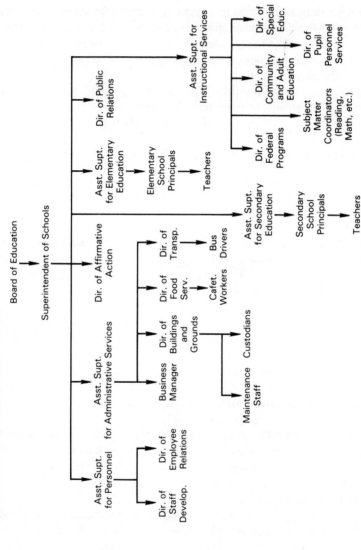

coordinator be assigned to administrators responsible to an assistant superintendent in charge of a particular function. Although it is in no way meant to be inclusive, Figure 1-2 represents a possible central-office organization that incorporates a line of authority from superintendent to assistant superintendents (cabinet positions) to directors and coordinators. The number of central-office administrators listed suggests that this could be the organizational structure for a school district with a pupil population of ten to twenty thousand. It was designed as a model exemplifying the scope of possible central-office administrative positions. Smaller-sized districts would compress central-office responsibilities into fewer positions. For example, a school district with two thousand students might be administered by a superintendent and an assistant superintendent, who share all responsibilities.

Organization of Individual School Buildings

Early in our country's development, the one-room schoolhouse was staffed by a teacher who was responsible not only for instruction but also for performing all tasks related to the maintenance of the building. This situation gradually changed in the 1800s, with the advance of education as a profession, so that the teacher's role was better defined. Finally, in the 1900s, education had advanced to the point where instructional materials, teaching techniques, licensing requirements, and job descriptions clearly established the expertise of the teacher, which includes the ability to take a body of knowledge and organize it into instructional units, or lessons. A second aspect of this expertise involves the skill to transmit these lessons such that students learn their content. More about the learning instructional process will be discussed in Chapter 8.

This specialization of the teacher's role was the catalyst that led to the creation of the modern-day principalship. While the teacher's role was evolving, there were many precursors of the building principal. As schools expanded, more teachers were employed, and one was usually chosen as headmaster or headmistress. This title was brought over from England, and, as the word indicates, the "head" or "lead" teacher was in charge of the school.

The contemporary public school is composed of an administrative staff, instructional staff, professional support staff, and classified employee staff. Each type of employee performs a vital service in helping to educate children and young people.

The elementary school. Figure 1-3 is an organizational chart for an elementary school with an enrollment of four hundred to seven hundred pupils. The pattern of grade-level organization could be kindergarten through grade five, grade six, or grade eight, depending on the organizational pattern of the secondary school program. The curriculum organization might be nongraded or traditional, with team teaching or undivided classroom teacher units. Likewise, the school building could utilize the open-space concept or self-contained classroom model. The professional staff can explain to the board of education the advantages and disadvantages of these grade level patterns and curricular organizations. The role, function and struc-

FIGURE 1-3: ELEMENTARY SCHOOL ORGANIZATION

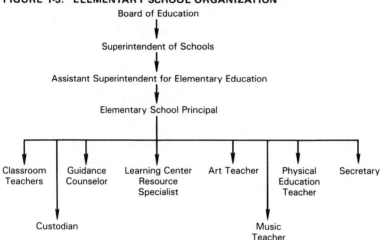

ture of the elementary school staff is of concern, because it is thus that questions and issues about the curriculum and grade-level patterns are addressed and resolved by the school board. School-board decisions should be based upon recommendations by the superintendent, who has been provided with information by the staff.

The principal is the administrative executive in the elementary school building. As an executive, it is his or her responsibility to provide leadership to effectively carry out the school's function, to educate the children in that particular building. The primary skill of the principal is to manage the human and material resources available. The role of the elementary school principal, therefore, is to perform the following tasks:

1. To formulate building-level policies and procedures that will clearly elucidate the duties and responsibilities of the professional staff, classified-employee staff, students, and parents in the school's attendance area;
2. To develop a personnel-planning forecast that will ensure that the right number of staff members with appropriate credentials is available;
3. To conduct an ongoing projection of pupil enrollment that will be used in personnel planning, budgeting, and facilities management;
4. To develop a building-level budget for supplies, materials, and equipment;
5. To create a facility maintenance and operations plan that will ensure that the building is energy-efficient and in good condition.

While the concept of the principal as a school executive is relatively new in many school districts, this role has become necessary because of the complexity of contemporary society. It does not nullify the principal's traditional role, but rather expands the scope of responsibilities. Traditionally, the principal evaluated teacher performance, handled chronic pupil disciplinary problems, and was the main line of communication with parents. Under the first item listed above, the building-level policies and procedures should clearly indicate that these are still a primary function of the building principal. However, principals will be more effective in dealing with teachers, students, and parents if they are truly chief executive officers of the elementary schools they manage.

The instructional staff is, of course, responsible for teaching basic skills to students. In the elementary school program, the expertise of the teachers lies in their ability to take the material to be taught, organize it, and present it to the children so that they learn it. Academic freedom in the elementary school consists of the right to organize and present the curriculum in the manner the teacher finds most effective with the children at a given point in time. Determining *what is to be taught* is the prerogative of the board of education, utilizing the central-office curriculum specialists as resources. The elementary school teacher should be well educated in child development and the psychology of learning, because it is through knowledge in these areas that lessons should be planned and presented.

Other professional staff members are charged with helping the teacher in the instructional process. In the model presented in Figure 1-3, these professionals include the guidance counselor, learning-center resource specialist, and fine arts and physical education teachers. All of these professionals, along with the classroom teachers and building principal, are responsible for pupil discipline and effective communication with parents. Appropriate education can occur only within an atmosphere of openness and mutual respect between all employees, students, and parents.

Classified employees, which includes building secretaries and custodians, are also a vital part of every elementary school. The tasks that they perform allow the professional staff to concentrate on the learning-instructional process. In addition, parents and students are constantly interacting with classified employees, making these individuals valuable public relations agents of the school district.

The secondary schools. Figure 1-4 is an organizational chart for a junior high school, middle school, or high school whose enrollment is between fifteen hundred and two thousand students. The pattern of grade-level organization might be (a) junior high school (grades 7–9) and high school (grades 10–12) or (b) middle school (grades 6–8) and high school (grades 9–12).

Middle schools, the subject of much research within the last decade, have proven to be an effective method of organizing the curriculum. Child-development theory appears to substantiate that the level of maturity of sixth-grade students is closer to that of seventh and eighth graders than to fifth graders. Likewise, ninth-grade students are closer in terms of maturity to tenth graders than to eighth-graders. The emphasis in middle school, as in elementary school, should be on learning as it relates to child development and the acquisition of basic skills rather than on mastering the rudiments of a discipline such as history or chemistry.

Junior high schools are structured to provide the student with a transitional period between elementary and high school. They more closely resemble the latter in terms of curriculum and instructional philosophy. However, a junior high school

FIGURE 1-4:   SECONDARY SCHOOL ORGANIZATION

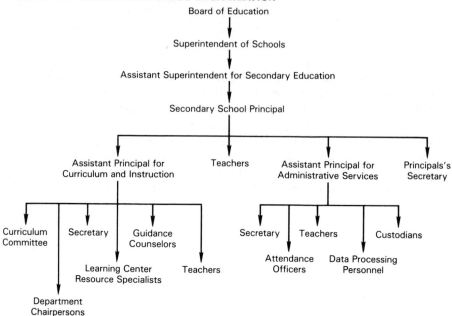

should never become a miniature senior high school. The emphasis should be on *preparing* the student for the high school experience.

Much of what has been said about the role and function of the elementary school principal, instructional staff, professional-support staff, and classified-employee staff can be applied to secondary school personnel. The principal, as the chief executive administrator of the building, is responsible for developing policies and procedures, personnel planning, projecting pupil enrollment, budget preparation, and management of facilities. The major difference lies in the fact that the principal usually shares this responsibility with an administrative team composed of assistant principals, who are assigned to specific areas of management. Figure 1-4 assigns administrative services to one assistant, while curriculum and instruction are assigned to a second assistant principal. Pupil discipline and communicating with parents are, of course, the responsibilities of all employees. Teacher evaluation is so important and time-consuming that most principals will divide the number of teachers to be evaluated equally between themselves and the assistant principals.

The instructional staff will be organized into departments, with a chairperson assuming much of the responsibility for helping the appropriate assistant principal to schedule and budget a particular department. While child development and the psychology of learning are important in all learning situations, the instructional program in a high school will focus on content mastery. Other building-level professionals such as guidance counselors, learning-center resource specialists, as well as district-wide professionals such as social workers and psychometrists, will assist the secondary school teachers with problems and issues that might affect classroom instruction.

The classified staff is more extensive in the secondary school and includes attendance officers and data-processing specialists. Their services are essential for the effective operation of the secondary school.

Chapters 5 through 12 present a thorough discussion of the role and function of central-office and building-level administrators.

SUMMARY

Our system of free and universal public education is a unique characteristic of American society. The school as an institution receives its mandate to exist from the society that it serves. Change is an integral part of this society. The content of our educational programs must address the fundamental principles of individual freedom, individual responsibility, and democratic government, yet must be flexible enough to cope with new developments and changing conditions.

Implementing educational objectives is the responsibility of the individual states. The authority of the state to create and govern public schools is embodied in the state constitution. The state legislature is the avenue through which this authority is exercised. The administrative arm of the state legislature is the department of education, which is usually governed by a board and administered by a commissioner or state superintendent. The legislature also delegates certain aspects of its authority to local units, boards of education. However, the state maintains some control over the local boards by establishing minimum educational program requirements, teacher-certification requirements, and providing funds to help finance education.

The federal government has increased its influence on education through congressional acts that provide funds for special programs, the regulations of the United States Office of Education, and Supreme Court decisions. However, in education, the federal government's power and influence is adjunct to the state's.

School districts are perhaps the most democratically controlled agency of government. The citizens of a community elect school-board members, who are charged with the adoption of policies to organize and administer the schools. The implementation of board policies is the responsibility of the administrative staff.

Administration is the process concerned with organizing human and material resources in order to accomplish educational objectives formulated as board of education policies. Therefore, administration is an executive activity distinct from policy making. This process is composed of various functions, including personnel administration, instructional-programs administration, and support-services administration. Each of these functions has objectives that are implemented through administrative processes, procedures, and techniques.

Functions are performed by administrators within a given organizational framework. The superintendent, as the chief executive officer of the school board, has full control of all school operations. These operations are so complex that his or her efforts must be simplified by a central-office administrative team, which is usually composed of assistant superintendents, who administer the major functions of the school system. These assistant superintendents form a cabinet that helps the superintendent formulate strategies and shares in the decision-making process. Directors and coordinators perform administrative tasks that support the major functions of the system; they report directly to assistant superintendents.

Today, individual schools are composed of an administrative staff, instructional staff, professional-support staff, and classified-employee staff. Members of each of these categories perform a vital service in helping to educate children and young people.

In addition to his or her traditional responsibilities—evaluating teacher performance, handling chronic pupil disciplinary problems, and communicating with parents—the building principal is the chief executive officer of the individual school. Thus, the role of the principal has expanded to include formulating policies and procedures for managing the building, developing personnel-planning forecasts, conducting pupil-enrollment projections, preparing a building budget, and managing the school plant.

The instructional staff is responsible for teaching the curriculum, which includes organizing the material and deciding on the most appropriate method of instruction based upon theories of child development and the psychology of learning. Other professional personnel, including counselors and learning-center resource specialists, provide valuable services that support the efforts of the classroom teacher. Maintaining good pupil discipline and open communication with parents is the responsibility of the building principal and the entire professional staff.

Classified personnel, which includes secretaries and custodians, perform tasks that relieve the professionals so they can concentrate on the learning-instructional process.

Finally, all school employees are public-relations agents for the individual school and the entire school district.

IMPLICATIONS FOR EDUCATIONAL ADMINISTRATORS

The structural framework of public education as discussed here has three implications for educational administrators.

First, administrators must remain informed about changes that will affect the type of curriculum required for students to become educated members of our community.

Second, administrators must be continually conscious of the organizational structure of public education in this country if they are to understand and carry out their role and function in local school districts.

Third, administrators must understand the difference between the management and governing function of the school board if they are to work effectively with its members.

SELECTED BIBLIOGRAPHY

CARLISLE, HOWARD M., *Situational Management.* New York: American Management Associations, 1973.

CUBBERLY, ELLWOOD P., *The History of Education.* Boston: Houghton Mifflin Company, 1920.

DALE, ERNEST, *Management: Theory and Practice* (3rd ed.). New York: McGraw-Hill Book Company, 1973.

DRUCKER, PETER F., *Management: Tasks, Responsibilities, Practices.* New York: Harper & Row, Publishers, Inc., 1974.

FROST, S. E., Jr., *Introduction to American Education.* New York: Doubleday & Company, 1962.

HANSON, E. MARK, *Educational Administration and Organizational Behavior.* Boston: Allyn and Bacon, Inc., 1979.

MORPHET, EDGAR., ROE L. JOHNS, and THEODORE L. RELLER, *Educational Organization and Administration: Concepts, Practices, and Issues* (4th ed.). Englewood Cliffs, N.J.: Prentice-Hall, Inc., 1982.

SERGIOVANNI, THOMAS J., MARTIN BURLINGAME, FRED D. COOMBS, and PAUL W. THURSTON, *Educational Governance and Administration.* Englewood Cliffs, N.J.: Prentice-Hall, Inc., 1980.

NOTES

1. National School Public Relations Association, "New Challenge for Schools: Age of Information." *Education USA,* 24, no. 19 (January 4, 1982), p. 141.

2. American Association of School Administrators, *The Federal Government and Public Schools* (Washington, D.C.: The Association, 1965), p. 3.

3. The National Council of Chief State School Officers, *Our System of Education* (Washington, D.C.: The Council, 1950), pp. 5–6.

4. Peter F. Drucker, *The Practice of Management* (New York: Harper & Row, Publishers, Inc., 1954), p. 111.

5. Steven J. Knezevich, *Administration of Public Education* (New York: Harper & Row, Publishers, Inc., 1975), p. 12.

6. American Association of School Administrators, *Profiles of the Administrative Team* (Arlington, Va.: The Association, 1971), p. 11.

The parents, students, teachers, administrators, and other constituents of a school district have a right to expect that individual board members will put aside personal ambitions and will conduct school district business in an open and efficient manner.

The Role and Function of the Board of Education

Who is the typical school-board member? What is the age, sex, religious affiliation, educational level, and so on, of this individual? There is no such thing as a typical school-board member. In addition, people make decisions to run for the board of education for a variety of reasons, all of which are so personal that they defy classification. For the purposes of this discussion, however, none of the above is important. Once an individual is elected to the board of education, he or she immediately assumes a mandate to govern the educational experience of children and young people, the effects of which are eminent and pervasive. It is an understatement to say that membership on a school board is the most important governmental position in our community, state, and nation. In the United States, it has always been understood that freedom and capitalism require an educated citizenry.

THE DYNAMICS OF SCHOOL-BOARD DECISION MAKING

When the members of a school board assemble to conduct business, there are numerous issues that underlie the proceedings. Because all actions of a school board involve a potential change in school district policy, the dynamics of change, in addition to the possible *hidden agendas* of members, coupled with the decision-making process, are variables at board meetings.

Change is a phenomenon that probably causes the most disruption in a school district. It does not matter if the change produces an improvement; the fact of the change itself is cause enough for people to be dissatisfied with the actions of a school board. There is no easy or right way for a school board to proceed to bring about change; however, the following aspects of the process, if taken into consideration, will lessen the unwanted reaction of the school district community.

Change is more acceptable when it is understood than when it is not.

Change is more acceptable when it does not threaten security than when it does.

Change is more acceptable when those affected have helped to create it than when it has been externally imposed.

Change is more acceptable when it results from the application of previously established impersonal principles than when it is dictated by a personal order.

Change is more acceptable when it follows a series of successful changes than when it follows a series of failures.

Change is more acceptable when it is inaugurated after prior change has been assimilated than when it is inaugurated during the confusion of other major change.

Change is more acceptable if it has been planned than if it is experimental.

Change is more acceptable to people new on the job than to people who have been there for a while.

Change is more acceptable to people who share in the benefits of change than to those who do not.

Change is more acceptable if members of the organization have been trained to accept change.[1]

Consequently, change can and should be a consideration of the school board when issues are brought before it for a decision. Timing is a legitimate variable that may dictate that a change, even a beneficial one, should be forestalled until the people most affected are prepared and ready for it. Closing a school because of declining enrollment is a classic example. Unless the parents, teachers, and students of a particular school understand the need to close their school, have been given ample time to speak their minds and participate in the accumulation of data to support the closing, and understand where the children will attend school the following year, this type of change has the potential of creating deep-seated resentment of the school-board members.

A second variable at work when a board of education meets to conduct business and make decisions concerning school district issues is the hidden agendas of school-board members. All groups operate on the surface level and the hidden-agenda level. Inexperienced school-board members are often confused by the actions and decisions of fellow board members when this is overlooked. Every member of the school board must face this and deal with it individually and as a corporate body. Some hidden agendas are even beneficial to the school district. For example, a school-board member may vote against a new teacher-evaluation policy because it is opposed by a local teachers' union, in order to gain the support of that group in working for an upcoming tax-levy election.

The following suggestions about how to handle hidden agendas are certainly relevant for most school boards:

1. Always remember that members of the school board are working on two levels at the same time, on the surface and at the hidden-agenda level. The board, therefore, may not move as fast as its members might expect.

2. Recognition is the first step in dealing with hidden agendas. Thus, be sensitive to the actions of board members and it will become clear when hidden agendas are hampering the work of the board.

3. At times, hidden agendas can be talked about by the school-board members, which should make it easier to handle them.

4. The school-board members should not be pressured in dealing with hidden agendas. These must be worked out in much the same way as obvious agendas. Hidden agendas should be given the attention necessary to accomplish the stated tasks of the board.

5. School-board members should spend some time evaluating how hidden agendas are handled and generate suggestions on how such agendas can be handled in the future.

Attention to these steps will minimize the disruption to the school district as an organization. A common criticism leveled against school boards is that they make decisions in isolation from the school district as a unit and hence run the risk of making decisions that are difficult, and at times impossible, to implement.

SCHOOL BOARD PROCEDURES AND OPERATIONS

The laws of most states are very clear about the fact that school boards are corporate entities and that, therefore, the board exists only when its members are meeting in a legally constituted session. Therefore, only the board of education as a corporate entity can conduct school district business and make decisions about issues. There are two aspects to the decision-making process: first, those logical steps that should be taken to insure that the best solution has been reached; secondly, those considerations that should be addressed within an organization when problems are being confronted by the school board.

Much has been written about the most effective way of handling issues and solving problems. There is no one way of acting that will guarantee the successful resolution of issues and problems all the time. The following eight steps, however, provides a framework that can be used by individual board members as they develop their own approaches to solving problems.

1. Identify all phases of the problem. Some aspects of an issue might be so obscure that a good deal of imagination will be required simply to find out what the problem is.

2. Deal separately with each component of the problem at first. This will help to identify its scope and magnitude.
3. Identify what data will help to clarify the problem and facilitate developing a plan of action.
4. Think through all possible solutions to the problem even if some appear to be unattainable.
5. Select the most promising solution to the problem and develop a plan of action.
6. Implement the plan of action.
7. Evaluate the effectiveness of the plan of action.
8. Modify the plan if it is necessary to be more effective.

It goes without saying that the jurisdiction of the school board extends only to the educational experience of children living within the legally constituted boundaries of the school district.

In governing the school district, the school board has two major roles: first, to create policies that will give the district's administrative staff the guidance necessary to educate children and young people; second, to evaluate through the administrative staff the programs of the school district and the personnel charged with implementing those programs. Both areas are complementary, because it will be impossible for a school board to create effective policies if the members of the school board are not informed about the progress of the district's programs and about the performance of school district personnel.

The policy-making process will be addressed later in this chapter. As with program and personnel evaluation, policies are formulated at board meetings. Program and personnel appraisal will be treated in later chapters. At present, we are concerned with those procedures that will insure that policy making and appraisal are addressed by the board of education in an orderly manner.

The School-Board Meeting

It is imperative for the effective governance of a school district that the board of education meet on a regular basis, probably once a month. There should be a board policy establishing the time and place of the regular meetings and a procedure for reminding board members of regularly scheduled meetings, facilitated by the superintendent's office.

Special meetings may need to be called from time to time for the purpose of handling problems and issues that cannot wait until the regular meeting or would be better dealt with apart from that meeting. Usually, a special meeting is called by the president of the school board or when a majority of its members request one. Notifying board members concerning the purpose, time, and place of special board meetings is the responsibility of the superintendent of schools.

The board of education should always meet in a school district facility, either at the central administrative office building or in a school building. The meeting place should be large enough to accommodate visitors who wish to attend. The room should be set up in such a way that visitors readily understand that they cannot participate in the proceedings unless invited to do so. A common practice in school districts with a permanent board of education meeting room is to have the board members and the superintendent seated at tables on a raised platform, with the central-office administrators and the recording secretary seated at a table on the side of the platform. Visitors can then be seated in rows of chairs in front of the platform. Because it is also common practice for the president of the board to ask visitors if they wish to address the board at a set time during the meeting, a table can be placed in front of the platform before the rows of chairs from which a presentation can be made.

Most state statutes have provisions that allow public bodies to meet in a closed executive session when certain issues arise. While the variety of provisions makes classification difficult, the following constitute appropriate reasons for holding an executive session: (1) the hiring, terminating, or promotion of personnel; (2) a proceeding involving scholastic probation, expulsion, and graduation; (3) litigation involving the school district; (4) the lease, purchase, or sale of property.

The School-Board Meeting Agenda

Board meetings will more than likely become disorderly and unproductive unless a formal agenda is prepared and sent to the board members with explanatory materials before the meeting. As the chief executive officer of the school board, the superintendent is usually charged with preparing the agenda, which will insure that the ordinary business of the school district can be addressed in a timely manner, such as paying invoices and approving contracts. In addition, school-board members could request the superintendent to add items to the agenda for discussion and action by all the members. In fact, it is a good practice for the superintendent to contact each individual board member before the agenda is prepared for this very purpose. The agenda, along with minutes from the preceding meeting, accompanied by pertinent reports and explanatory materials, should be received by board members at least three days before the meeting, to give them sufficient time to prepare for the meeting. They should be encouraged to contact the superintendent before the meeting if clarification or additional information is needed concerning items on the agenda.

The agenda should be constructed in such a manner that it can also serve as the order of business to be followed at the board meeting. While the order of business will be dictated by the items to be dealt with at the meeting, the following order should suffice at most meetings.

1. *Call to Order.* The president of the board calls the meeting to order. If the president and vice-president are both absent, the secretary should preside; the treasurer does so in the secretary's absence. A *quorum* is necessary to transact business, and is usually defined as two-thirds members of the board.
2. *Scheduling Visitors' Presentations.* It has become common practice in recent years for boards of education to allow visitors a place on the agenda to address the board. The board may and should limit the number of individuals

allowed to speak and set a time limit on presentations, to facilitate the transaction of the business.

3. *Approval of the Agenda.* The members present may also change the agenda by adding or deleting items. Even if there are no changes in the agenda and no visitors who wish to address the board, the agenda must be formally adopted through the normal *motion* process.

4. *Approval of the Warrants.* The board of education must approve the checks that are issued to pay the bills of the district and the payroll. The *warrants* list check numbers, to whom the checks are written, and the reason for each check. Once the board approves the warrants—usually the day after the meeting—the checks may be signed and mailed. The signature of two board members—usually the president and the treasurer—is commonly required on the checks. A facsimile plate and check-signing machine may be used to facilitate this. Through a resolution, the board may authorize the paying of certain bills in advance of the board meeting, such as utility bills, but these checks must be included on the warrants for the purpose of information. Payroll checks can also be handled in the same manner when a contract exists between an employee and the board, because the contract itself is authorization to issue the checks.

5. *Unfinished Business.* If the board of education did not complete action on a previous item on the agenda or requested additional information from the superintendent about it at a previous meeting before taking action, this is the appropriate time to address the issue(s).

6. *New Business.* The superintendent, upon the request of the president, may make preliminary remarks about the items to be discussed and acted upon. There is no appropriate order for these items. However, it might be more beneficial to place noncontroversial issues before those that will take considerable time, for the sake of accomplishing as much as possible and in order not to carry items over to the next meeting.

7. *Superintendent's Report.* The superintendent can use this time to inform the school board about certain programs and issues that are not only important but should be made public. The actual report may be given by other administrators, teachers, or staff members. A budget-operating summary is very important and should be a regular part of each meeting. Other reports could include an explanation of curriculum programs, the district's standardized testing program, and any other aspect of school district operations.

8. *Adjournment.* This procedure, as well as all other aspects of the board meeting, should be accomplished through parliamentary rules and regulations.

Minutes of the Board Meetings

All official actions of a school board must occur at a board meeting, for such actions to be legally binding. The minutes of the board meetings, therefore, are essentially the formal and legal medium through which the board of education communicates and documents its decisions and actions. Courts have traditionally admitted only the minutes of board meetings in reviewing the actions of school boards when such actions are relevant to litigation. It goes without saying that minutes must be absolutely accurate in reflecting the intent and actions of the board of education.

The minutes of board meetings are public documents and must be open to review by all interested citizens. It is customary to keep the minutes in the central office and in a container, vault, or room that is fireproof, secure, and safe from vandalism. The minutes may be kept in a loose-leaf form and bound into a volume at the end of each year or kept in some other orderly manner. Some school districts microfilm the minutes and keep the microfilm in a different place from the original records, significantly increasing security from possible loss due to fire, theft, and the like.

The minutes should be available to the public during the regular working hours of central-office personnel. Copies of the minutes could be made available by charging a nominal fee to offset duplication costs.

It is also desirable for the director of community relations to summarize the minutes after they are approved by the school board and to send this summary to internal and external groups such as teacher unions and the press.

Most state statutes have provisions that permit the minutes of executive sessions to be closed to public inspection. Therefore, such minutes must be bound under separate cover and kept in a secure place.

The contents of the minutes for all school board meetings should include the following:

1. Identification data, which include the time and place of the meeting; the board members and staff members in attendance; the approval of minutes from the preceding meeting; and the purpose of the meeting if it is a special one or an executive session.
2. Identification of who made the motions at the meeting; who seconded the motions; a record of how each member voted by name unless the vote was unanimous; and a statement that the motion passed or failed.
3. Identification of all other matters brought before the school board and the disposition of these matters if the board did not take an action.

Parliamentary Procedures

Because the board of education is a legislative body with the authority to organize its procedures and to transact business, it is essential to the orderly conducting of this business that specific parliamentary procedures be adopted, and/or adapted to the needs of each school board. With no standards for conducting business, the board of education is subject to an informality that will surely result in a waste of time and energy. On the other hand, definite procedures will provide a framework that will allow for the courteous and efficient handling of issues.

There is a danger, however, that a school board will formulate very complex and technical procedures that may tend to confuse rather than facilitate business.

Officers of the School Board

Different state statutes may provide for the organizational structure of the school board. However, a few generalizations may be made that will apply to all boards of education. First, a president or chairperson must be elected by the board members, who will preside at the board meetings and act as the spokesperson for the entire board when it is necessary to make a public statement concerning an issue facing the board. The president signs the official documents of the school district, including contracts, and a facsimile of his or her signature should appear on all school district bank drafts. It is desirable to elect a vice-president or vice chairperson who will assume these duties in the absence of the president/chairperson.

A treasurer of the school board should be elected, who will be responsible for monitoring the financial affairs of the school district. This in no way means that the treasurer conducts the business operations of the district, which is an administrative responsibility. The budget-operating summary presented at the monthly board meeting should be of particular concern and should be scrutinized by the treasurer. A facsimile of the treasurer's signature should appear on all school district bank drafts.

The secretary of the school board, who is also elected by the other board members, is responsible for monitoring the accurate recording of school-board meetings, the safekeeping of official school district records, and attesting by signature to the accuracy of official school district reports. The secretary also attests to all contracts by signature. A recording secretary, who is an employee of the district, usually the superintendent's personal secretary, is responsible for handling the mechanics of the secretary's duty.

School-Board Consultants and Advisory Committees

Like contemporary society, the issues and problems facing boards of education are very complex. It has become common practice for school boards to hire consultants with an expertise that can be used to deal with problems that arise. These consultants fall into two broad categories: those providing ongoing services and those providing occasional services when a specific problem occurs. Every school district will need the assistance of an attorney and a certified public accountant, both of whom should be employed on a continual basis, because it will be beneficial to the school district for them to have an in-depth understanding of its operations. It is important to review annually the quality of service rendered by the district's auditor and attorney as well as their fee schedule; but once an attorney and C.P.A. auditor are hired, it is not advisable to change, unless the quality of performance diminishes and/or the fee structure becomes out of line with others in the profession.

When the school district is in need of occasional services from other professionals such as a property appraiser or an architect, the following procedure could be used to contract them: (1) the superintendent advertises that portfolios are being accepted by the district, which should include the professional's credentials, experience, references, and a fee schedule or structure; (2) the superintendent compares the credentials and experience of all applicants; (3) the superintendent contacts the references; (4) the superintendent compares fee structures in relation to individuals' experience and skills; (5) the superintendent presents a summary and recommendation to the school board regarding who to hire; (6) the board of education contracts for the services. This procedure is also most appropriate when hiring an attorney and a C.P.A. auditor.

By having the assistance of school district citizens and patrons when the board studies certain issues and problems, valuable information can be obtained and good public relations result. Citizens' advisory committees, when specifically charged with studying and collecting data for the board about such issues as student discipline, the criteria to be used in closing a school, and declining enrollment, can save the administration a great amount of time and energy in addition to providing the school board with a basis upon which to make a decision. The key to the successful use of a citizens' advisory committee lies in the following two principles: first, the school board should make the charge to the citizens' advisory committee very specific and establish guidelines that the committee can use to formulate the desired report; second, the committee should work in cooperation with the superintendent of schools, because he or she is the chief executive officer of the school board and should be continually informed about the committee's progress.

School-Board Self-Evaluation

Boards of education demand accountability by the teachers, administrators, and staff members of their respective school districts. Performance-evaluation procedures and instruments are commonly employed by school boards in demonstrating and implementing accountability principles. However, few school boards have a self-evaluation procedure to ascertain their own level of performance.

Developing an evaluation procedure could help a school board assess its successes and failures in addition to ensuring that the board has ethical standards and is avoiding abuses of power.

The evaluation process is basically the same as that for any personnel or program appraisal. The school board needs to set goals and objectives for itself, must decide on an assessment technique and instrument for measuring its progress in attaining these goals, should carefully review the data generated by the assessment process, and, finally, should formulate new goals for the next year.

The superintendent of schools should research and present to the board those assessment instruments and techniques, which the school board might adopt and/or modify to evaluate its performance.

While there is some controversy about whether the results of the evaluation should be made public, it is probably better for a school board to use the results only for its own information. Because school boards are political entities, making such an evaluation public could become a political liability for certain board members, and might discourage school boards from engaging in evaluation altogether.

BOARD-STAFF RELATIONS

Members of school boards are elected public officials and as such are subject to all the political pressures that partisan public officials find themselves confronted with. Teachers, administrators, staff members, and classified employees, as well as students, parents, and other citizens are concerned about the potential decisions of school boards and how they will handle issues that have an impact on their lives. Teacher unions and organizations have been the most politically active employees of school districts.

It should not be surprising that school-board members, particularly those newly elected, will be personally contacted by employees from all levels of the school district, not only about policy-level issues but also about problems they are facing in their work for the school district. They will want the board members to intervene on their behalf, either directly or indirectly, perhaps by contacting the administrative staff or the individuals with whom they are experiencing difficulty.

The most appropriate response is for the board member to refer the employee to his or her immediate supervisor in order to resolve the problem. The decision can then be appealed, all the way to the board of education if necessary. Obviously, this requires that the board of education create a grievance policy that the administration can develop to ensure fair and impartial treatment of all employees who are experiencing difficulty on the job.

A sympathetic response and simply being listened to by a board member may ease an employee's anxiety. The old cliché, "There are two sides to every story," is true. However, it is not the responsibility of a board member to listen to both sides. School-board members must always remember that they enjoy no jurisdiction as individuals and can act only at a legally-called board meeting.

SCHOOL BOARD POLICY DEVELOPMENT

In exercising their authority to govern schools, boards of education should carefully formulate and adopt policy statements. This very difficult task cannot be successfully accomplished without guidance from the professional-educational staff and, at times, an attorney. Many factors affect board decisions today; Figure 2-1 illustrates these influences on policy formulation.

Some advantages for developing policies have been outlined in *The School and Community Relations* and may serve as a rationale for school boards.

> Policy facilitates the orientation of new board members regarding relations between the school and community.
> Policy facilitates a similar orientation on the part of new employees in the school system, both professional and nonprofessional.

FIGURE 2-1:   INFLUENCES ON POLICY FORMULATION

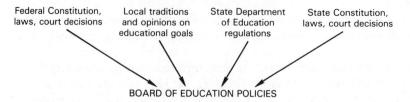

Policy acquaints the public with the position of the school and encourages citizen involvement in educational affairs.

Policy provides a reasonable guarantee that there will be consistency and continuity in the decisions that are made under it.

Policy informs the superintendent what he may expect from the board and what the board may expect from him.

Policy creates the need for developing a detailed program in order that it may be implemented.

Policy provides a legal reason for the allocation of funds and facilities in order to make the policy work.

Policy establishes an essential division between policy making and policy administration.[2]

School-board policies should not be confused with administrative rules and regulations, which constitute the detailed manner in which policies are to be implemented. Rules and regulations explicate who does what, when, and where. In other words, they apply policy to practice. In fact, many rules and regulations may be required to implement one policy.

A properly conceived and phrased board of education policy has the following characteristics:

It is stated in broad, general terms but clear enough to allow executive discretion and interpretation.

It reveals the philosophy of the board of education as members understand the desires of the community pertaining to the matters.

It provides purpose and rationale for the subject about which a policy is being made.

It suggests how the matter is to be carried out; in a few instances, it may indicate who should execute the policy.

It is never executive in substance or tone.

It covers situations which are likely to occur repeatedly.

It is usually brief but may be lengthy on a few concerns of the board.

It is always subject to review by the board with the objective of improvement in accordance with changing conditions.

Likewise, the policy should:

Provide support and authority for all school programs and activities.
Be brief, clear, concise, and complete.
Be stable even during personnel changes.
Have adequate provisions for review and amendment.[3]

The policies of the school board must be incorporated into a manual if they are to be effective in governing the school district. The following steps can be used in developing such a manual.

First, identify and code all existing policy decisions of the school board. These policies may be found in various publications, such as faculty and student handbooks, in addition to the minutes of school-board meetings and formal negotiated agreements. See Figure 2-2 for additional sources of existing school-board policies.

FIGURE 2-2   SOURCES OF EXISTING BOARD POLICIES

1. The present board policy manual and the state education code
2. The present book of administrative rules and procedures
3. The last several years' board minutes
4. The current compensation guide and contracts with professional and nonprofessional staffs
5. Currently active administrative memoranda
6. Current annual budget documents, particularly if they incorporate program goals and objectives, as in a program budget
7. Current teachers' and students' handbooks
8. Board approved staff committee reports
9. Board approved citizens' advisory and consultation reports
10. Board approved cooperative agreements with other districts, federal projects and foundations (these documents will have "guidelines" that have the force of policy)
11. Board approved building program and education specifications
12. Copies of the superintendent's and staff contract forms
13. Purchasing guides, requisition forms, purchase orders, etc.
14. Emergency operating procedures
15. School calendar
16. Use-of-school facilities forms
17. Organization charts
18. Job descriptions

SOURCE: Missouri School Boards Association, *A Manual for Missouri School Board Members* (Columbia, MO.: The Association, 1981), pp H7–H8.

Second, separate board-of-education policies from administrative rules and regulations. In the daily operations of a school district, policies and rules sometimes overlap in handbooks and manuals.

Third, identify and eliminate board-of-education policies that are obsolete or contrary to state and federal laws.

Fourth, identify and update board policies that contradict each other and are written in ambiguous language.

The administrative staff under the supervision of the superintendent may be charged with the responsibility of codifying and developing a policy manual. If a school district does not have a large administrative staff, it may be difficult to free an administrator to handle the policy manual project. In such a case, the National School Boards Association and many state school board associations may be contracted with to provide this service.

Once a policy manual has been created, the immediate concern is to keep it updated. The superintendent should develop an administrative procedure by which newly created board policies are incorporated into the policy manual. Many districts update their policy manual once each year, using the board-of-education meeting minutes as a resource document.

There are various formats a school board may use in formulating policies. A common one is the resolution style on which the school board takes action. Equal Employment Opportunity and Affirmative Action policies are usually adopted in this style. A second format sets forth the rationale for the policy and establishes broad goals that are implemented through administrative rules and regulations. A third style identifies who is responsible for implementing the policy. This is a common practice with policy formulation that addresses a specific function, such as collective bargaining. The policy might identify the director of employee relations as the chief negotiator for the school board and establish the parameters within which he or she will function. A fourth format is used when the school board wishes to eliminate possible misunderstanding about how the policy is to be implemented. This type of style, therefore, will incorporate administrative rules and regulations.

SUMMARY

There is no typical school board member. People make decisions to run for the board of education for a variety of reasons, all of which are so personal that they defy classification. Membership on a school board is the most important governmental position in our community, state and nation, for we have always understood that freedom and our economic system demand an educated citizenry.

Because all actions of a school board involve a potential change in school district policy, the dynamics of change must be understood and addressed by each member of the school board. Change probably causes the most disruption to a school district. Timing is a legitimate variable that may dictate that a change, even a beneficial one, should be forestalled until the people most affected are prepared and ready for it.

A second variable at work when a school board meets to conduct business and make decisions is the hidden agendas of school board members. Each member must be sensitive to them if the board is to be effective as an entity in providing for the educational needs of the children in the school district.

A final consideration in terms of school-board dynamics is how decisions are reached. Problem solving has two aspects: (1) logical steps in reaching a solution, and (2) organizational considerations—who does what in the school district.

School boards are corporate entities, and, as such, can function only at a legally constituted board meeting. Board members have no authority as individuals. The role and function of the school board in governing the school district is two-fold: to (1) create policies and (2) evaluate programs and those people charged with implementing them.

For the effective governance of a school district, the board of education must meet on a regular basis, probably once a month. Special meetings may be called from time to time for the purpose of handling problems and issues that cannot wait until the regular meeting or that would be better dealt with separately. Most state statutes have provisions that allow public bodies to meet in executive session on certain issues, usually concerning personnel, property, lawsuits, and student discipline.

Board meetings will become disorderly and unproductive unless a formal agenda is prepared by the superintendent, with input from the board members, and mailed to them before the meeting. The agenda should be organized in the following manner: (1) call to order, (2) approval of the agenda, (3) scheduling visitor presentations, (4) approval of warrants, (5) unfinished business, (6) new business, (7) superintendent's report, and (8) adjournment.

All official actions of the school board must occur at a board meeting. The minutes of the meeting are the formal and legal medium through which the board communicates and documents these actions. The minutes are public documents and must be open to review by all interested citizens.

Because the board of education is a legislative body, parliamentary procedures must be adopted so that business can be conducted in an orderly manner. Likewise, it is necessary to elect officers who will be charged with carrying out school-board operations. Typically, these offices include president, vice-president, treasurer, and secretary.

From time to time, school boards will need the assistance of regular and occasional consultants. An attorney, C.P.A., auditor, property appraiser, and the like, should be hired according to a process that will ensure that the most qualified professional is employed. Valuable assistance can also be obtained through citizens' advisory committees if the board is careful to give the committee a specific charge, including guidelines with the understanding that it should work in cooperation with the superintendent.

The demands of the public for accountability should alert boards of education to investigate the desirability of conducting an annual self-evaluation of their successes and failures.

Members of the school board will be contacted from time to time by school district employees who will want the board member to intervene on their behalf regarding a problem at work. It behooves board members to refer these individuals to their immediate supervisors and to encourage them to appeal the grievance all the way up to the board if the employee so wishes. Of course, this procedure is predicated on the existence of a school employee grievance policy.

In exercising their authority to govern schools, boards of education should carefully formulate and adopt policies. School board policies should not be confused with administrative rules and regulations, which are detailed procedures for implementing these policies. The policies of the school board must be incorporated into a manual if they are to be effective in governing the school district.

IMPLICATIONS FOR EDUCATIONAL ADMINISTRATORS

There are three implications for educational administrators resulting from this presentation of the role and function of the board of education.

First, the superintendent of schools should remind school-board members that the daily operations of the school system are the responsibility of the administrative staff. School-board members have no authority as individuals and can exercise their jurisdiction as board members only at legally constituted board meetings. When board members attempt to become involved in daily operations, the superintendent and his or her administrative staff must tactfully correct this situation so as not to damage the working relationship with members of the board.

Second, the superintendent of schools and the administrative staff must help the board of education facilitate the conducting of business at school-board meetings. Many school boards will need advice about constructing meeting agendas, monitoring and keeping accurate board-meeting minutes, and the proper use of parliamentary procedures.

Third, the superintendent of schools and the administrative staff are responsible for making policy recommendations to the board of education. Too often, school boards become concerned with making decisions about current problems and neglect to formulate policies that address the broader, underlying issues creating the problems.

SELECTED BIBLIOGRAPHY

EDUCATIONAL RESEARCH SERVICE, "Local Boards of Education: Status and Structure," Circular No. 5, 1972.

IANNACCONE, LAWRENCE and FRANK W. LUTZ, *Politics, Power and Policy: the Governing of Local School Districts.* Columbus, Ohio: Charles E. Merrill, 1970.

KOWALSKI, THEODORE J., "Why Your Board Needs Self-Evaluation," *The American School Board Journal,* 168, no. 7 (July 1981), 21–23.

MANN, DALE, *Policy Decision-Making in Education: An Introduction to Calculation and Control.* New York: Teachers College Press, 1975.

MISSOURI SCHOOL BOARDS ASSOCIATION, *A Manual for Missouri School Board Members* (rev. ed.). Columbia, Mo.: The Association, 1981.

UNDERWOOD, KENNETH E., WAYNE P. THOMAS, TONY COOKE, and SHIRLEY UNDERWOOD, "Portrait of the American School Board Member," *The American School Board Journal,* 167, no. 1 (January 1980), 23–25.

ZIEGLER, L. HARMON, M. KENT JENNINGS, and G. WAYNE PEAK, *Governing American Schools: Political Interaction in Local School Districts.* North Scituate, Mass.: Duxbury Press, 1974.

NOTES

1. R. M. Besse, "Company Planning Must Be Planned," *Dun's Review and Modern Industry,* 74, no. 4 (April 1957), 62–63.

2. Leslie W. Kindred, Dan Bagin, and Donald R. Gallagher, *The School and Community Relations* (Englewood Cliffs, N.J.: Prentice-Hall, Inc., 1976), p. 30.

3. Missouri School Boards Association, *A Manual for Missouri School Board Members* (Columbia, Mo.: The Association, 1981), p. H-3.

APPENDIX A:
A CODE OF ETHICS FOR SCHOOL BOARD MEMBERS

I. As a member of my local board of education, representing all the citizens of my school district, I recognize
   1. That my fellow citizens have entrusted me with the educational development of the children and the youth of this community.
   2. That the public expects my first and greatest concern to be in the best interest of each and every one of these young people without distinction as to who they are or what their background may be.
   3. That the future welfare of this community, of this State, and of the nation depends in the largest measure upon the quality of education we provide in the public schools to fit the needs of every learner.
   4. That my fellow board members and I must take the initiative in helping all the people of this community to have all the facts all the time about their schools, to the end that they will readily provide the finest possible school programs, school staff, and school facilities.
   5. That legally the authority of the board is derived from the State which ultimately controls the organization and operation of the school district and which determines the degree of discretionary power left with the board and the people of this community for the exercise of local autonomy.
   6. That I must never neglect my personal obligation to the community and my legal obligation to the State, nor surrender these responsibilities to any other person, group, or organization; but that, beyond these, I have a moral and civic obligation to the Nation which can remain strong and free so long as public schools in the United States of America are kept free and strong.
II. In view of the foregoing considerations, it shall be my endeavor
   1. To devote time, thought, and study to the duties and responsibilities of a school board member so that I may render effective and creditable service.
   2. To work with my fellow board members in a spirit of harmony and cooperation in spite of differences of opinion that arise during vigorous debate of points at issue.
   3. To base my personal decision upon all available facts in each situation; to vote my honest conviction in every case, unswayed by partisan bias of any kind; thereafter, to abide by and uphold the final majority decision of the board.
   4. To remember at all times that as an individual I have no legal authority outside the meetings of the board, and to conduct my relationships with the school staff, the local citizenry, and all media of communication on the basis of this fact.
   5. To resist every temptation and outside pressure to use my position as a

school board member to benefit either myself or any other individual or agency apart from the total interest of the school district.

6. To recognize that it is as important for the board to understand and evaluate the educational program of the schools as it is to plan for the business of school operation.

7. To bear in mind under all circumstances that the primary function of the board is to establish the policies by which the schools are to be administered, but that the administration of the educational programs and the conduct of school business shall be left to the employed superintendent of schools and his professional staff and non-professional staff.

8. To welcome and encourage active cooperation by citizens, organizations, and the media of communication in the district with respect to establishing policy and proposed future development.

9. To support my State and National School Boards association.

10. Finally, to strive step by step toward ideal conditions for most effective school board service to my community in a spirit of teamwork and devotion to public education as the greatest instrument for the preservation of our representative democracy.

SOURCE: National School Boards Association, *A Code of Ethics for School Board Members* (Washington, D.C.: National School Boards Association, May 2, 1961).

3

Educational management is the art of synthesizing data and correlating this information with political, social, and human-relations variables in creating the organization necessary to accomplish a definite mission.

A Theory of Educational Administration

In 1983, The National Commission on Excellence in Education issued a report that was not very complimentary to public education in the United States. Allegations centered on the mediocrity of instruction and the low expectations for achievement by students and the schools. Much of the cure for these ills prescribed by government officials and the citizenry was simplistic, and, at times, clearly demonstrated a lack of understanding about the very essence of how public education is delivered to students. An extended school day and school year, along with merit pay for teachers, have been proposed as the means by which the quality of education can be raised to the level enjoyed in the "good old days." The problem, of course, is that instruction to children is no longer given in a one-room schoolhouse by an individual who also triples as the principal and custodian.

The advances in life-style enjoyed by U.S. citizens and created by American business and industry have been made possible by the education the general population has received as a consequence of free public education. We now expect increased services to children and an opportunity for all citizens to have a more advanced education. We can also see how the micro-chip has revolutionized our way of life, and it has far-reaching implications for schools, which must prepare children to take advantage of the benefits offered by microcomputers. This phenomenon is what prompted Peter Drucker to state: "That America's schools will improve—radically and quite soon—is certain . . . the economic rewards for knowledge and skill, after a half century of steady decline, are going up sharply—and so are the penalties for their absence."[1]

Instruction has gradually evolved into a very complex process because of our expectations and because of technological advances. Effective instruction, therefore, can only occur within an organization that is responsible for analyzing the needs of future generations and for creating delivery systems that will meet these needs. Thus, what follows is a treatment of the nature of educational organizations. Further, the manner in which educational organizations are managed will determine the level and quality of instruction; therefore, this chapter also contains a treatment of the nature of management.

THE NATURE OF EDUCATIONAL ORGANIZATIONS

In any organization, there is a central issue that takes precedence over others, because it is the *raison d'être* of an organization. This issue can be reduced to a single question: "What is the mission of the organization?" To the casual observer, that question might appear easy to answer, but, in reality, it is most difficult. The difficulty lies in the fact that "mission" is an organic entity that is subject to periodic change.

For educational organizations, the obvious but misleading answer is: "To educate children, adolescents, and young people." So far, so good! However, what does "to educate" really mean? Does it mean to provide transportation and food services to children, or just classroom instruction in the "basics"? Should statistics be a part of the high school mathematics program? Should foreign language be taught in the elementary school? Should all students learn to use microcomputers? Obviously, there is no pat answer to these questions. However, "mission" is the only justifiable reason to create an organization and its only reason for remaining in existence.

Therefore, a school district, as an organization, must devise a process by which its mission is continually under review for the purposes of refining and defining the nuance of that mission. Consequently, mission is viewed as the detailed and specific goals that direct the governance and management of the school district. For example, one goal might be to provide a sequential learning experience from kindergarten through twelfth grade that allows each student to acquire reading and language skills commensurate with that student's ability. A second goal might be to provide each student who lives over one mile from school with transportation services within half a mile from home. It is desirable for a board of education to outline the mission of the school district in policy statements that are readily available to its constituents.

The Structure of Educational Organizations

Most organizations fall into one of two categories, service rendering or production. The former can be further divided into private-sector and public-sector organizations. The criteria for classifying an organization are its mission and the manner in which it is financed.

The overall mission of the Chrysler Corporation is to manufacture automobiles; the company generates a profit through the sale of these automobiles (production organization). Arthur Andersen and Company is a firm that provides auditing services and generates a profit by charging a fee for them (service-rendering private-sector organization). School districts provide educational services to children that are financed by the taxing authority of the state and local districts (service-rendering public-sector organization). Municipal governments, sewer districts, water districts, police districts, and fire districts are additional examples of service-rendering public-sector organizations, because they all provide unique services financed by some form of taxation.

Characteristics of an Educational Organization

The following characteristics of an organization have proven to be a good guide in analyzing its effectiveness.

1. *Single Executive.* The organization has a single executive responsible for the overall management of the organization.
2. *Unity of Purpose.* The organization has a clear definition of its mission.
3. *Unity of Command.* Every person in the organization knows who his supervisor is and what his or her responsibilities are.
4. *Delegation of Authority and Responsibility.* Starting with the chief executive officer, authority is delegated to subordinates who carry out the daily operations of the organization.
5. *Division of Labor.* The organization encourages division of labor and task specialization.
6. *Standardization.* Standardized procedures have been developed for routine daily operations.
7. *Span of Control.* Each administrator in the organization is assigned no greater number of employees than he or she is capable of supervising.
8. *Stability.* Policies and programs are continued until results can be evaluated.
9. *Flexibility.* The organization makes provision for change and innovation.
10. *Security.* Members of the organization believe that they have security in their position.
11. *Personnel Policies.* The organization has effective personnel policies that provide for the proper selection, compensation, evaluation, and termination of employees.
12. *Evaluation.* The organization has a procedure for staff and program evaluation.[2]

The Role of the Individual Employee in Educational Organizations

The individuals who are employed to carry out the mission of a given organization are its building blocks. Their roles should be delineated in such a manner that it is readily apparent who has what responsibility and who supervises whom. This is traditionally accomplished by the pyramidal structuring of employees. In a school district, the superintendent of schools, as the chief executive officer of the school board, occupies the pinnacle of the pyramid. Immediately underneath are the assistant superintendents, followed by the building principals, who supervise the teachers. Employees such as curriculum directors, who provide support to the line administrators, are scattered throughout the pyramid. Line administrators have supervisory responsibilities that eminate from the superintendent down through the pyramid to the building level.

While many different models have been used, this is the most successful and effective in school districts. It is interesting to note that during the French Revolution, everyone was considered *equal* before the government and given the title "citizen." However, after the revolution ended, some in the French army were called "citizen general" and others "citizen private." We believe that human nature requires a clear delineation of authority. This does not mean that administration should be autocratic, as the following discussion will demonstrate.

A significant development has occurred within the last five years concerning the role of the individual employee in production organizations that has implications for educational organizations. The development originated in Japan, and has been dubbed *Theory Z* management.

For the last fifteen years, the quality of Japanese products has been recognized as superior to those made in the U.S. Many U.S. corporations have spent considerable sums of money studying the reason for this and have produced much data on Japanese corporate organizations.

Basically, Japanese corporations assume that workers have good ideas. If the organization listens to its employees and attempts to implement their ideas, these employees will be motivated to higher levels of productivity. The vehicle for involving the employees in formulating strategies to improve production is called *quality circle*. Groups of workers are organized to study and discuss methods for improving production, but in a very structured, step-by-step manner that requires sophisticated techniques of group relations that improve employee performance.[3]

The essence of Theory Z is that organizations must reverse their priorities if the mission of the organization is to be effectively and efficiently carried out.

United States corporations have traditionally considered the stockholder as most important in the hierarchy of corporate priorities, which is reflected in most companies' concern with increasing the value of stock and/or the amount of dividends paid to shareholders. The next priority in line is the customer, to whom the company wishes to offer a superior product. The welfare of the employees is the last priority in the typical corporate structure. The effect of this model has been decreasing employee productivity and other personnel problems such as high absenteeism.

FIGURE 3-1: PRIORITY-SETTING MODELS

U.S. Corporations
   1. Stockholders
   2. Customers
   3. Employees
Japanese Corporations
   1. Employees
   2. Customers
   3. Stockholders
Public School Districts
   1. Students
   2. Parents
   3. Employees

Many Japanese firms have reversed this model, and made the welfare of employees their top priority, with the customer next, and the stockholder last in line. The effect of this model has been increased productivity and a commitment by Japanese workers to the company that is unparalled in the United States business community. Because of this, the customer receives a superior service or product, and the stockholder, over the long term, receives an increase in stock value and/or dividends. In essence, by reversing the company's priorities, the Japanese model delivers what the United States corporate model hopes to accomplish.

The implications for an educational organization are clear. Make the welfare of the administrators, teachers, and other employees the first priority of the school system. Staff members who believe that they are respected, trusted, and appreciated by the school board will be productive employees. In turn, the students and parents will receive a higher level of service (see Figures 3-1 and 3-2).

The external manifestation of placing the welfare of employees first in a school district is best demonstrated through creating a *rewards* system that meets

---

**FIGURE 3-2: APPLICATION OF JAPANESE MODEL
TO PUBLIC SCHOOL DISTRICTS**

a. *Priorities → Increases Employee Productivity → Increases benefit to*
   1. Employee   *students and parents*
   2. Student
   3. Parents
b. Productivity increases because of:
       Emphasis → We Respect You!
c. Requires a change in:
       Job Description → Participate in Decision Making *→ We Trust You!*
       Rewards System → Direct and Indirect Rewards *→ We Appreciate You!*

personal, career, and professional needs. Chapter 9 presents a treatment of compensation that reflects this concept.

Political and Social Influences on Educational Organizations

Like private-sector and other public-sector organizations, school districts do not operate in a vacuum, but, rather, reflect social and political trends. In fact, the schools are called upon to prepare children to take an active role in American society. Thus, school districts are required to analyze and translate the expectations of its constituents into goals.

Some educators believe that academic pursuits should be untainted by political and social trends. Of course, not only is this impossible, but it shows a lack of understanding about public education. The schools were created by, are financed by, and belong to the people. Educational organizations should not ignore social and political trends, but rather decipher and meet their challenges by incorporating concepts from them in the curriculum. An example of a trend that has political and social implications is the current interpretation of free-enterprise capitalism.

THE NATURE OF MANAGEMENT IN EDUCATIONAL ORGANIZATIONS

For some reason, educators prefer to speak about *administration* rather than *management* when referring to the functions of and tasks performed by superintendents, assistant superintendents, principals, and so on. Perhaps educators believe that *management* as a term and concept is more appropriately applied to business and industry, while *administration* is better applied to the educational enterprise. Here we will use the terms interchangeably, because the current literature tends to blur this distinction.

Our initial consideration is to define what is meant by the term *management.* Since the Egyptians built the pyramids, people have attempted to define what it is that someone does who is in command of something that results in a desired outcome. Management can be defined as controlled action that leads to an outcome.

Management in educational organizations can be viewed in the same way, but somewhat more elaborately. It is controlled action because the mission of a school district can only be achieved through the management of other professionals. That controlled action has the following characteristics:

First, administrators must decide what they want the professionals whom they supervise to do.

Second, they must decide which professionals are to perform which functions and tasks.

Third, administrators must establish performance standards for the professionals they supervise.

Fourth, administrators must review these performances to determine whether the mission of the organization is being realized.

Fifth, by creating processes and procedures, administrators must control how functions are implemented.

Sixth, rewards and incentives must be developed by administrators if they hope to increase the level of performance of their subordinates.

The desired outcome of management in educational organizations is to provide services to the children in the school district. Thus, we see the necessity for professionalism in education and administration.

Competency Model

What the foregoing treatment demonstrates is that proper and effective management requires competent administrators. Competency means that an administrator has the knowledge and skills necessary to manage the people and resources (what people need to fulfill their responsibilities) to attain a desired outcome. Having good intentions and being a successful teacher do not necessarily make an individual a competent administrator.

It has been assumed in most states that an administrator must take certain courses or have a degree from a graduate program in educational administration. The course work usually involves three areas of administration: management (school law, finance, personnel administration, collective negotiations, buildings and sites, and the like); supervision of professional personnel; and curriculum development. The American Association of School Administrators has published a set of guidelines for the preparation of school administrators that addresses the knowledge necessary to meet the issues now facing school districts. A common core of requirements for all administration programs is:

1. Administrative, organizational, political, and learning theory
2. Technical areas of administrative practice
3. Behavioral and social sciences
4. Foundations of education
5. Research
6. Advanced technologies
7. Ethical principles of the profession[4]

The skills necessary to be an effective educational administrator involve abilities that must be exercised in three areas. These are:

1. The skill to manage oneself
2. The skill to manage others
3. The skill to manage operational functions

In the final analysis, the competency model rests on the theory that management is an *art*. It is true that scientific knowledge and learned skills are essential. However, no one can be an effective administrator by applying a set formula to all types of situations. Even the advocates of a systems approach to management will admit that there is an intangible that gives order to the system.

The "A" factor in management is an administrator's ability to analyze and interpret the variables involved in making a decision and to make that decision because of past managerial experience. Inherent in analyzing and interpreting variables is the ability to foresee the various consequences that different decisions will create and to choose the consequence that will produce the most desired effect.

The course work and programs offered by schools of education will give an individual the opportunity to acquire the knowledge and skills necessary to be an administrator. The art of management can be learned only from personal experience and by practicing its principles.

The Dynamics of Leadership

There are many levels and degrees of leadership that a superintendent, principal, curriculum coordinator, and the like can achieve, based upon the perimeters of the job and one's desire to become a "high performer." It is important to understand from the outset that "leadership" is not a characteristic that can be acquired, but is rather the result of performance. Someone can become a leader in his company because he is the best salesperson, or a principal can be a leader in her school district because of her achievement in administration. In each case, a high degree of performance is what gives the individual a position of leadership.

The very basic level of leadership is derived from certain job positions. The superintendent of schools is in a position of leadership by virtue of his or her authority and responsibility. The decisions he or she makes can have an effect upon every student in the school district and every teacher and staff member. This is true of all line executive positions and, thus, is also applicable to building-level principals. If someone is sitting on the corner of a two-story building, he or she can see the automobile traffic on the two adjacent streets. If two automobiles are traveling at extremely high speeds in the direction of the intersection at the corner of the building, the person sitting at the pinnacle will be able to anticipate a potential accident involving both vehicles. Because of his or her physical position, that person knows more than either driver. Thus, certain jobs give those who occupy these positions information and data that no other single individual can perceive. These individuals, therefore, possess a degree of leadership that is theirs simply by having that position.

Those who are leaders because of high performance are easily recognized. They outperform their colleagues because of the way in which they set goals for themselves, solve problems, manage stress, and take risks. In the last decade, there has been a great deal of research in psychology concerning why some individuals outperform others. The Soviets call this research *anthropomaximology.*

There are six characteristics that mark high performers:

1. They transcend previous levels of accomplishment.
2. They avoid feeling too comfortable with their present level of performance.
3. They work for the "art of it" and are motivated by compelling internal goals.
4. They attempt to solve problems rather than place the blame on other persons or events.

5. They take risks after carefully investigating all possible consequences.
6. They are capable of mentally rehearsing coming actions or events.[5]

Thus, one would be mentally prepared for every facet of an activity, such as making a presentation to the board of education. The truly high performer is not a workaholic, but, rather, a person who takes vacations, manages stress, and does not get entangled in details at work. Further, such an individual knows the value of delegating authority.

Effective time management is vital for those in leadership positions and those who strive to become high achievers. Time management means that you do not allow others or events to dictate what you will do at work. Further, it means that you do not spend your time on unnecessary or unproductive tasks. Thus, it is critical to have an agenda that maps out blocks of time for handling daily routines such as making telephone calls and for keeping appointments. At the same time, your agenda should be flexible enough to allow for unexpected situations or emergencies. Finally, some time each day should be devoted to planning activities.

A final note on leadership: Some administrators experience personal conflicts because they have not come to terms with the realities of management. What people consider the "right way" to accomplish a task or the way they expect others to act often falls short of what is possible or how people actually operate. It is very difficult to be a successful administrator unless one is flexible enough to accept the reality of events and to allow the people one supervises to make their own mistakes and lead their own lives. Administrators should only be concerned if the behavior of their subordinates affects performance, and then they must be careful not to make value judgments. Rather, such individuals should be counseled regarding how to change the undesirable behavior.

The Administrative Team Management Concept

In a pyramidal structure, the chief administrative officer, superintendent of schools in educational organizations, is responsible for the overall management of the organization. Obviously, it is impossible in all but the very smallest school district for the superintendent to manage all major functions alone. Personnel management, secondary school management, elementary school management, curriculum services management, and administrative support services management, for instance, are delegated to assistant superintendents in most districts. This does not necessarily mean that the superintendent believes in the team management approach to school district administration.

The chief executive officer has the responsibility and authority to manage the school district. Team management refers to the participation of other administrators in setting administrative policies (not to be confused with board-of-education policies) and of translating these policies into administrative strategies. Administrative policies are goals that the management believes are necessary to fulfill the mission of the school district, which is reflected in board-of-education policies. The administrative goals are translated into strategies, the "game plan" for achieving them. These strategies are used by the administrators charged with managing a delegated function. They are implemented through the establishment of processes and procedures for daily operations.

Thus, the superintendent conferring with the assistant superintendents at a cabinet meeting about a new board-of-education policy on affirmative action might ask the assistant superintendent for personnel to draft a list of appropriate goals regarding the recruitment of minority candidates for job vacancies; this would be discussed at the next cabinet meeting. When these goals are presented, all assistant superintendents could discuss how they (administrative policies) can be achieved in their respective areas of management (strategies). The assistant superintendent for personnel would then meet with his or her staff and discuss how the strategies can be realized, asking, "What procedures can be utilized in the recruitment process to attract minority candidates?" Contacting placement offices at colleges and universities that have large minority populations could be one procedure, while advertising in newspapers could be a second one. Finally, all internal divisions of the school district could be notified of vacancies. The assistant superintendents managing these divisions might have decided at the cabinet meeting that another strategy was to nominate qualified candidates whom they were already supervising.

The team management approach is applicable to each level within the school district. An assistant superintendent managing a district function would want to formulate division policies and strategies with staff members. Each division chief should then involve his or her staff in establishing division policies and strategies.

The team management concept is also very effective at the building level, where assistant principals could constitute the "principal's cabinet." The assistant principals can in turn set up the same situation with the staff members from the departments in the school that they manage.

The advantages to the team management approach are obvious. First, team management makes good use of the talent that is present in most organizations. Second, change is more likely to be implemented with minimal resistance if decisions are made cooperatively. Third, all levels within an organization are forced to identify administrative policies and strategies that are compatible and have the same ultimate objectives.

Evaluating the Members of the Administrative Team

A natural development in initiating and utilizing the team management concept is devising a method to evaluate the performance of the members of the administrative team. Performance evaluation is discussed throughout this book. Chapter 5 treats the evaluation of the superintendent of schools; Chapter 9 discusses performance evaluation in general and presents a detailed treatment of the consequences of chronically improper performance, termination; and Chapter 12 contains a section on managing the professional staff that includes a discussion of supervision and evaluation. The brief treatment here must be considered in relation to the other discussions to gain a complete understanding of performance evaluation.

The objectives for the performance evaluation of administrators include: to improve the performance of administrators, to encourage self-improvement, to identify staff development needs, to determine if an individual administrator should be retained, to determine the salary increase for administrators, and to help in the placement and/or promotion of administrators.

A significant aspect of the evaluation process is measuring an administrator's performance against the responsibilities of the job. Thus, each chapter dealing with the role and function of specific administrators contains a job description that can be used as a guide in establishing appropriate job responsibilities.

Appendix B contains a sample building-level administrator evaluation form that incorporates not only skills that an administrator should possess in the areas of administration, instruction, supervision, and community relations, but personal qualities as well. It also includes a section concerning priorities that, in essence, reflect a "results" approach to performance appraisal. Each administrator is responsible for developing priorities (objectives) against which performance in attaining these objectives will be measured.

Compensating the Members of the Administrative Team

Perhaps the most difficult task for a superintendent of schools is to create a compensation program for administrators. This is so difficult because the compensation program must be structured in such a manner as to demonstrate to administrators that the school district recognizes their worth and is compensating them fairly.

The fundamental concept behind compensation development is that salary is not the only method of compensation. The term *compensation* is much broader in scope and encompasses fringe benefits and even certain working conditions. Chapter 7 contains a section entitled "Rewarding Performance" that presents a detailed discussion of intrinsic and extrinsic rewards. Extrinsic rewards are usually divided between direct compensation, which is salary or wages; indirect compensation, frequently referred to as fringe benefits; and nonfinancial rewards, such as the services of a private secretary or a reserved parking space.

The most common fringe benefits available to administrators are those required by law. They include social security, state retirement programs, unemployment insurance, and workmen's compensation, in addition to voluntary fringe benefits such as medical, dental, term life, and errors and omissions insurance.

Appendix C contains a salary plan that incorporates two variables used in determining the appropriate wage to be paid to various levels of administrators: position factors and incumbent factors. Position factors refer to supervisory, leadership, and administrative responsibilities, and conditions of employment. Incumbent factors are professional education and experience and the performance of the administrator. This salary plan includes merit pay, which is rapidly becoming the norm for administrators throughout the country because of an attempt to improve the quality of educational services.

Whatever compensation program is devised, it must incorporate the following characteristics if it is to be effective:

1. *Equity.* People are paid similar amounts for similar jobs.
2. *Competitiveness.* The plan competes with other school districts in attracting and retaining competent administrators.
3. *Performance.* The plan appropriately rewards the performance of administrators.
4. *Rationality.* The plan reflects the responsibilities of the various levels of administrators in the organization.
5. *Responsiveness.* The plan retains the administrator's purchasing power over time.[6]

SUMMARY

Educating children has evolved into a very complex process because of the expectations of the American people and because of advances in technology. Instruction as a key component of the educational services provided to children can effectively occur only within an organization charged with the delivery of these services.

In educational organizations, the mission is to provide an education to children and youth living within the jurisdiction of a given school district's boundaries. A school district must, therefore, devise a process by which its mission is continually under review for the purpose of refining and defining the nuances of that mission. This mission is viewed in practice as the detailed and specific goals that direct the governance and management functions of the school district.

Most organizations fall into one of two categories, service rendering or production. Service-rendering organizations can be further divided between those in the private and those in the public sector. The criteria for classifying an organization are its mission and the manner in which it is financed. School districts are service-rendering public-sector organizations because they provide educational services to children that are financed by state and local taxes.

The following characteristics have proven to be a good guide in analyzing the effectiveness of an organization: (1) single executive, (2) unity of purpose, (3) unity of command, (4) delegation of authority and responsibility, (5) division of labor, (6) standardization, (7) span of control, (8) stability, (9) flexibility, (10) security, (11) personnel policies, (12) evaluation.

The building blocks of an organization are the individuals who are employed to carry out its mission. It should be readily apparent who has what responsibility and who supervises whom. This is traditionally accomplished through the pyramidal structuring of employees.

A significant development in contemporary Japanese corporations concerning the role of the individual has implications for school districts. The basic assumption is that workers have good ideas, and that if these are implemented, the workers will be motivated to higher levels of performance. This demands a reversal of priorities for school districts that makes the welfare of staff members the primary concern of the district.

Administrators must also recognize that school districts do not operate in a vacuum but reflect the social and political trends of the times.

Implementing the mission of an organization is the responsibility of the school district's management. Thus, management may be defined as controlled action that leads to an outcome. This function requires competent administrators. Competency means that an administrator has the knowledge and skills necessary to manage people and resources in order to attain a desired outcome. The knowledge requirement has been interpreted in most states to mean a set of courses or graduate program leading to administrative licensing. The skill requirement means that administrators can manage themselves, others, and operational functions. In the final analysis, the competency model rests on the theory that management is an art, because an administrator must possess the ability to analyze and interpret the variables involved in a decision based upon past experiences.

There are multiple levels of administrative leadership. The basic one is derived from the job position; others are determined by the level of performance that an individual achieves. Leadership qualities are necessary for an educational administrator.

Team management refers to participation by administrators at all levels within the organization in setting administrative policy and in translating this policy into administrative strategies. This approach makes good use of available talent, reduces resistance to change, and allows for continuity of purpose.

A natural development in initiating and utilizing the team management concept is to devise a method to evaluate the performance of the members of the administrative team. The objectives are: to improve performance, to encourage self-improvement, to identify staff development needs, to determine who should be retained, to determine salary increases, and to determine placement and promotions.

Rewarding performance with an adequate compensation program for administrators is a very important task of the superintendent of schools. Compensation includes salary, fringe benefits, and working conditions. The following are characteristic elements of an effective compensation program: equity, competitiveness, performance, rationality, and responsiveness.

IMPLICATIONS FOR EDUCATIONAL ADMINISTRATORS

There are three implications for educational administrators if one adheres to the theories presented here.

First, excellence in education and superior instruction are products of a very complex organization, the school district. Administrators will never upgrade the quality of educational services unless they strive to understand, accommodate, and modify the goals of the organization. This requires a profound understanding of the political and social influences on these organizations.

Second, management is the vehicle by which educational services are delivered. These services will be mediocre at best unless school districts are managed by competent administrators who possess the knowledge and skills necessary to coordinate people and resources such that quality service can be delivered.

Third, competent administrators are attracted and retained by school districts if the management has initiated an evaluation process and compensation program that rewards performance.

SELECTED BIBLIOGRAPHY

AMERICAN ASSOCIATION OF SCHOOL ADMINISTRATORS, *Guidelines for the Preparation of School Administrators,* Arlington, Va.: The Association, 1979.

AMERICAN ASSOCIATION OF SCHOOL ADMINISTRATORS AND THE NATIONAL SCHOOL BOARDS ASSOCIATION, *The Administrative Leadership Team.* Arlington, Va.: The Associations, 1979.

——— , *Compensating the Administrative Team.* Arlington, Va.: The Associations, 1981.

——— , *Selecting the Administrative Team.* Arlington, Va.: The Associations, 1981.

HANSON, MARK E., *Educational Administration and Organizational Behavior.* Boston: Allyn and Bacon, Inc., 1979.

JACKSON, JOHN H., and CYRIL P. MORGAN, *Organization Theory: A Macro Perspective for Management* (2nd ed.). Englewood Cliffs, N.J.: Prentice-Hall, Inc., 1982.

MORPHET, EDGAR L., ROE L. JOHNS, and THEODORE L. RELLER, *Educational Organization and Administration* (4th ed.). Englewood Cliffs, N.J.: Prentice-Hall, Inc., 1982.

MOUZELIS, NICOS P., *Organization and Bureaucracy: An Analysis of Modern Theory.* Chicago: Aldine Publishing Co., 1968.

ROBBINS, STEPHEN P., *Organization Theory: The Structure and Design of Organizations.* Englewood Cliffs, N.J.: Prentice-Hall, Inc., 1983.

SERGIOVANNI, THOMAS J., MARTIN BURLINGAME, FRED D. COOMBS, and PAUL W. THURSTON, *Educational Governance and Administration.* Englewood Cliffs, N.J.: Prentice-Hall, Inc., 1980.

STONER, JAMES A. F., *Management* (2nd ed.). Englewood Cliffs, N.J.: Prentice-Hall, Inc., 1982.

NOTES

1. Peter Drucker, "Quality Education: The New Growth Area," *The Wall Street Journal,* (New York), July 19, 1983, p. 24.

2. Edgar L. Morphet, Roe L. Johns, and Theodore L. Reller, *Educational Organization and Administration: Concepts, Practices, and Issues,* 4th ed. (New Jersey: Prentice-Hall, Inc., 1982), pp 69–73.

3. David A. Nichols, "Can 'Theory Z' Be Applied to Academic Management?" *The Chronicle of Higher Education* (September 1, 1983), p. 72.

4. American Association of School Administrators, *Guidelines for the Preparation of School Administrators* (Arlington, Va.: The Association, 1979), pp. 3–10.

5. Charles A. Garfield, "Why Do Some People Outperform Others? Psychologist Picks Out Six Characteristics," *The Wall Street Journal* (New York), January 13, 1982, p. 25.

6. American Association of School Administrators, *Compensating the Administrative Team* (Arlington, Va.: The Association, 1981), pp. 10–13.

APPENDIX A:
ADMINISTRATOR'S BILL OF RIGHTS

The administrator's Bill of Rights is comprised of ten distinct, but sometimes overlapping and interrelated, rights. Their development depends more upon the profession of school administration than the state of present law governing the employment contractual relationship of school administrators and school districts. To make the school administrator's Bill of Rights work, it must be agreed to by all levels of the profession. And it must be respected by school boards.

1. The right to a specific and complete written description of the professional duties and responsibilities expected to be fulfilled.
2. The right to a full and impartial evaluation of professional performance on a regular and continuing basis.
3. The right to constructive counseling on a regular and continuing basis to up-grade performance.
4. The right to participate in an administrative staff "in-service" training program to improve professional performance in the present position and establish a basis for increased responsibilities in the future.
5. The right to be furnished a list of reasons when dismissal, demotion, or non-re-employment is proposed.
6. The right to a fair, but private hearing before the school board prior to dismissal, demotion, or non-re-employment.
7. The right to a private review by the professional school administrator association of all the facts and judgments resulting in a proposal to demote, dismiss, or not to renew employment.
8. The right to adequate compensation for providing the socially important, complex and learned professional services.
9. The right to a voice in district administrative policy making consistent with the management position and unique individual experience and expertise.
10. The right to be accorded the respect and dignity due a member of an honorable and learned profession and an individual, sensitive, human being.

SOURCE: American Association of School Administrators, *Administrator's Bill of Rights* (Arlington, Va.: The Association, 1979).

APPENDIX B:
ADMINISTRATOR EVALUATION REPORT

ADMINISTRATOR _____ YEAR _____

POSITION _____ SCHOOL _____

YEARS IN PRESENT DISTRICT'S ADMINISTRATION _____

PURPOSES

Evaluation is to ensure that the administrator displays adequate management skills and leadership among the students, staff, and community. The evaluation process will assure that the administrator has goals appropriate to his level of responsibility and in line with overall school system goals. This process will aid the administrator in the improvement of his performance and provide a basis for merit pay adjustment.

IMPLEMENTATION

1. The Superintendent will evaluate all building principals.
2. Evaluation of grade principals and assistant principals will be made by the building principal. The Superintendent will review these evaluations and confer with the principal prior to the formal evaluation.
3. The Evaluator will receive appropriate input from all Central Office Administrators prior to completing the evaluation.
4. Administrators will be evaluated on the standards and expectations of (name of school district).
5. The evaluation will be made on a scale of one to nine ranging from improvement needed to consistently outstanding.
6. The overall rating will not be adversely affected by items marked not applicable.
7. The formal evaluation will take place following the close of the school year.

ADMINISTRATIVE SKILLS

Consistently Outstanding — Needs Improvement — N A

1. Has implemented procedures for budget preparation and accounting methods for monitoring the budget . . . .
2. Has implemented a plan for the effective cleaning and maintenance of the facility . . . .
3. Has implemented a process for inventorying, acquiring, and replacing of equipment . . . .

Consistently Outstanding · Needs Improvement N A

4. Has implemented safety and energy conservation procedures . .

5. Has established procedures for the use of student, teacher, and parent feedback . . . .

6. Has developed and followed procedures for administrative scheduling and reporting . . . .

7. Has completed written communications accurately and on schedule . . . .

Total points _____ ÷ _____ number of items marked = _____ average marking.

INSTRUCTIONAL LEADERSHIP

1. Has demonstrated knowledge of curricular issues in various subject areas . . . .

2. Has assisted classroom teachers in the implementation of the curriculum. . . . .

3. Has monitored and evaluated the instructional program and used the results to plan program improvements . . . .

4. Has demonstrated knowledge of good teaching methods and assisted teachers to improve diagnostic skills and teaching strategies. . . . .

5. Has carried out procedures to evaluate and maintain an effective teaching-learning environment . . . .

Total points _____ ÷ _____ number of items marked = _____ average marking.

SUPERVISION

1. Has coordinated the work of special and support personnel with the programs of the school. .

2. Has conducted a program of faculty and staff supervision that included periodic visits, conferences and evaluation of all personnel. . . . .

3. Has carried out a procedure for the orientation and supervision of all new personnel . . . .

	Consistently Outstanding							Needs Improvement	N A

4. Has developed and implemented procedures to maintain effective school discipline. . . . .

5. Has maintained a system of supervision of all co-curricular and extra curricular activities. . . . . .

Total points _____ ÷ _____ number of items marked = _____ average marking.

SCHOOL AND COMMUNITY

1. Has promoted good relationships between the school and community through positive interpretation and implementation of district policy . . . .

2. Has conducted a comprehensive and effective system of communication with the students of the school . . . .

3. Has conducted a comprehensive and effective system of communication with the parents of the school . . . .

4. Has conducted a comprehensive and effective system of communication with the staff of the school . . . .

5. Has coordinated and maintained a volunteer program in the school. .

6. Has participated in various civic, service, and community groups and community functions to help assure public knowledge and understanding of the school program . . . .

7. Has provided support and guidance to P.T.O., Mothers' Club, and other parent groups . . . . . .

Total points _____ ÷ _____ number of items marked = _____ average marking.

PERSONAL QUALITIES

1. Has exhibited professional growth through in-service activities, conferences and conventions, membership in and participation in professional organizations, and continuing formal education. . . .

2. Has displayed appropriate decision making skills by recognizing

	Consistently Outstanding							Needs Improvement	N A

problems, evaluating facts, and
implementing decisions. . . . . . .

3. Has displayed good personal relationships with administration,
faculty, staff, parents, and
students . . . .

4. Has evidenced personal and
professional ethics in all relationships . . . .

5. Has shown sustained effort and
enthusiasm in the quality and
quantity of work accomplished . .

Total points _____ ÷ _____ number of items marked = _____ average marking.

BUILDING PRIORITIES

Each building priority is rated separately on a combination of the following criteria:

1. Building priorities are identified with input from teachers, students, and/or parents.
2. The written design to meet each priority is clearly written with definitive steps and timetable.
3. Periodic review of progress toward accomplishing each priority is carried out and necessary adjustments made during the year.
4. Accomplishment of building priorities involves participation and input from the school faculty and other affected groups where appropriate.
5. Priority is completed according to the timetable and definitive steps in the original written design. Deviations from that design will be stated and explained.

Priority I _____

Priority II _____

Priority III _____

Priority IV _____

Priority V _____

Priority VI _____

Priority VII _____

Total points _____ ÷ _____ number of items marked = _____ average marking.

RATING SYSTEM

1. Each item is marked from one to nine or NA.
2. The item markings in each area are added and the sum is divided by the number of items marked.

3. The average marking is multiplied by the percentage weight given that area.
4. The weighted scores for each area are added. The sum will fall in a range from one to nine. The total score will be carried out to the third decimal place.
5. The sum of the weighted scores is applied directly to the merit portion of the administrators salary schedule.

	AVERAGE MARKING		PERCENTAGE WEIGHT	WEIGHTED SCORE
Administrative Skills	_____	X	.10	_____
Instructional Leadership	_____	X	.20	_____
Supervision	_____	X	.20	_____
School and Community	_____	X	.10	_____
Personal Qualities	_____	X	.10	_____
Building Priorities	_____	X	.30	_____
			TOTAL	_____

EVALUATOR'S COMMENTS:

ADMINISTRATOR'S COMMENTS:

Evaluator's Signature _____ DATE _____

Administrator's Signature _____ DATE _____

SOURCE: Lindbergh School District, *Administrator Evaluation Report* (St. Louis: The District, 1983).

APPENDIX C:
ADMINISTRATOR SALARY PLAN

Philosophy

This salary plan has been developed with the following general concepts in mind:

1. The plan should attract and retain the most competent administrative staff possible.
2. All district administrative personnel should be included in the salary structure.
3. The salary structure should include an individual performance factor.
4. Levels of responsibility should be taken into account in the salary structure.
5. The salary structure should set forth a salary range for any given position.
6. The salary structure should minimize compression between positions and contain factors to eliminate compression where it previously existed.
7. The salary structure should include qualifications necessary for any given position, i.e., academic preparation, certification, and experience.
8. The salary structure should take into account areas of special knowledge or preparation not covered by certification or college preparation.
9. The salary structure should be responsive to the current state of the economy and its impact on the buying power of personnel under the plan.
10. The salary structure should be simple to compute and easy to understand.

The salary plan is based upon the above concepts. These concepts are generally principles which forward looking private and public sector organizations consider foundations for administrative salary plan.

The Plan

The salary plan consists of two factors. First, the *position factor* is determined entirely from the nature of the particular administrative position. This position factor changes only when the job responsibilities are changed. The position factor is composed of the following sub-factors:

1. Supervisory responsibility. This factor refers to—
   a. number of persons over whom the administrator exercises supervisory responsibility
   b. closeness of supervision or degree of independence of those supervised
   c. nature and difficulty of work performed by persons being supervised
2. Leadership responsibility. This factor refers to—
   a. participation in policy and program determination
   b. extent and nature of public contacts
   c. independence of action in significant functions which are performed

3. Administrative responsibility. This factor refers to—
   a. number, variety, and complexity of administrative functions for which the person is responsible
   b. breadth of work knowledge required to appraise and make decisions with respect to administrative functions
   c. depth of work knowledge required to appraise and make decisions with respect to administrative functions performed.
4. Conditions of employment. This factor refers to—
   a. length of work year
   b. length and nature of work week taking into account the number and regularity of working hours.

The second factor is the *incumbent factor* which is determined entirely from the qualifications and performance of the person in the job. The incumbent factor changes only when the incumbent changes or when the qualifications or performance of the incumbent change. The incumbent factor is composed of the following sub-factors:

5. Professional education held by the incumbent. This factor refers to the scope of formal professional study in preparation for this position.
6. Professional experience of the incumbent. This factor refers to the length and nature of administrative experience in this school district.
7. Performance of the incumbent. This factor refers to the quality of services performed. (This is the only factor which depends upon substantially subjective judgment.)

The position and incumbent factors are assigned numerical values and then combined to produce an overall index of salary for an individual administrator. This index is then multiplied by a normative minimum administrative salary. This minimum salary would be considered for adjustment annually to reflect changes due to inflation, changes in the district's revenues, changes in the going rate for administrators in comparable districts in the area, and other variables.

Normative Minimum Administrator Salary: $35,000

POSITION FACTOR

Elementary School Principal	1.00
Middle School Assistant Principal	1.04
High School Grade Principal	1.08
Director of Buildings & Grounds	1.06
Middle School Principal	1.12
High School Principal	1.20
Assistant Superintendent	1.26
Associate Superintendent	1.28

INCUMBENT FACTORS

Professional Education
Masters + 30 hours	.02
Masters + 60 hours	.04
Doctorate	.06
Quality of Performance	.00-.09

PROFESSIONAL ADMINISTRATIVE EXPERIENCE

1 yr. = .00	11 yrs. = .135	21 yrs. = .185
2 yrs. = .02	12 yrs. = .14	22 yrs. = .19
3 yrs. = .04	13 yrs. = .145	23 yrs. = .195
4 yrs. = .06	14 yrs. = .15	24 yrs. = .20
5 yrs. = .08	15 yrs. = .155	25 yrs. = .205
6 yrs. = .09	16 yrs. = .16	26 yrs. = .21
7 yrs. = .10	17 yrs. = .165	27 yrs. = .215
8 yrs. = .11	18 yrs. = .17	28 yrs. = .22
9 yrs. = .12	19 yrs. = .175	29 yrs. = .225
10 yrs. = .13	20 yrs. = .18	30 yrs. = .23

Administrative Salary Ranges

The salary plan provides for a minimum salary for each position as well as a maximum salary. It is expected that all salaries will fall within the position range; however, the plan does permit 15 percent of the administrative staff to exceed the maximum salary level.

	LOW	HIGH
Elementary Principal	$35,000	$45,000
Middle Assistant Principal	$36,000	$46,000
Director of Buildings & Grounds	$37,000	$47,000
High School Grade Principal	$38,000	$48,000
Middle School Principal	$39,000	$49,000
High School Principal	$40,000	$50,000
Assistant Superintendent	$41,000	$51,000
Associate Superintendent	$42,000	$52,000

The following are examples of the calculations involved in determining the salary for two administrators.

EXAMPLE #1

Middle School Principal	1.12
Masters + 60 hours	.04
Quality of Performance	.05
Administrative Experience—5 yrs.	.08
Total Index	1.29
Normative Minimum Salary	× $35,000
Salary	$45,150

EXAMPLE #2

Elementary Principal	1.00
Masters + 30 hours	.02
Quality of Performance	.05
Administrative Experience—2 yrs.	.02
Total Index	1.09
Normative Minimum Salary	X $35,000
Salary	$38,150

SOURCE: Lindbergh School District, *Administrator Compensation Plan* (St. Louis: The District, 1983).

School administrators are held accountable for
their responsibilities through the
American judicial system.

Legal Considerations for Educational Administrators

Many school districts have experienced an increase in litigation over the last decade, partially because sovereign immunity has been abrogated by many state legislatures. Sovereign immunity is the common-law principle that protects government officials from lawsuits resulting from the performance of their duties. School districts are governmental subdivisions of the state operating on the local level, and thus, school-board members have been protected from such lawsuits. However, over twenty-eight states have taken away this cloak of immunity, and the 1990s may see most of the remaining states in a similar position.

The ripple effect from this situation has caused many school administrators to become more vulnerable to judicial review of their decisions and actions than their colleagues were a decade ago. Even if they act in good faith and with reasonable deliberation, administrators may find themselves defending their actions in court.

It is, therefore, imperative that school administrators have a rudimentary understanding of the American judicial system and are capable of carrying out their daily responsibilities in such a manner that they can legally defend themselves if they are sued.

The following discussion is meant to provide administrators with a better understanding of their potential liabilities.

THE AMERICAN JUDICIAL SYSTEM

There are two systems of law that must be addressed from the beginning of this presentation in order to understand the American judicial system. The first system is known as *civil law* and is decended from Roman law, which attempts to establish all law in the form of statutes enacted by a legislative body. Our federal law is basically derived from statutes enacted by the United States Congress.

The second system is known as *common law* and is the basic approach used in England. It was adopted in theory by most of the states in our country. Under this system, the decisions rendered by a court become a guide or precedent to be followed by the court in future cases.

Consequently, the system of law found in the United States is mixed, using principles of both civil and common law.

Sources of Law

Three major sources of law form the foundation of our judicial system: constitutions, statutes, and case law.

Constitutions are bodies of precepts that provide the framework within which government carries out its duties. The federal and state constitutions contain provisions that secure the personal, property, and political rights of citizens.

School districts are continually confronted with constitutional issues, many of which have resulted in lawsuits. Some of these issues have dealt with compulsory education, academic freedom, the rights of students, and censorship of books.

Statutes are the enactments of legislative bodies, more commonly called *laws.* Thus, the U.S. Congress or state legislature may enact a new law or change an old law by the passage of legislation. These statutes may be reviewed by the courts to determine if they are in violation of the precepts set forth in the state and federal constitutions.

The presumption is that the laws enacted by legislative bodies are constitutional, and proving otherwise occurs only through litigation. Thus, if a state legislature passed a law requiring school districts to provide free bus transportation to parochial-school children living within the boundaries of their respective districts, a citizen or group of citizens could initiate a lawsuit asking the supreme court to consider the new law's constitutionality. The basis for the lawsuit might be a provision in the state constitution for the separation of church and state.

Because public schools are state agencies, the legislatures of every state have created statutes governing school districts. School operations, therefore must comply with such statutes, and it is the responsibility of school superintendents and their administrative staffs to ensure compliance. Further, the board of education cannot establish policies that are in conflict with state statutes and, of course, the acts of the U.S. Congress; in addition, these policies must not be in conflict with either the federal or state constitution. If a school board, therefore, creates a policy prohibiting handicapped children living in its district from attending school with other children, this policy would be in violation of Federal Public Law 94-142, probably violates the due process guaranteed by the Fourteenth Amendment to the U.S. Constitution, and, perhaps, the state constitution, stipulating that a free education must be provided for all children.

A third source of law is *common law,* more properly called case law, because it is derived from court decisions rather than from legislative acts. Past court decisions are considered to be binding on subsequent cases if the situation is similar. This is the doctrine of *precedent.* Lower courts usually adhere to the precedent (rule of law) established by higher courts in the same jurisdiction. The United States Supreme Court and state supreme courts can reverse their own previous decisions and thereby change the rule of law. Thus, a state circuit court may apply a rule of law established by a state supreme court as to what constitutes proper teacher supervision of children in a case alleging negligence that resulted in injury to a child. In a later case, the supreme court may redefine proper supervision and thus change the rule of law.

There are two additional sources of law that affect the practice of educational administration even though they are not traditionally considered primary sources: administrative law and attorney-general opinions.

Administrative law has developed through the creation of state and federal boards and commissions charged with administering certain federal and state laws by the establishment and application of rules and regulations. At the federal level, administrators are likely to be affected by the regulations of the Social Security Administration; while on the state level, central-office administrators may interact with the Employment Security Administration or the Workmen's Compensation Commission. Of course, the actions of these boards and commissions are subject to review by the courts.

A second and frequently used legal procedure is to request an opinion by a state attorney general regarding the interpretation of a certain statute. In the absence of case law, this opinion can be used by school boards and administrators in governing and managing the affairs of the school district.

Major Divisions of Law

Law may be divided into two major categories: civil and criminal law. This distinction arises out of the rights that are protected under the law. Civil law protects the rights of individuals and corporations. It is concerned with resolving disputes between these entities. The state is usually not a party to the dispute but, through the court system and the judge, acts as an impartial arbiter. Many subdivisions of civil law are familiar to most people; they include the following: contracts, real estate, divorce, wills and estates, and torts.

A dispute may arise between the superintendent of schools and the board of education over the terms of the superintendent's contract. The superintendent may allege that a due process clause in his contract was not followed in his dismissal by the board of education. Because the school district is a state agency and because the dispute involves a contract, the lawsuit would be filed by the superintendent's attorney in the state circuit court. This is an example of civil law.

Criminal law protects the rights of society. An individual who commits a crime is violating a law enacted by Congress or a state legislature to protect society. Thus, when a person is arrested and charged with committing a crime, the federal or state government prosecutes the individual and bears all the costs.

In certain cases, a civil and criminal wrong can coexist. If a school bus driver is intoxicated and causes an accident that injures certain children riding on the bus, the state may prosecute him for drunken driving and causing injuries. Further, the parents of the injured children may bring suit against the school district for damages, alleging that the bus driver was not properly supervised and that this negligence resulted in the accident.

The Court Structure

The federal and state constitutions provide the framework for the establishment of our court systems. On the local level, municipal courts deal with the enforcement of city ordinances and handle such problems as traffic and housing-code violations.

At the state level, the primary court is generally prescribed by the state constitution, which also gives the state legislature the power to create new and additional courts. Most states have four categories of courts: courts of special jurisdiction, circuit courts, courts of appeal, and supreme courts.[1]

Courts of special jurisdiction are limited and may hear only certain types of cases. Examples of these special courts include juvenile, probate, divorce, and small claims.

Circuit courts are usually considered to be the court of original jurisdiction. All major criminal and civil cases are tried before this court. It is of particular significance to school administrators, because most disputes involving contracts, tenure, and torts will be tried here. In like manner, because education is a state function, the state court system, rather than the federal system, has jurisdiction over the resolution of most issues.

Appellate courts are found in all fifty states and are commonly referred to as *supreme courts.* In some states, there are intermediate courts of appeal that have jurisdiction to hear and terminate certain types of cases on appeal from the circuit court.

At the federal level, the United States Constitution provides for the establishment of a supreme court and gives Congress the authority to create inferior courts.[2] This power has been exercised by Congress, with the resultant establishment of special jurisdiction courts, district courts, and the United States Court of Appeals. The federal courts of special jurisdiction, like the state courts of special jurisdiction, are limited to hearing certain types of cases. A few of these courts with which many are familiar include: Tax Court, Court of Claims, Bankruptcy Court, Court of Custom and Patent Appeals.

The Federal District Court, like the state circuit court, is a general court of original jurisdiction. It is the trial court that hears litigation between citizens from

FIGURE 4-1: STRUCTURE OF THE COURTS

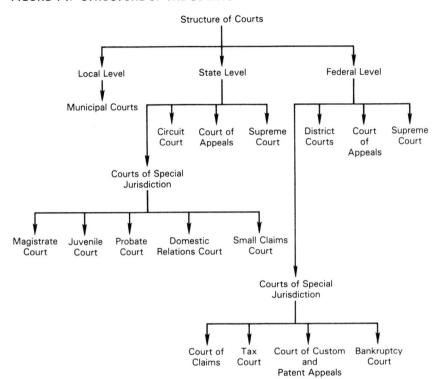

two or more states, cases involving federal civil or criminal statutes, and those involving the Federal Constitution.

The decisions of a Federal District Court may be appealed to the United States Court of Appeals or, in certain cases, directly to the United States Supreme Court. The United States Supreme Court is, of course, the highest court in the country, beyond which there is no appeal.

There is a distinction in the manner by which certain courts can hear cases that is very important for educational administrators to understand. Certain issues are traditionally tried in "equity" by the state circuit courts and Federal District Courts. The most familiar to school administrators are injunctions. Because teachers are state employees, a school board may go to a state circuit court to ask for an injunction directing a group of teachers to leave the picket line and return to the classroom if there is a state statute prohibiting strikes by teachers. Obviously, if the parties named in an injunction fail to obey the court order, they are in contempt of court and may be punished by a fine or jail. Thus, the same court may sit in law or in equity, depending upon the remedy sought.

TORTS AND EDUCATIONAL ADMINISTRATORS

The term *tort* refers to a civil wrong, other than the breaking of a contract, that is committed against a person or a person's property.[3] Torts are so varied that it is difficult to categorize them. However, for the sake of demonstrating how tort litigation could affect the practice of educational administration, three types of torts will be explained.

Actions a person takes that interfere with another person or with his or her property that are also usually crimes are intentional torts. Assault, battery, and defamation are the most common forms of personal interference. It is hoped that administrators will not be accused of an assault, which is a threat to physically harm someone, or a battery, which is the actual carrying out of a threat. There are two situations, however, in which administrators may find themselves involved and that may result in a lawsuit charging assault and battery. If two students fight, it may be the responsibility of the principal to break it up. The result might be such that an injured student could accuse the principal of assault and battery. The administrator will have an easier time defending his or her actions if only that force necessary to restrain the two students was used.

The second situation involves the administration of corporal punishment. The school district should have a policy that details how and for what purposes corporal punishment may be used. Such a policy should include the following provisions at a minimum:

1. Corporal punishment should be administered only in the presence of another administrator or teacher.
2. Corporal punishment should not be applied by an administrator of the opposite sex as the child. Another administrator or teacher of the same sex as the child should be enlisted to carry out the punishment.
3. The purpose for using corporal punishment should be to correct inappropriate behavior, not to harm the child.

Defamation occurs when a person communicates something about another individual, either by word of mouth (slander) or in writing (libel), that is false and

FIGURE 4-2: CLASSIFICATION OF TORTS

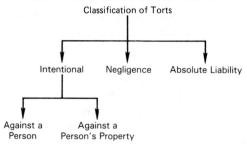

makes that person hated or ridiculed and also harms the individual in some way. Defamation is an area of potential litigation for school administrators, particularly in regard to personnel matters. If employees are not performing at an acceptable level, it is the responsibility of their immediate supervisors to inform them of their deficiencies and give them an opportunity to correct their behavior. For example, if a principal indiscriminately discusses the performance of a teacher with his or her secretary, with other teachers or administrators, that administrator may end up in court with a defamation lawsuit, particularly if that teacher's employment is subsequently terminated. The teacher could allege that the principal lied about his or her performance and indiscretely told other people these lies, which ultimately resulted in his or her being fired.

There might be a similar set of circumstances involving student discipline. The principal could be accused of slandering a student by discussing his or her school behavior indiscriminately with others, with the result that the student was expelled from school.

Thus, it is critical for an administrator to consider privileged all information about the behavior of teachers, staff members, students, and other administrators. Such information, of course, may be shared in writing or in discussions with others who have a legal or professional responsibility that requires having such information.

Chapter 11, "The Role and Function of the Curriculum and Pupil Personnel Administrators" contains a detailed treatment of students' property rights. This, in essence, deals with the most common situations found in schools, in which an administrator can be accused of a tort involving a person's property.

A second classification of torts is usually referred to as *absolute liability*. For example, when a person keeps a wild animal as a pet, and that animal escapes and injures someone, the owner is liable simply by virtue of having kept the animal in a residential area. A more relevant example for school administrators concerns recognized hazardous activities. If a central-office administrator requires custodians to use highly toxic chemicals for pest control or cleaning without the proper equipment or training, and if an injury occurs, the administrator has absolute liability. Further, if that administrator had made this activity required of custodians and it was an accepted school district practice, the injured person could enjoin other line administrators, up to and including the superintendent, in the lawsuit. All those who have supervisory responsibilities could share the liability, because they should have found out about the hazardous practice.

This example overlaps with the third category, negligence, which involves a person's conduct falling below an established standard so that injury to another person results. For instance, it is usually the principal's responsibility to supervise the conduct of elementary school children as they get off the bus in the morning and board the bus in the afternoon. The principal may not personally supervise this activity but may assign teachers to perform it. A prudent and responsible elementary school principal may do the following to insure student safety:

1. Develop written guidelines for the unloading and loading of school buses that require teachers to explain these guidelines to the students during the first week of school.
2. Send home a copy of these guidelines to parents asking them to impress upon their children the importance of following them.
3. Assign an adequate number of teachers to supervise the activity.
4. Periodically observe the unloading and loading of school buses to determine if the teachers are adequately fulfilling this responsibility.
5. Reinforce the importance of good student conduct by taking specific disciplinary actions when students violate the guidelines.

All elementary school principals know that children run, push, and shove one another as they get on and off the school bus. Not to supervise this situation is both unprofessional and carries legal liability. The question that will be raised in a lawsuit by the attorney for the parents of the injured child is whether a reasonable person could have prevented the injury. The concept of a "reasonable person" has a very specific application in a tort. He or she is defined as someone who:

1. Possesses average intelligence
2. Possesses the knowledge specific to being an elementary school principal
3. Possesses the same level of experience as the defendant
4. Possesses the same physical limitations as the defendant

Thus, the conduct of the principal involved in the lawsuit is compared with the conduct of a mythical reasonable person. The jury or judge must decide if the defendant was negligent when compared with this reasonable person. Therefore, all administrators should examine their professional responsibilities to determine if their conduct in fulfilling these responsibilities can withstand the test of the "reasonable person."

In a civil lawsuit that results in a decision for the plaintiff, the defendant will usually be required to pay actual damages, which is the amount of money that the injury cost. A broken arm could result in thousands of dollars in physician and hospital bills.

If it can be demonstrated in court that a person deliberately caused the injury, punitive damages may also be levied by the court against the defendant. This dollar amount is a punishment for intentionally bringing about the injury. In some cases, punitive damages may equal or supersede the actual damages assessed by the court.

It should be clear from this presentation that each and every school administrator must be protected by errors and omissions liability insurance. Sources for obtaining such coverage include professional school administrator associations and the school district's insurance underwriter. Many large insurance companies provide such protection under a group policy for school districts that may be extended to cover school-board members, central-office administrators, principals, teachers, and other employees. Finally, it should be remembered that most errors and omissions liability insurance policies do not cover punitive damages, because this would amount to condoning an act that was deliberately perpetrated.

THE ROLE OF THE SCHOOL DISTRICT'S ATTORNEY

The school district's attorney is a key person when a lawsuit is brought against the district, board members, or other district employees. An attorney is also usually consulted when the school board enters into a business contract or when the board authorizes a tax-levy or bond-issue election. Condemnation of property for the purpose of constructing a school building is a very complex legal process that always requires the assistance of an attorney.

A common misconception about the role of the attorney in a lawsuit is that he or she will handle the litigation without much involvement from board members, administrators, or other district employees. Even in litigation that is initiated to challenge a present law, input from board members and school administrators is necessary in the preparation of legal briefs.

Attorneys basically perform three functions when litigation is involved. First, they analyze the issue to determine the facts and real questions involved. Second, they research court cases and statutes for the purpose of deciding what law is involved. Finally, they put together a workable solution to the issue in relation to the material facts and the law. Obviously, there may be a number of alternative solutions to the same issue.

The superintendent of schools should, therefore, initiate a process for selecting an attorney to represent the school district that significantly emphasizes proven performance in litigation.

However, in the last ten to fifteen years, a set of circumstances has arisen that requires school attorneys to possess competencies beyond the technical skills necessary to practice law. These competencies reflect the emerging role of the school attorney, as a consultant on school district governance and educational administration.

In this new role, the attorney must be an expert on government, understanding not only the functions of the legislative, judicial, and executive branches of local, state, and federal governments but also how these three branches impinge upon the governing and managing of school districts. For example, the policies enacted by boards of education have a legal character, and the effects of these policies on students and employees is subject to review by state courts and, in certain instances, the federal court system. A considerable amount of time and money may be saved by school boards if they consult their attorney in the creation of district policies.

Likewise, administrative procedures initiated by the superintendent and other school administrators in implementing the policies of the board could become more legally defensible if they are reviewed by the school attorney. Potential litigation can thus be minimized and administrators can be spared the unpleasant experience of being sued, which, of course, infringes upon their regular duties.

A final consideration about the school-board attorney involves the avenue of communication he or she has with the board of education. Difficulties have arisen in some school districts where the school attorney reported directly to school-board members. Because the superintendent is the chief executive officer of the school board, the attorney must operate in conjunction with and through the superintendent's office. The only exception to this occurs when the board of education needs the advice and counsel of an attorney in the selection or termination of the superintendent.

ANATOMY OF A LAWSUIT[4]

Although lawsuits do not follow a set pattern, there is enough commonality in civil litigation for us to be able to make a few general observations.

A lawsuit is initiated when a person or persons files a petition with a court, setting forth a cause that is an allegation. For example, parents could allege that faulty playground equipment caused their child to sustain a fall resulting in a broken leg. A summons is then delivered by the court to the defendant, who, in this case, might be the principal of the school, because that individual is responsible for periodically having the playground equipment at his or her building inspected for defects. The principal or his or her attorney will be required to appear in court on a given date for the purpose of answering the allegation set forth in the petition.

If the principal states that he or she is not guilty of negligence, the next step involves clarifying the allegation and the material facts that support it. This may be accomplished by the taking of depositions, a formal procedure in which the parties to the lawsuit are required to answer questions posed by the respective attorneys. Written questions may also be required in lieu of or in addition to the depositions.

If the principal's attorney believes that the material facts do not appear to support the allegation, a motion may be filed to dismiss the case. If the judge does not do so, a trial date is set. In civil cases involving such issues as tenure, a business contract, or a tort, the defendant usually has the option of a jury trial or of having the judge render the decision.

If the decision is rendered in favor of the plaintiff, a remedy is assessed against the defendant that may involve a number of options, depending on the nature of the case. In tenure cases, teachers may be reinstated in their teaching positions with the school district and be reimbursed for lost wages. In a tort liability case, the school district may be required to pay the hospital bill and other related expenses for the child who sustained an injury because of a fall from faulty playground equipment.

There are certain circumstances under which the decision in a trial may be appealed to a higher court for review. Most commonly this occurs when a question arises regarding the law or the impartiality of the trial proceedings. For example,

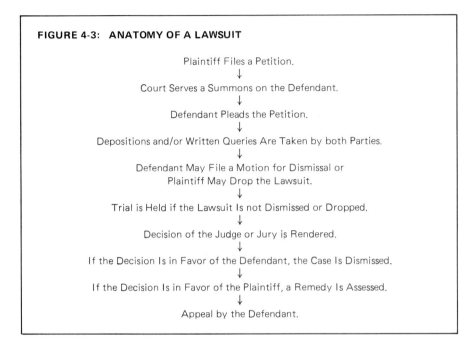

FIGURE 4-3: ANATOMY OF A LAWSUIT

Plaintiff Files a Petition.
↓
Court Serves a Summons on the Defendant.
↓
Defendant Pleads the Petition.
↓
Depositions and/or Written Queries Are Taken by both Parties.
↓
Defendant May File a Motion for Dismissal or
Plaintiff May Drop the Lawsuit.
↓
Trial is Held if the Lawsuit Is not Dismissed or Dropped.
↓
Decision of the Judge or Jury is Rendered.
↓
If the Decision Is in Favor of the Defendant, the Case Is Dismissed.
↓
If the Decision Is in Favor of the Plaintiff, a Remedy Is Assessed.
↓
Appeal by the Defendant.

a higher court could reverse the decision of a lower court because the higher court believes that the state statute on tenure was not properly applied by the lower court. In like manner, if the judge in the lower court demonstrated a prejudice against the defendant, a higher court might declare a mistrial.

The defendant in a civil lawsuit is determined by the nature of the case. In a tenure or teacher-contract dispute, the board of education as a corporate body is usually the defendant, because the school board approves all personnel contracts. In a tort case, an individual such as the building principal may be named as the defendant. A more common occurrence is for all individuals with line authority to be named as defendants. In the case of the child who was injured as a result of faulty playground equipment, the principal, assistant superintendent for elementary education, and superintendent may be named as defendants. However, the last decade has witnessed the inclusion of the board of education as a defendant in most lawsuits, including tort cases, because the board, as the legal governing body of the school district, has greater resources to pay damages. School districts, of course, carry various types of insurance that should cover the damages assessed in a lawsuit.

Conclusion

The purpose of this chapter is to heighten the sensitivity of administrators to the potential risk of being sued. It is in no way meant to be all-inclusive. However, it is hoped that administrators will use this material as a basis for further investigating their legal liability.

SUMMARY

School districts have experienced an increased involvement in lawsuits over the last decade. In addition, school administrators are far more vulnerable today to judicial review of their decisions than administrators of a decade ago. It is imperative, therefore, that school administrators have a rudimentary understanding of the American judicial system and are capable of making decisions that are legally defensible.

There are basically two systems of law. The first, civil law, attempts to establish all laws in the form of statutes enacted by a legislative body. The second is common law, which is used in England and was adopted in theory by most of the fifty states. Under this system, the decisions rendered by a court set a precedent to be followed by the court in dealing with future cases. The legal system in the United States is a mixture of both civil and common law.

There are three major elements that form the foundation of the American judicial system: constitutions, statutes, and court cases. Constitutions are bodies of precepts that provide the framework within which government carries out its duties. Statutes, or laws, are the enactments of legislative bodies. Common law emanates from the decisions of courts rather than from legislative bodies.

There are two additional sources of law that affect the practice of educational administration even though they are not traditionally considered primary: administrative law and attorney-general opinions. Administrative law consists of those regulations set forth by agencies established by Congress and state legislatures. In the absence of case law, the state attorney general may be requested to render an opinion on the interpretation of a certain statute.

Law may also be categorized according to the rights that are being protected. Civil law attempts to protect those rights existing between individuals, corporations, or between an individual and a corporation. Criminal law protects the rights of society.

The judicial system is composed of municipal, state, and federal courts. Most states have four categories of courts: courts of special jurisdiction, circuit courts, courts of appeal, and supreme courts. Similarly, there are four types of federal courts: special jurisdiction courts, district courts, the United States Court of Appeals, and the United States Supreme Court.

Our American judicial system also preserves the concept of equity. The state circuit and United States district courts may handle both law and equity issues. Certain issues are traditionally tried in equity, the most common being injunctions.

Tort litigation has become a serious issue for boards of education over the last decade. A tort is a civil wrong committed against a person or a person's property, and may fall into one of three categories: intentional, absolute liability, and negligence. Negligence involves conduct falling below an established standard that results in an injury to another person or persons. If the plaintiff receives a favorable judgment in a tort case involving an injury, the defendant will usually be required to pay the costs incurred as a result of the injury. If it can be demonstrated in court that a person deliberately caused the injury, punitive damages may also be levied by the court.

The last ten to fifteen years have ushered in a set of circumstances that require school attorneys to have competencies beyond the technical skills necessary to handle litigation. Today, school attorneys must also be counselors to boards of education and administrators regarding school district governance and administration.

Litigation does not follow a pattern. However, civil lawsuits are similar enough to allow administrators to make general observations that should be helpful as they administer the affairs of their schools and districts.

IMPLICATIONS FOR EDUCATIONAL ADMINISTRATORS

This discussion of legal liability has five implications for educational administrators.

First, ignorance of state and federal legislation and court decisions is no excuse for initiating administrative procedures that are in conflict with such legislation and case law.

Second, school administrators should, therefore, attend workshops, seminars, and convention programs dealing with legal issues. State school administrator associations and the American Association of School Administrators have convention programs and offer other services to administrators that address the legal implications of school administration.

Third, the superintendent of schools and central-office staff should keep the board of education informed about relevant state and federal legislation and court decisions. The school attorney will be a valuable resource in fulfilling this responsibility.

Fourth, school administrators must be active in promoting state and federal legislation that supports the educational goals of public education.

Fifth, it is imperative that school administrators be protected through errors-and-omissions liability insurance.

SELECTED BIBLIOGRAPHY

ALEXANDER, KERN, RAY CORNS, and WALTER McCANN, *Public School Law: Cases and Materials.* St. Paul, Minn.: West Publishing Co., 1969.
—— , *1975 Supplement to Public School Law: Cases and Materials.* St. Paul, Minn.: West Publishing Co., 1975.
BOLMEIER, EDWARD C., *The School in the Legal Structure,* American School Law Series. Cincinnati: The W. H. Anderson Co., 1968.
HAZARD, WILLIAM R., *Education and the Law* (2nd ed.). New York: The Free Press, 1978.
MORRIS, ARVAL A., *The Constitution and American Education.* St. Paul, Minn.: West Publishing Co., 1974.
REZNY, ARTHUR A., *A Schoolman in the Law Library* (2nd ed.). Danville, Ill.: The Interstate Printers and Publishers, Inc., 1968.

NOTES

1. Kern Alexander, Ray Corns, and Walter McCann, *Public School Law: Cases and Materials* (St. Paul: West Publishing Co., 1969), p. 9.

2. Ibid, p. 10.

3. Edward C. Bolmeier, *The School in the Legal Structure* (Cincinnati: The W. H. Anderson Company, 1968), p. 110.

4. Ronald W. Rebore, *Personnel Administration in Education: A Management Approach* (Englewood Cliffs, N.J.: Prentice-Hall, Inc., 1982), p. 324.

5

The Role and Function of the Superintendent of Schools

No position within the educational profession has received more attention in the news media over the past decade than the superintendency. "The job is much more political than ever before" appears to be the reason there is such tremendous turn-over among superintendents; it rivals that among baseball managers.[1] Declining enrollment, teacher layoffs, dwindling financial resources, labor-union strikes, and falling achievement-test scores constitute some of the major problems facing contemporary public schools. The individual who is often singled out as contributing to these problems rather than solving them is the superintendent of schools. He or she becomes the target for criticism when the real culprits are too elusive to be found.

The quality of the relationship that exists between a board of education and the superintendent will directly affect the quality of education received by the children and youth in the district's schools. A good board of education will demand a good superintendent of schools. This may also be reciprocal. The school community will, over time, be able to perceive the school board's attitude toward the superintendent, and the superintendent may influence the community's perception about individual board members. Thus, it is critical for the superintendent to establish a good working relationship with the school board, which will enhance rather than detract from the district's function, to educate children.

This chapter addresses a number of key issues concerning the superintendency that should help to delineate its function. First, the job description for the superintendency should clarify the relationship of the superintendent to the school board and the other administrators, teachers, and staff members. Second, the board of education from time to time will be required to hire a superintendent of schools. If improperly handled, this could result in the selection of an individual who does not meet the needs of a specific school system. Third, the school board must create a compensation plan for the superintendent that will reasonably reward performance and become an incentive for a good superintendent to remain with the district. Fourth, the board of education must establish an evaluation process that will continuously monitor the superintendent's performance and insure that the school community has the kind of leadership necessary to meet the challenges it faces.

JOB DESCRIPTION FOR THE SUPERINTENDENT OF SCHOOLS

Job Summary

The superintendent of schools is the chief executive officer of the board of education. As such, he or she is responsible for establishing and maintaining an effective two-way communication system between all levels of the school district.

Organizational Relationship

The superintendent has a line relationship with all school personnel and employees—the assistant superintendents, director of affirmative action, and director of community relations all report directly to him or her. It is to these assistants that the everyday operations of the school system are delegated by the superintendent.

The superintendent is responsible and reports directly to the board of education.

Organizational Tasks

The superintendent of schools acts as the chief advisor to the school board on all matters that affect the school system. Thus, the superintendent is responsible for providing the board with reports, data, and information that will help the school-board members make decisions. The superintendent should initiate such reports and information not only at the request of the board but also when he or she perceives that such information is necessary for the effective governance of the school district.

The superintendent of schools is the chief executive officer of the school board and is responsible for implementing its policy decisions. In this capacity, the superintendent is responsible for the following:

1. Formulating and recommending policies to be adopted by the board of education.
2. Establishing administrative rules and regulations necessary to carry out the policy decisions of the board of education.
3. Preparing and submitting an annual budget to the board of education.
4. Directing the expending of the approved budget in accordance with school-board policies.
5. Recommending all candidates for employment to the board of education.
6. Formulating and administering a program of supervision for the instructional process.
7. Submitting an annual report to the board of education regarding the operations of the school system.

The superintendent of schools is also responsible for assuming a leadership role with professional educators, not only within the school system, but at the state and national level as well. This will help the superintendent to be informed about current issues in education, which in turn should be communicated to the board of education and the school community.

Job Requirements

In terms of education and experience, the superintendent of schools should possess:

Appropriate state administrator certification.
A doctorate in educational administration.
Formal course work in the areas of curriculum, finance, school law, public relations, personnel administration, and central-office administration.
Experience as a superintendent of schools or as a central-office administrator in a school system of comparable size.

It is important to point out that this job description clearly defines the superintendent as the chief executive officer of the school board, not the head teacher, lead administrator or instructional leader of the school district. He or she is first and foremost the chief executive officer of the board. This is not to imply that the superintendent should not be an instructional leader, or be identified with the teaching and administrative staff. However, to avoid the confusion that exists on the part of some educators and school-board members who make a dichotomy between the superintendent and the school board it is critical to understand that the superintendent performs a function integral to governance.

SELECTING AND HIRING A SUPERINTENDENT OF SCHOOLS

There are nine steps that, if followed by a board of education, will result in the selection of a superintendent who has a reasonable probability of being successful in a given school district. This is, of course, the major purpose of all personnel-selection processes: to minimize the possibility of hiring the wrong person and to maximize the district's potential to attract highly qualified applicants. Some school boards have, in many cases, used haphazard and ineffective methods of choosing the educational leader for the district. The following steps will provide a model that can be adapted to a particular school district and will increase both the tenure and effectiveness of superintendents.

Step 1: Appoint a Selection Committee

The school board should begin the process of selecting a superintendent by appointing a committee that will be charged with monitoring the entire process, recruiting and screening candidates, and recommending several individuals to the board of education for final selection.

The committee should consist of several board members, teacher representatives, parents, secondary school students, central-office and building level administrators, other community representatives, and classified employees. It is important to have a committee that is not so large as to nullify its effectiveness but is large enough to be truly representative of the entire school community. Each segment of that community should recommend representatives to the school board for appointment to the committee. For example, the various teacher organizations and unions should recommend their representatives, the PTA should recommend the parent representatives, and the high school student council should recommend the student representatives to the school board.

It is common practice for the school board to hire outside consultants to assist in recruiting and screening applicants; these assistants may be a superintendent from another school district, a professor from a school of education, or a professional consultant. Sometimes school boards use consultants in lieu of a committee. These individuals are charged with seeking input from various segments of the school community before making recommendations to the school board.

Myron Lieberman warns: "No shortage of ways exists to manipulate a list of finalists to make sure one of the consultant's favored candidates gets the job."[2] In order to insure against this and other abuse, he makes the following suggestions:

1. Make sure you don't pay for busy work. Have a clear idea of what the board wants, and get right to the point with the consultant. Debate his qualifications on your time, not his.

2. Try to employ consultants whose chief or only business is personnel selection, or whose other activities suggest few or no conflict-of-interest problems.

3. If the consultant's billing is on a per diem basis, define what a day's work is, and have the consultant list the number of days worked. Also make sure the consultant is willing to sign a statement affirming that he is not billing the board for time or work allocated to any other employee.

4. Have the consultant state any financial or professional relationship with any of the candidates submitted to the school board for selection. If you are asked to hire the consultant's brother-in-law, you ought to know about the relationship.[3]

Outside consultants can be very helpful, and the possibility of abuse will be minimized if the consultant works with and supports a selection committee. The primary responsibility of a consultant should be to educate and advise the selection committee about how to perform its responsibilities, as outlined in the following steps.

Step 2: Establish a Budget for the Selection Process

The board of education must recognize that selecting and hiring a superintendent can be a very expensive process. The school board should decide on a reasonable dollar amount that will get the job done but will not become an embarrassment to the board.

The cost of printing a recruitment brochure and application forms along with postage to mail these items to applicants is a minor expense, as is the cost of advertising the position in professional journals and local newspapers. All these expenses combined might cost one to two thousand dollars.

The real expense comes from transporting and housing finalists coming to be interviewed by the selection committee and the school board. Some school boards will also want all or a few of their members to travel to the finalists' home school districts for the purpose of interviewing colleagues, parents, and students there.

The assistance of a consultant will be an added expense, which can be very costly, depending on the scope of the consultant's responsibilities.

A rule of thumb in establishing a budget for the selection process is that the total cost should not exceed one-third of the anticipated first year's salary for the newly-hired superintendent. If the school board expects to offer the chosen finalist between fifty and sixty thousand dollars, the total cost for the selection process should not exceed twenty thousand dollars.

Step 3: Establish a Calendar for the Selection Process

A detailed calendar should be established by the board of education so that the selection committee will understand the time constraints under which it will function. Such a calendar can also designate responsibilities, which should insure the timely selection of a superintendent. Table 5-1 presents a model calendar of events and activities that addresses the major considerations in the selection process. This model calls for the selection to be completed within six months. Because of the importance of the superintendency, it is necessary for the school board to establish a time period that will enhance rather than hinder the process. It is questionable whether an effective selection can be made in less than six months.

Step 4: Identify Qualifications for the Superintendency and Selection Criteria

There are several reasons for identifying desired qualifications and establishing selection criteria. This information (1) should be included in the recruitment

TABLE 5-1   Calendar of Events and Activities

MONTHS	ACTIVITY	RESPONSIBILITY
1st	Appointment of a selection committee	Board of Education
	Advertise, accept, and evaluate proposals from potential consultants	Board of Education
2nd	Hire a consultant or consultant firm	Board of Education
	Initial discussions concerning the philosophy, process, and procedures for selecting a superintendent	Board of Education Selection Committee Consultant
	Begin to identify qualifications for the superintendency and selection criteria	Selection Committee Consultant
	Begin to develop a recruitment brochure and an application form	Selection Committee
3rd	Have recruitment brochures and application forms printed	Consultant
	Approval of qualifications and selection criteria	Board of Education
	Establish a deadline for receiving applications	Selection Committee Consultant
	Advertise position vacancy in professional journals, association bulletins, and newspapers	Consultant
4th	Initial screening of applicants against qualifications	Selection Committee Consultant
5th	Final screening of applicants, planning for interviews of top 5–10 candidates	Board of Education Selection Committee Consultant
	Investigating credentials and references of top 5–10 candidates	Board of Education Consultant
6th	Interviewing top 5–10 candidates	Board of Education Selection Committee
	Recommendation of top 3 candidates to the school board	Selection Committee
	Visiting the home school districts of the top 3 candidates by a committee of the school board	Board of Education
	Notify selected candidate, negotiate contract, and establish transition-period activities	Board of Education Candidate
	Notify unsuccessful candidates and school committees, identifying the successful candidate	Board of Education Consultant

brochure, (2) will facilitate the work of the selection committee and consultant in screening applicants, and (3) will insure the objectivity of the selection process.

The following qualities identify appropriate qualifications for the contemporary superintendency.

1. *Leadership.* He (or she, in all references) inspires teamwork, maintains high morale, directs the school system toward given objectives, and helps others grow on the job. The community sees the superintendent as an educational leader, and the superintendent raises community expectations of its schools.

2. *Scholarship.* He is scholarly and analytical but not pedantic; he is widely read and understands the need for empirical support for recommendations; he keeps abreast of current educational trends.

3. *Judgment.* The superintendent's actions and decisions reflect knowledge and use of common sense.

4. *Alertness.* The superintendent is intellectually and intuitively able to interpret and respond effectively to new conditions, situations, problems and opportunities as they arise.

5. *Initiative.* He can originate and/or develop ideas and "sell" them to board and staff. In the language of the early Sixties, he's a self-starter.

6. *Cooperation.* He has the ability and desire to work with others in a team situation; authority, role and power are not his paramount considerations.

7. *Drive.* The superintendent's continuing urge is to improve the educational program without frightening others.

8. *Self-confidence.* He's self-reliant and tactful.

9. *Communications.* The superintendent expresses himself clearly and concisely as a writer and speaker.

10. *Flexibility.* He adapts to new situations and does not regard his own opinion as inviolate.

11. *Stability.* The superintendent remains calm and poised under pressure; he appreciates but is not bound by tradition and custom.

12. *Reliability.* He performs according to promise on matters within his control.[4]

These abstract qualities can then be translated into specific qualifications, as outlined in Appendix A, Model Recruitment Brochure for the Position of Superintendent of Schools. Successful experience and expertise in financial management, human relations, curriculum development, program planning, personnel management, and public relations are a few of the qualifications necessary for the superintendency. Each of the identified qualifications can then be weighted or ranked by the selection committee and consultant, from the most important to the least important. In essence, these become the selection criteria, which will be compared against the credentials submitted by interested candidates.

It is the responsibility of the board of education to give final approval to the qualifications and selection criteria recommended by the consultant and the selection committee.

Step 5: Develop a Recruitment Brochure and an Application Form

The recruitment brochure in Appendix A can serve as a model for a selection committee and consultant as they proceed with the very important task of developing a brochure. This brochure provides potential candidates with extensive information, enabling them to better ascertain if they wish to apply for the position and whether they possess the minimal requirements.

The format for such a brochure will vary, but certain information is usually provided. The most important includes the announcement of the vacancy, the procedure for applying, a description of qualifications, information about the community served by the school district, and data about the district, which normally includes financial, personnel, and curricular information.

The recruitment brochure and application form should be mailed to individuals inquiring about the position.

Applications for positions are generally of two types. The first emphasizes detailed and extensive factual information about the individual, with little or no attention given to the person's attitudes, opinions, and values. The second, conversely, emphasizes the applicant's attitudes, opinions, and values and asks for little factual information.

It is more appropriate to utilize the application form to ascertain the objective qualifications of potential candidates and to use the interview to obtain an understanding of the candidates' attitudes, opinions, and values. Body language and an applicant's manner of addressing questions dealing with such issues as values can better assess these intangibles than the written word, which can be calculated. Thus, application forms such as the one in Appendix B, requesting detailed factual information, are more helpful to a selection committee and consultant. The model application in Appendix B also incorporates those features that will insure that the application forms meet affirmative action and equal employment opportunity requirements consistent with current legislation and legal decisions.

The basic principle in constructing application forms is to ask only for information you need to know. Most information requested on applications falls under one of the following headings: personal data, education and professional information, work experience, and references. Such information should be sufficient to screen out those applicants who do not meet minimal qualifications. It is the responsibility of the selection committee and consultant to construct the application form or to choose one that has proven an effective screening instrument.

Step 6: Advertise the Vacant Position

The search for a new superintendent must not be limited to the local community or state in which the school district is located. Rather, national advertising will give talented individuals across the country an opportunity to become candidates, which in turn will increase the school board's chances of hiring a good educational executive. Many professional administrator associations have job bulletins, which will prove to be a valuable source of applicants. In addition, the vacancy should be announced in all major professional journals, in national and local newspapers, and at the placement offices of major universities with nationally renowned schools of education. The consultant is usually charged with writing and placing the announcement.

Step 7: Screen Applicants

The selection committee and consultant must carefully screen all the applications that have been received by the deadline specified in the announcement. The screening process involves comparing the information on the application forms with the selection criteria in order to find the five to ten most-qualified candidates.

The selection committee and consultant should then meet with the school board and report on the screening process, indicating the number of applications received and outlining how the screening was conducted, along with giving any additional information requested by the board. The consultant can then plan and initiate a schedule in which the school board and selection committee can interview the candidates.

Step 8: Interview Candidates

The school board and selection committee should separately interview the top five to ten candidates. Four areas should be addressed in the interviews: (1) the applicant's opinions on the relationship between the school board and the superintendent, particularly in regard to policy and administrative matters; (2) the applicant's views on current issues in public education; (3) the applicant's opinions on managing the curriculum, personnel, community, and pupil relations; and (4) the applicant's understanding of public school finance.

Some school boards and selection committees tape-record the interviews so that they can later be studied and compared in greater depth. Finally, the selection committee should recommend three candidates to the school board. Of course, the board is in no way obligated to accept this recommendation, and may find none of the candidates recommended satisfactory. This is most unlikely, but it is for this reason that both the school board and selection committee should interview the candidates.

Step 9: Hire the Best Candidate

It is a common practice for the school board or a committee of board members to visit the home school districts of the finalists. The colleagues, students, parents, and other individuals in the school districts can be questioned by the board members about the abilities and performance of each finalist.

The consultant, under the direction of the school board, can at this time begin to verify the credentials of the finalists and to contact the references given on the applications.

Once a decision is reached, the successful candidate should meet with the entire board to negotiate a contract. The board of education should, at this time, communicate with the school community about the newly-hired superintendent. The board of education or consultant is responsible at this point for notifying all applicants that the position has been filled and by whom.

COMPENSATING THE SUPERINTENDENT OF SCHOOLS

Compensation includes such fringe benefits as multiple forms of insurance and, in some cases, an expense account and the use of a district-owned automobile. The compensation package developed by a given board of education should be defensible. In other words, the superintendent of schools should be compensated in a manner that is suitable, considering the school district and the community.

Gathering data from neighboring school districts, from municipal governments, and from private institutions such as hospitals will help a school board assess the appropriateness of its compensation plan for the district's superintendent. It is obvious that the financial condition of the school district will also have a significant effect upon the ability of the district to compensate the superintendent in a manner comparable to that given the chief executive officers of other school districts and comparable to similar positions in the community. It is most unlikely that a school district will attract and be able to retain a qualified superintendent if the compensation package is not comparable at least to other school districts in the region.

The major component of the compensation package is, of course, wages. It is common practice also to offer the superintendent the following types of insurance: major medical and hospitalization, dental, term life, errors and omissions liability, accidental death and disability, and annuity programs. Some states have mandatory retirement programs, which must be paid into by the superindendent and the school district. Offering some of these insurance coverages to the family of the superintendent is also a common practice, especially major medical, hospitalization, and dental insurance.

It has become more common within the last five years to help pay the moving expenses for a new superintendent living outside the immediate region. The use of a district-owned automobile and an expense account, along with the payment of membership dues in professional associations, are typical fringe benefits in medium- and large-sized school districts. Attendance at state and national conferences, workshops, and conventions is important in order to keep the superintendent informed about current educational problems and issues. Therefore, the expenses incurred in attending these meetings are also usually paid by the school district.

It is important for the superintendent to request that the school board put the components of the compensation package in writing, in the form of a contract. Many school boards include only the wages and neglect to include the fringe benefits in the superintendent's contract.

The contract should also serve as a communications tool between the superintendent and school board, addressing such items as (1) the authority and responsibilities of the superintendent, (2) an evaluation procedure along with a due-process clause, and (3) a procedure to renegotiate the contract.

It is most appropriate to offer the superintendent a multiple-year contract, usually for three to five years, depending upon state statutes and local practices. The ability of a newly-hired superintendent to make significant changes in school district operations will require a minimum of three years.

EVALUATING THE PERFORMANCE
OF THE SUPERINTENDENT OF SCHOOLS

More than at any other time in the history of public education, the superintendent of schools today has come under attack for a variety of problems and issues. Pressures upon superintendents that may ultimately cause many good individuals to reconsider their careers in education are summarized below.

1. Too many school board members want to run the show. They overlook the specialized training and competencies that superintendents have for handling administrative tasks effectively and efficiently.
2. Budget cuts, accompanied by shrinking tax revenues, are increasing with alarming frequency. This places the superintendent in a pincer. On the one hand he searches his imagination for ways to find more money; on the other he turns a sympathetic ear toward staff who complain chronically about the skimpiness of their work environment.
3. It's becoming more hectic to coordinate information in order to complete reports on deadline.
4. Dissension among school board members gobbles time and causes serious, sometimes lasting rifts.
5. Declining enrollments are matched inversely with increasing expenditures, mainly because operating costs are rising fast—as are installations of new programs mandated by law or public fancy.
6. Taxpayers are starting to sour on teachers; it's those strike patterns and salary demands that annoy.
7. Union tactics are growing stronger and more refined.
8. Special interest groups make more noise these days, and they're gaining substantial headway in their appeals.
9. Students have changed—admittedly, an understatement. Their altered philosophies and actions place particular strains on families and schools; this trend is reflected by the upsurge in the number of school vandalism and discipline cases.
10. The news media want headlines. Their banners—whether oral or written—often convey an erroneous impression of what actually is happening in schools.
11. The processing of local, state, and federal regulations creates carloads of paperwork and weekends of overtime.[5]

However, the demise of many superintendents stems from a lack of sophisticated communication and organizational skills needed to work effectively with school boards, the staff, and the community. David Fultz lists some of the major reasons superintendents lose their jobs that exemplify these professional and personal deficiencies.

1. *Weak rapport with the board poses the biggest threat.* This is a reiteration of the central point mentioned earlier, but it bears repeating because of its importance. So: A school board is irked most by refusal of an administrator to seek and accept criticism; by his lack of demonstrated effort to work in

harmony with the board; by his failure to support board policy and follow the board's instructions.

2. *Lack of staff respect bodes ill for the superintendent.* The school administrator needs firm backing from his staff. Without such respect and support his days are numbered, because he has no cohesion within his chain of command to get work accomplished on time and in good order.

3. *Poor communications up and down the line present problems.* Failure to make himself understood readily and clearly puts an administrator at a serious disadvantage. It places him in a particularly precarious position with school personnel, board members, and the community. In addition, he must make an effort to excel at public speaking, since this counts as an art of communication and figures prominently in his survival, according to findings that were included in the study.[6]

Some superintendents fail to recognize the imminence of their demise, which in many cases stems from the fact that they are not formally evaluated by their respective boards of education. The decline in effective performance often occurs at an accelerated rate and may catch the superintendent off guard. As alluded to earlier, an evaluation process with due-process considerations should be written into the superintendent's contract. The purpose of the selection process for hiring a superintendent and the reason for developing an attractive compensation plan is to hire and retain the best possible educational executive for the school district. Consequently, the evaluation process should encourage the professional growth of the superintendent and provide that individual with the opportunity to stay with the school district as long as he or she is an effective administrator. Considering the turmoil in public education, stability in leadership will help alleviate numerous problems and issues that have become common in so many districts.

The superintendent is responsible for developing the evaluation process, which includes the following steps:

First, the superintendent annually prepares a list of objectives to be accomplished during the school year. Such a list might include improving his or her understanding of the community or might center on improving communications with the school board. These objectives, along with all aspects of the evaluation procedure, should be submitted to the board for consideration at an executive session. A list of five to ten objectives each year would be reasonable.

Next, the superintendent develops a plan of action to carry out these objectives. A plan to improve communications with the school board might include sending the board members a weekly newsletter outlining current issues and problems facing the district. This would help board members answer the questions of parents, students, employees, and other citizens as they are encountered, without first contacting the superintendent, a procedure that would help board members to demonstrate to their constituents that they are on top of problems. This plan of action is normally presented to the school board along with the objectives.

Third, the superintendent prepares an interim report to the board, which is usually made approximately halfway through the school year, on his or her progress in meeting the approved objectives. At this time, revisions and/or new objectives and action plans can be developed.

Finally, the superintendent prepares a self-evaluation report on how effectively the objectives have been met and submits supportive documentation to the school board. The board is responsible for assessing the results and will begin to prepare a written evaluation of the superintendent's performance in meeting the objectives along with suggestions on how to improve it and on the type of objectives that should be developed by the superintendent for the next year.

If the superintendent's performance is unacceptable, the school board should include in the evaluation report a specific list of deficiencies, a time limit regarding expected improvement, and suggestions about how to improve performance. The board of education, of course, always has the option not to renew the superintendent's contract, but the foregoing due-process procedure is a humane way of handling deficiencies in performance. It is also mandatory if the board decides that the superintendent's poor performance necessitates termination of employment.

This, of course, is not the only way to evaluate the performance of the superintendent. A number of more objective methods have been developed by the American Association of School Administrators. Appendix C presents one of many alternatives to the approach described in this chapter.

SUMMARY

No position within the educational profession has received more attention in the news media over the past decade than the superintendency. Declining enrollments, teacher layoffs, dwindling financial resources, labor strikes, and falling achievement-test scores by pupils constitute some of the major problems facing contemporary public schools. The superintendent of schools is often the target of criticism as a school district deals with these problems.

The quality of relationship that exists between a board of education and the superintendent will directly affect the quality of education received by those enrolled in the district's schools. The following responsibilities of the school board form the basis upon which an effective working relationship will function between the board and the superintendent: selecting and hiring a superintendent, creating a compensation package for the superintendent, and establishing an evaluation process for measuring the superintendent's performance.

There are nine steps in an effective selection process for hiring a superintendent of schools:

Step One	Appoint a selection committee.
Step Two	Establish a budget for the selection process.
Step Three	Establish a calendar for the selection process.
Step Four	Identify qualifications for the superintendency and selection criteria.

Step Five	Develop a recruitment brochure and application form.
Step Six	Advertise the position.
Step Seven	Screen applicants.
Step Eight	Interview candidates.
Step Nine	Hire the best candidate.

Compensation constitutes more than salary, and includes many types of fringe benefits. The compensation package created by the school board for the superintendent should be suitable to the school district and the community. One method of insuring suitability is for the school board to gather data on the compensation packages offered by neighboring school boards to their respective superintendents. In addition, the compensation packages offered to local hospital administrators and the chief executives of municipal governments also provide useful comparative data.

It is a common practice in many districts to offer the superintendent multiple types of insurance, in addition to the use of a district-owned automobile and an expense account in some medium- to large-sized school districts. Many districts also pay the moving expenses for a newly-hired superintendent living outside the district's immediate region. Paying the superintendent's membership dues to professional associations and the expenses of attending conferences, conventions, and workshops are also common fringe benefits.

It is important for the board of education to put in writing components of the superintendent's compensation package, in the form of a contract. Multiple-year contracts are appropriate, and should set forth the scope of the superintendent's authority and responsibility and procedures to evaluate performance, for due process, and to renegotiate the contract.

The demise of many superintendents stems from a lack of sophisticated communication and organizational skills needed to work effectively with school boards, the staff, and the community. Many superintendents fail to recognize the imminence of their demise. A formal evaluation of the superintendent's performance by his or her respective school board would provide the superintendent with the opportunity to grow professionally, which, in turn, would help the school system to progress.

There are four steps in the evaluation process: the superintendent (1) prepares a list of objectives, (2) develops a plan of action for carrying out the objectives, (3) prepares an interim report on progress in meeting the objectives, and (4) prepares a self-evaluation report on how effectively those objectives have been met.

If the superintendent's performance is unacceptable, the school board should include in its written assessment of the superintendent's performance a specific list of deficiencies, a time limit on when improvement is expected, and suggestions on how to improve performance.

IMPLICATIONS FOR EDUCATIONAL ADMINISTRATORS

This presentation concerning the superintendent of schools has two implications for educational administrators.

First, the effectiveness of a school system is directly influenced by the professional performance of the superintendent of schools, because he or she is the individual who sets the tone and atmosphere within which all other administrators will function. Educational administrators should encourage the most qualified members of their ranks to become candidates for superintendency vacancies. Those who have the qualifications to be candidates should feel that their responsibility to the profession warrants applying for such positions.

Second, the board of education is responsible for establishing a selection process, devising a compensation package, and developing an evaluation procedure that will insure that the best qualified individual is hired and retained as the superintendent of schools. The administrators in a school district should ask the board of education to have administrators represented on a selection committee when the board initiates the search for a superintendent.

SELECTED BIBLIOGRAPHY

AMERICAN ASSOCIATION OF SCHOOL ADMINISTRATORS, *Compensating the Superintendent.* Arlington, Va.: The Association, 1979.
—— , *Evaluating the Superintendent.* Arlington, Va.: The Association, 1980.
—— , *Selecting a Superintendent.* Arlington, Va.: The Association, 1979.
—— , *The Superintendent's Contract.* Arlington, Va.: The Association, 1979.
EISENBERGER, KATHERINE E., "How Much Should You Involve Your Community in Picking Your Next Superintendent?" *The American School Board Journal,* 162, no. 11 (November 1975), 33-34, 64.
FOWLER, CHARLES W., "How to Let (and Help) Your Superintendent be a SUPERintendent," *The American School Board Journal,* 162, no. 9 (September 1975), 19-22.
—— , "Twelve Earmarks of a SUPERintendent," *The American School Board Journal,* 162, no. 9 (September 1975), 19-22.
FULTZ, DAVID A., "Eight Ways Superintendents Lose Their Jobs," *The American School Board Journal,* 163, no. 9 (September 1976), 42, 51.
HELLER, MEL, "Subjectivity Beats Objectivity Every Time in Picking a Superintendent," *The American School Board Journal,* 162, no. 10 (November 1975), 32-33.
JOHNSON, CARROL F., "How to Select a Superintendent," *The American School Board Journal,* 162, no. 11 (November 1975), 27-33.
LIEBERMAN, MYRON, "The Case against Letting a Moonlighting Professor Pick Your Next Superintendent," *The American School Board Journal,* 165, no. 4 (April 1978), 35-36, 46.
ROELLE, ROBERT J., and ROBERT L. MONKS, "A Six-Point Plan for Evaluating Your Superintendent," *The American School Board Journal,* 165, no. 9 (September 1978), 36-37.

NOTES

1. National School Public Relations Association, *Education USA,* 22, no. 47 (July 21, 1980), 347.

2. Myron Lieberman, "The Case Against Letting a Moonlighting Professor Pick Your Next Superintendent," *The American School Board Journal,* 165, no. 4 (April 1978), 36.

3. Ibid, p. 46.

4. Charles W. Fowler, "Twelve Earmarks of a SUPERintendent," *The American School Board Journal,* 162, no. 9 (September 1975), 20.

5. Edward P. Travers, "Eleven Pressures That Squeeze Superintendents," *The American School Board Journal,* 165, no. 2 (February 1978), 43.

6. David A. Fultz, "Eight Ways Superintendents Lose Their Jobs," *The American School Board Journal,* 163, no. 9 (September 1976), 42.

APPENDIX A:
MODEL RECRUITMENT BROCHURE
FOR THE POSITION OF SUPERINTENDENT OF SCHOOLS

POSITION AVAILABLE
SUPERINTENDENT OF SCHOOLS
GOODVILLE SCHOOL DISTRICT

An Equal Opportunity and
Affirmative Action Employer

Announcement of Vacancy

The Board of Education of Goodville School District is seeking a superintendent of schools.

The salary of the superintendent selected will be determined by his or her professonal preparation and by his successful experience in educational administration, as well as by other qualifications.

Professional assistance for the initial screening of applicants has been acquired. It is a special consultant committee consisting of:

A superintendent for a neighboring school district

Dean, School of Education, Goodville University

All letters of application, nominations, inquiries, credentials, and copies of legal proof of administrative qualifications should be mailed to the President of the Goodville School Board.

To receive consideration, applicants must submit the following by January 1:

1. A formal letter of application indicating a desire to be a candidate for the position.
2. Up-to-date confidential credentials from your university, up-to-date resume, and a listing of your educational accomplishments by title.
3. Submit legal proof or other evidence showing qualification to be a superintendent.

The Person Needed

The Board of Education of the Goodville School District and the community it serves are committed to the continuing development of high-quality schools. They are seeking a person who has had successful administrative experience as a superintendent or a central-office position with comparable responsibilities. The superintendent they are seeking should have a thorough understanding of and a prime interest in public school education; a concern for the welfare and motivation of students is of prime importance. By experience, knowledge, and stature, he or she must reflect credit upon himself or herself and upon the district.

The superintendent selected must be skilled in providing educational leadership, and must be a goals-oriented educator with proven success in the continuing development of teamwork among the administrative/teaching staff, board of education and community.

Although no candidate can be expected to meet all qualifications fully, preference will be given to candidates with capabilities and/or potential as follows:

Successful experience in financial management, budgeting, and fiscal responsibility, with the ability to evaluate the financial status of the district and establish a management plan based on projected future revenues and curriculum programs.

In the area of human relations, the ability to work with the public, students, and staff, thus leading to good school-personnel management. This process should also include evaluation of and in-service training for staff.

An "educational manager" who delegates responsibility, yet maintains accountability, through the management-team concept.

Ability to exercise leadership and decision making in selection and implementation of educational priorities—a person with a realistic and responsible educational philosophy.

The ability to objectively select, evaluate, and assign staff.

Willingness to help formulate, review, and effectively carry out board policies, and to communicate and relate openly and honestly with the board of education, keeping members informed about issues, proposals, and developments within the district.

Ability to maintain desired student behavioral patterns.

Successful administrative experience in a comparable district.

A strong academic background in and a constant evaluator and planner of proper curriculum and programs; one who constantly keeps in view the present and future financial status of the district.

Skillful educational leadership in the development of long- and short-range district goals and objectives—a "management-type" educational leader.

The Community

The Goodville School District is currently serving the educational needs of nearly 22,000 residents in a geographic area of great growth potential. It covers 90 square miles—one of the largest school districts in the state.

The district is highly diverse, with a rich cultural background and diversity of life-styles. Approximately 25 percent of our residents live in a rural setting, with the remaining 75 percent located in suburban communities. Our district is enriched by a broad range of ethnic and racial groups.

Since we are located just 15 miles south of a major metropolitan area, many of our residents can conveniently commute to and from the city to work.

Local employment continues to be enhanced by the growth of many industrial parks.

As a microcosm of life-styles and cultures, the school district encourages unique opportunities in community living and education.

It is a district of parks, churches, schools, shopping centers, and excellent recreational facilities. We are served by two local newspapers, in addition to a large daily newspaper and a local radio station. Goodville State University is located in our district, and many other colleges and universities are within driving distance.

The Schools

The Goodville School District enrolls approximately 5,000 pupils in K-12. Additionally, the district offers services for preschool, special education, and adult education programs. Currently there are four K-5 elementary schools; one middle school, 6-8; and one high school, fully accredited and recognized. The school system is supported by approximately 275 certified staff and 100 support personnel.

Concern and support for the teaching of basic skills has been recognized equally by the school board and administrative staff. In addition to basic skills, however, many innovative services and programs are provided to teachers, parents, and students. An alternative education program for secondary students is recognized as the finest in the county. In addition, major steps have been taken toward identification of pupils' educative styles and the proper mode of instruction to enhance these styles.

Extracurricular activities have always been a vital part of the school curriculum. The district prides itself on its athletic programs and its band and orchestra activities for both boys and girls.

Philosophy of the Board of Education

Policy-making body. The Board of Education is primarily a policy-making body and shall maintain an organization to operate the schools efficiently with the funds available, shall constantly strive to improve all phases of the school system, and shall keep the public well informed of its problems.

Education of the child. The Board believes that the education of each child in the district is the heart of the entire school operation, and that administration, business management, building construction, and all other services should be appraised in terms of their contributions to the progress of instruction. It shall be the goal of the Board to offer each child the opportunity to develop his or her potentialities to the maximum. It shall be the intention of the Board of Education to provide for equality of educational opportunity for all children regardless of race, color, creed, or national origin.

Staff

Administration:
    1 Superintendent
    2 Assistant Superintendents

          6 Principals
          3 Assistant Principals
          1 Business Manager/Treasurer
Staff:
          243 Classroom Teachers
          7 Counselors
          6 Library/AV Specialists
          5 Special Education Classroom Teachers
          4 Nurses
          5 Learning Disabilities Classroom Teachers
          5 Speech Correctionists
          20 Paraprofessionals
          35 Secretarial/Clerical Employees
          45 Custodial/Maintenance Employees
Student Composition:
          500 Black, Non-Hispanic
          120 Hispanic
          30 Asian or Pacific Islander
          2 American Indian or Alaskan Native
          4,348 White, Non-Hispanic
          5,000 Total Enrollment
Supportive Programs:
          60 Title I

Financial Data

Assessed Value	$235,000,000.00
Tax Rate	$4.50
Bonded Indebtedness	$4,000,000.00
Budget Expenditures	$15,000,000.00

APPENDIX B:
SAMPLE APPLICATION

APPLICATON FOR THE POSITION OF SUPERINTENDENT OF SCHOOLS
GOODVILLE SCHOOL DISTRICT

Date _____

I. Personal Information:

Name _____
           Last   First   Middle

Date of birth _____ Age _____

Social Security Number _____

Present Address _____
                             Street

_____ Phone _____
    City   State   Zip

General condition of health _____

Are you willing to take a physical exam? _____

Community Activities and Honors _____

_____

II. Professional Information:

List Administrator Certificates held _____

_____

Membership in professional organizations _____

_____

List your professional achievements, awards, and honors _____

_____

_____

III. Teaching and/or administrative experience:

List experience in chronological order (starting with first position held), and account for each school year since you began your professional career.

No. Yrs. Exp.	Inclusive Dates From To	Name of School District	Number of Pupils in District	Location City or County	State	Position	Annual Salary

In your present position list the number of people responsible to you _____

Indicate the annual budget for the school district in which you are currently employed _____

List the major accomplishments you have achieved in your present position _____

IV. Educational Information:

Total Number of Hours to Date _____ Undergraduate _____

Graduate _____ Major _____ Number of Major Hours _____

Minor _____ Number of Minor Hours _____

Name of Instit. Attended	State	Dates Attended		Time in Yrs. and Fractions of Yrs.	Graduation		Subjects	
		From	To		Date	Degree	Major	Minor
A. College or Univ.								
B. Graduate Work								
C. Additional Education								

V. Professional References:

Location of confidential placement file _____

It is the responsibility of the applicant to have his/her placement file and college/university transcripts sent to the school district.

Please list three people who have firsthand knowledge of your work performance. Have these individuals send a letter of reference to the President of the School Board. One of the three reference letters must be from your current or last immediate supervisor.

Name	Official Position	Present Address

Use the back of the application to provide additional information to the school board about your qualifications for the superintendency.

Signature: _____

APPENDIX C:
BOARD'S ASSESSMENT OF SUPERINTENDENT'S PERFORMANCE

Superintendent's Name: _____ School Year: _____

Directions: After individual board members have discussed superintendent's performance in each of the following Major Areas of Responsibility, complete an assessment reflecting the composite judgment of the board. Check the appropriate symbol in the assessment column. If some aspect of the superintendent's performance merits particular praise or if improvement is needed in some area, indicate it in the appropriate Comments space below.

Assessment Symbols:

> C—Commendation (Performance exceeded expectations)
> M—Performance Met Expectations
> NI—Needs Improvement (Needs explanation in Comments section.)

Major Areas of Responsibility

	OVERALL ASSESSMENT		
	C	M	NI
100—Board Relations			
200—Community-Public Relations			
300—Staff Personnel Management			
400—Business and Fiscal Management			
500—Facilities Management			
600—Curriculum and Instructional Management			
700—Management of Student Services			
800—Comprehensive Planning			
900—Professional and Personal Development			

Comments (Use this space to cite praiseworthy achievements and/or areas that should be improved):

Signatures (Superintendent's signature does not necessarily indicate concurrence):

President of Board _____ Date _____

Superintendent _____ Date _____

RESPONSIBILITY CRITERIA

100—Board Relations
     101—Preparation of reports and materials for the board
     102—Presentation of reports to board
     103—Recommendations to the board
     104—Responding to requests from the board
     105—Keeping the board informed about operations in district
     106—Implementation of board actions
     107—Other (specify)
200—Community-Public Relations
     201—Contacts with media
     202—Interpreting district problems and concerns to community and public
     203—Interpreting the educational program to the community
     204—Responding to concerns of community
     205—Periodic communications (publications, reports, newsletters, etc.) to community
     206—Other (specify)
300—Staff Personnel Management
     301—Employment of personnel
     302—Utilization of employed personnel
     303—Administration of personnel policies and procedures
     304—Administration of salary and benefits program
     305—Direction of employee relations program
     306—Administration of personnel evaluation programs
     307—Other (specify)
400—Business and Fiscal Management
     401—Determination of educational needs of district
     402—Forecasting financial requirements
     403—Budget preparation
     404—Management of budget allocations
     405—Cost accounting and cost effectiveness management
     406—Procurement of equipment, materials, supplies, etc.
     407—Financial reporting
     408—Other (specify)
500—Facilities Management
     501—Planning and providing physical facilities
     502—Management of maintenance of buildings and grounds
     503—Providing for the security and safety of personnel and property
     504—Planning for and managing modifications, renovations, expansions, and discontinuation of facilities
     505—Directing the utilization of facilities
     506—Other (specify)
600—Curriculum and Instructional Management
     601—Keeping current with trends and developments in curriculum and instruction

602—Initiating new programs, modifying existing ones, and discontinuing others
603—Direction of supervision of instruction
604—Monitoring effectiveness of instructional programs
605—Assessment of effectiveness of instructional programs
606—Planning and direction of in-service and staff development
607—Management of state and federal programs and projects
608—Other (specify)
700—Management of Student Services
701—Providing comprehensive student personnel services
702—Management of enrollment and attendance policies and procedures
703—Management of student behavior and discipline
704—Providing for health and safety of students
705—Liaison with community agencies concerned with student services
706—Other (specify)
800—Comprehensive Planning
801—Developing and implementing short- and long-range planning
802—Developing management systems (example: MBO)
803—Training administrators and supervisors in planning
804—Accountability procedures
805—Evaluation of planning results
806—Other (specify)
900—Professional and Personal Development
901—Keeping self current professionally
902—Representing district at local, state, and national meetings of interest to education
903—Contributions to profession by writing and speaking
904—Participation in local, state and national professional organizations
905—Other (specify)

SOURCE: American Association of School Administrators, *Evaluating the Superintendent* (Arlington, Va.: The Association, 1980), pp. 42, 43, 44, 49, 50.

6

*The legal and political structure of public education
clearly attests that the mission of the public schools
is derived from the people. Therefore, ongoing
communication should occur between the school
and the public.*

The Role and Function of the Community-Relations Administrator

All public and even private institutions and organizations have relations with their various publics. Thus, the school district's administrative staff must develop an approach for addressing the various publics who make up the school district. The options are few, but their impact can have a significant effect on how well the school district is able to achieve its primary objective, educating students. Basically, the administration can choose to let its relationship with the community develop by chance or develop a systematic, organized, ongoing program.

The basic principle upon which an effective community-relations program must rest is the public character of the schools. The schools are brought into existence, financed, and governed by the people. The state legislature, which is composed of the elected representatives of the people, creates school districts by and through the laws of the state; school districts receive their revenue through taxation; and school board members are elected by the people.

Because of this basic principle, a community-relations program in the public sector is viewed very differently than a public-relations program in the business community. A community-relations program is not a "sell job" or a "publicity program" aimed at developing an image of the district that will bring a favorable response from the community. Rather, a community-relations program is an ongoing, two-way communications program between the school district and the various publics that make up the school community. This community must not be limited to students and parents but must include senior citizens, parochial-school parents, public officials, taxpayers without children, and so on. In effect, all those who reside within the boundaries of the school district are its constituents and must be part of community-relations activities.

Even from a pragmatic perspective, the effects of a good school district are invaluable for all citizens. It is sometimes said, for example, that people without children in school have no need of the services provided by the public schools; therefore, they often vote against tax levies and/or bond issues. One common response to such a statement is to note that our future physicians, architects, artists, entrepreneurs, political officials, and the like will be educated in our public schools. In a much more immediate way, a good school district will increase real estate values by 10 percent. Ask any real estate agent to verify this! From a philosophical point of view, the public schools are the vehicle by which our American culture and heritage are transmitted from generation to generation. In fact, our free, republican form of government and capitalist economy are dependent upon the quality of education received by our citizens.

Therefore, two-way communication is the foundation of an effective community-relations program. All publics must be included, the various segments of the community must understand the importance of the public school, and the input of all publics must be sought by the board of education and administration.

STEPS IN DEVELOPING A COMMUNITY-RELATIONS PROGRAM

Creating a Community-Relations Policy

The effective development of all programs in a school district is dependent upon the support of the school board. In fact, because it is the governing body in the district, no program has official status until it is authorized by the board of education. The traditional method by which the board mandates and sanctions programs is through the creation of policies that set the direction and determine the scope of the programs.

Many formats can be used by a school board in the development of policies; these were addressed in Chapter 2. It is critical, however, that board-of-education policies be put in writing and made known to the public. Having appropriate written policies is not a major problem. There are many model community-relations policies available from state school board associations and from the National School Boards Association that can be used in developing individual district policies. Figure 6-1 represents a sample policy that would meet the needs of most school districts.

The major problem is making the public aware of the community-relations posture of the school board. This is generally accomplished not by distributing

**FIGURE 6-1: SAMPLE BOARD OF EDUCATION
SCHOOL-COMMUNITY RELATIONS POLICY**

The Board recognizes that intelligent, informed public support of the school district is dependent upon full knowledge, understanding, and participation in the efforts, goals, problems, and programs of the district. The Board is also aware of its responsibility to provide the public with information and opportunities leading to participation in the establishment of programs and policies.

Therefore, the Board and the school district will strive:

To develop intelligent citizen understanding of the school system in all aspects of its operation.

To determine how the public feels about the school system and what it wishes the school system to accomplish.

To develop citizen understanding of the need for adequate financial support for a quality educational program.

To foster public understanding of the need for constructive change and solicit public advice on how to achieve educational goals.

To earn the good will, respect, and confidence of the public with regard to school staff and services.

To promote a genuine spirit of cooperation between the Board and community in sharing leadership for the improvement of the community.

The achievement of these goals requires that the Board and the staff, individually and collectively, express positive attitudes toward the district in their daily contacts with students, parents, patrons, and one another. They must also make a systematic, honest, and continuing effort to discover what the public thinks, what patrons want to know, and to interpret the district's programs, problems, and accomplishments to the public. Finally, they must take an active interest in the community, in working toward the improvement of both the educational programs and making the community a better place in which to live.

SOURCE: Missouri School Boards Association, *A Manual for Missouri School Board Members* (Columbia, Mo.: The Association, 1971), pp. F-10, F-11.

---

the policy statement, but, rather, through the activities of a community-relations program.

Establishing a Community-Relations Administrative Position

The second step in developing a community-relations program is to establish an administrative central-office position, usually called Director for Community Relations. This staff member should report directly to the superintendent of schools. Because the superintendent is the chief executive officer of the school board, it is important for the board as a whole and for individual board members to channel all official communications through the superintendent's office. At that point, the superintendent can inform the director for community relations about the issue to be communicated, and the director, in turn, can select the appropriate media for delivering the message to the public.

Most school districts with enrollments of three thousand or more students should employ a full-time director. If a district has more than ten thousand students, it will be necessary to establish a community-relations department and to employ a number of assistant directors.

Very small school districts and those faced with severe financial problems will have the same needs as other districts for the services of someone to direct their community-relations program. However, they will be forced to search for alternatives to the full-time director we have described. These alternatives include (1) assigning community-relations duties to an administrator with a communications background; (2) decreasing the teaching load of a teacher with a background in journalism, English, or communications in order to allow that person to assume some community-relations duties; (3) looking for someone in the community with public-relations skills or a newspaper reporter to volunteer some time or be hired part-time to work on community-relations tasks; (4) hiring a consulting firm to handle a limited number of community-relations duties.[1]

Learning About the School District Publics

A third step in developing a community-relations program is collecting data about the various publics that make up the constituents of a school district. Data about the community that are pertinent to a community-relations program include:

1. The needs and expectations of citizens in relation to the school district
2. The formal and informal power structures in the community
3. Immediate and long-term problems
4. Identifying the most appropriate channels of communicating with the public
5. Identifying groups and individuals who are friendly and unfriendly toward the school district.
6. Identifying the type and number of service and civic organizations in the community.[2]

A sociological survey of the community is the most appropriate vehicle for gathering these data. The survey should concentrate on customs, and traditions, population characteristics, economic conditions, leadership in the community, political structures, social issues, and communication channels.[3]

Conducting the research into these areas may involve a number of different techniques, for no single one will provide all the answers. Therefore, it is most advantageous to choose complementary approaches that will ultimately provide the school board with a total view of the community.

Some of the most common opinion research methods are: (1) forums and conferences, (2) advisory committees, (3) telephone surveys, (4) written questionnaires, and (5) direct interviews.[4]

The indirect power structure in a community should be mentioned here. The influence of the individuals who make up this group must not be underestimated by the board of education and school district administration. Unless these individuals are identified and dealt with, the best efforts of the board and administration are doomed to failure. Members of the indirect power structure in a community can influence political and economic decisions by reason of their financial, family, political, or labor connections. These individuals are usually intelligent people who possess genuine leadership abilities and are members of powerful clubs and organizations. They usually develop a system of rewards and punishments as the primary vehicle for wielding their influence. For example, those who make large financial contributions to political candidates generally have an opportunity to provide input that those politicians will consider before they make political decisions.

Developing Techniques for Communicating

The fourth step in developing a community-relations program is to identify and initiate appropriate techniques for communicating with various publics. Each school district will find that certain techniques are more effective than others for its particular community.

Printed materials.   The basic advantage to using publications is that detailed data and concepts become available to a large number of people at a minimal cost. Like all other methods of communicating, it is essential to identify the audience to be addressed by the various publications. A publication prepared for parents might have as an objective to increase parents' knowledge of education programs or to educate parents about selected school problems and issues. On the other hand, the objective of a publication aimed at the general public might be to inform citizens about the policies and practices of the school district or to thank individuals and groups for supporting the cause of public education.

The district newsletter, which is mailed to all citizens, perhaps on a monthly basis is commonly used. Another publication with across-the-board appeal is the superintendent's annual report, which highlights the accomplishments of the school district along with the financial condition of the district and objectives for the future. Figure 6-2 presents a listing of internal, external, and joint-purpose publications commonly employed by school districts. No one district, of course, will use all of these publications.

The press.   Newspapers play a significant role in the school district's community-relations program. They are widely read and provide the entire community with an ongoing account of those issues and problems facing both public education and specific school districts. It is, therefore, imperative that the director of community relations use the newspapers as a primary method of communication with the various publics in a school district.

The key to successful news coverage is the relationship that is developed by the director for community relations with the reporters who are assigned to your

FIGURE 6-2: TYPES OF PUBLICATIONS

Internal Publications

Employee Manual: To acquaint all employees with rules and regulations, district policies, etc.

Specialized Employee Manual: To familiarize special employee groups—secretaries, bus drivers, etc.—with the requirements of their job.

New Employee Bulletin: To help new employees adjust to their first weeks on the job.

Handbook for Substitutes: To inform substitute teachers of the required procedures.

Telephone Communications Bulletin: To assist secretaries and other employees in dealing with the public on the phone.

Student Handbook: To acquaint students with school rules and regulations.

Parent-Teacher Conference Booklet: To show teachers how to conduct a successful conference.

Resource Center Brochure: To let faculty and staff know what materials are available for their assistance.

Field Trip Booklet: To provide help to teachers and helping mothers on field trips.

Board Briefs: To inform faculty and staff of actions taken by the board at its meetings.

Pay Envelope Stuffer: To provide various informational items to employees when they receive their pay checks.

Curriculum Idea Exchange Bulletin: To familiarize teachers with successful teaching practices used by other district teachers.

Communications Guidebook: To inform staff members of the district's communications program and suggest how they might help.

Article Reprints: To keep employees informed of recent news and feature articles in local news media.

External Publications

Rumor Control Bulletin: To help quell rumors with facts. Sent to opinion leaders and key communicators.

Welcome Leaflet: To welcome new residents into the district with school facts and registration procedures.

Report Card Stuffers: To provide parents with information and special announcements.

Wallet-Size Calendar: To familiarize residents with important dates and vital school information.

Recruitment Brochure: To attract high quality faculty and administrators to the district.

Parent Handbook: To acquaint parents with important school information.

Guidance Booklet: To suggest to parents how to help children adjust to important educational periods in their lives.

Curriculum and Special Service Brochure: To explain to residents the various programs offered.

Work-Study Report: To familiarize prospective employers with the vocational and career oriented programs in the high school or vocational school.

Special Purpose Publications: To solve specific problems as they arise. This category might include a drug abuse booklet, a brochure on busing, etc.

Internal and External Publications

Annual Report: To acquaint the board, staff, and public with the district's efforts for the year.

Budget and Bond Issue Publications: To gain public and staff acceptance for budgets and building programs.

Facts and Figures Booklet: To provide in pocket-size format vital facts about the district.

SOURCE: Don Bagin, Frank Grazian, and Charles Harrison, "PR for School Board Members," *AASA Executive Handbook Series,* XIII (Arlington, Va.: American Association of School Administrators, 1976), 31–33.

school district. Reporters have a job to perform, which they will do with or without your help. It is obviously more productive to be of assistance to reporters, because you gain the opportunity to provide accurate information and an interpretation of data.

Almost every school activity or event will have some newsworthy aspects. The director for community relations must keep the press informed about upcoming events, organize information about them, and be willing to answer questions to clarify the information. News conferences are another vehicle for providing reporters with an opportunity to clarify issues and problems of interest to the community.

The cardinal principle in working with the press is *honesty.* Never try to mislead or interfere with the press. Be open with and available to reporters, and the school district will have a better chance of receiving good, accurate coverage. Figure 6-3 presents a number of tips that experience has proved are excellent guidelines in working with the press.

From time to time, a school district may receive radio and/or television coverage, especially when controversial issues are facing the school board, such as schools closing due to decreased pupil enrollment or when teachers are on strike. Of course, the same concepts and principles that pertain to relationships with the press are applicable to all members of the news media. The director for community relations must not neglect newscasters and interviewers when establishing those relationships that will allow for communication via radio and television.

In addition, the Federal Communications Commission, in licensing radio and television stations, usually requires all stations to devote some air time to public-service broadcasting. If a school district does not have a well-defined process for requesting coverage of school events and requesting appearances by board members, administrators, teachers, and staff members on public-service programs, the radio and television stations may overlook your district.

Special activities. Community relations is sometimes viewed narrowly to include only utilization of printed material and the news media. There are, however,

FIGURE 6-3:   DEALING WITH THE MEDIA

The amount and type of publicity you receive frequently will depend on your relations with the local media and how well you are able to meet their respective needs. "Media" generally is defined as newspapers (daily, bi-weekly, weekly, etc.), radio and television stations, and sometimes specialized publications such as magazines. Here are some suggestions for working with news media:

1. Maintain all elements of a professional relationship with the news media. Get to know your local editors and broadcast news directors. In a small town this will normally be a relatively simple procedure. In larger areas it is considerably more difficult but still well worth the effort.

2. Whenever possible, deliver news releases and other information to the media personally. This will permit you to get to know editors and news directors, building good rapport and credibility.

3. On the first visit, make an effort to sit down with the editor or news director and mutually decide on operating policy, preparpation of news stories, deadlines, types of photos needed, and other necessary information. From then on, a planned program for keeping on good terms with the news media is essential.

4. Learn as much as possible about the newspaper or broadcast facility, politically and philosophically. Get to know the personal idiosyncrasies of those you will be working with.

5. Know deadlines and be prompt in meeting them. Bring news items in advance. They will have a better chance of being used.

6. Use good glossy black and white photos with your news releases whenever possible. Articles with good accompanying pictures will get better use.

7. Be fair among the news media. Don't play favorites.

8. Be the only person from your group to contact the news media. Two people calling the same editor or news director will only cause confusion.

9. Try to understand the journalistic temperament. Like educators, they are professionals and should be treated as such. Qualities of candidness, frankness, honesty and openness will go far in establishing your credibility and in obtaining fair and accurate news coverage for your group. Don't try to "cover up" for the press. Stress the positive. Tell what's right with education. However, if a journalist asks a question about a "sticky" subject, give an honest answer. If you can't answer a question, send them to the person who can or the place where they can research the topic.

10. Respect the journalist's time, especially around deadlines.

11. Publicity is not news to a journalist. Therefore, don't ask for "publicity" about a given topic. Explain that you have some information and you think it might make a good story.

12. Keep in mind, members of the press are always invited guests. Never ask them to buy tickets or pay admission. Arrange a special press table for large events.

13. Use the telephone to report information that is extremely timely. When time or logistics do not permit you to take news releases to the media personally, it is acceptable to use the mail.

14. Write in journalistic style. If a story is not in journalistic style, it must have content that is extremely important or the editor will file it in the wastebasket. Stories written in journalistic style are many times set in type "as is." If the infor-

mation is not extremely important to the editor, it still may get into the paper because it took minimum effort to get it ready for print.

15. There are basically two kinds of stories—straight news and feature. Straight news answers who, what, when, where, why, and how. A feature gives the facts, but adds the human interest angle. Write simply. Use a minimum of adjectives and few superlatives.

16. Check facts, figures, dates, grammar, spelling, and titles in your stories. Be concise, clear, timely, and objective. Attribute subjective statements.

SOURCE: Missouri State Teacher's Association, *Tip Sheet* (Columbia, Mo.: The Association, 1981).

many different activities that can significantly benefit a community-relations program. This discussion will center on four publics and the kinds of activities that can be used with the publics for the purpose of community relations.

First, the public most important to a school district is the student body. The education of pupils enrolled in our schools constitutes the primary reason for a school district's existence. Many programs and activities geared toward student participation will enhance the instructional program and, at the same time, act as a community-relations vehicle. Student advisory committees, suggestion boxes, and student council activities are a case in point. Further, public performances by the music, drama, and forensic departments in addition to interscholastic sports demonstrate how well the school district has been able to develop the talents and skills of the students. Student newspapers and other student-generated publications will spread the word about the quality of the educational programs. Finally, alumni associations help to continue interest in and support for the school district.

Second, the parents are a vital source of support for the school district. Visits to the school and to classrooms, parent conferences with teachers, PTA and/or PTO organizations, room mothers, club booster organizations, and parent volunteer programs are examples of how parents can be brought into the schools. Such participation is certain to have a beneficial effect, in gaining the support of parents when a school district is faced with such issues as the financial support of public education or pupil discipline.

Third, school district employees can play a role in community relations, depending on how they interact with students, parents, citizens, and those who have a business relationship with the district. The school district, on the other hand, must demonstrate to employees that they are vital to it and are respected members of the staff. Internal advisory committees, recognition of accomplishments, functions, and internal publications help to get this message across not only to teachers and administrators, but also to cooks, custodians, secretaries, and the like.

Fourth, community groups can provide the school district administration with both input necessary to help evaluate the effectiveness of the community relations program and invaluable expertise. The citizens' advisory committee can be employed successfully by a school district to study such issues as school closings and attendance-area consolidation, the financial condition of the school district, and the need to upgrade the facilities. The more the involvement, the greater the support.

Almost every activity has a community-relations effect. How the administration handles a parental complaint, the appearance of the buildings, and even how the board meetings are conducted can generate negative or positive feelings about the school district.

Tax-levy and bond-issue campaigns. Economic conditions have caused many school districts to seek additional revenue through an increase in property taxes. Inflation and decreased federal and state revenues are the major factors that have created the need to cut back school district staff members and programs. When this retrenchment seriously affects the quality of education, often the only answer is to ask the taxpayers for more money. Tax-levy election campaigns have, therefore, become commonplace, but their success rate has been negligible.

Some school districts are also in need of new school buildings, renovating existing facilities, and/or making other buildings energy-efficient. Capital improvements are traditionally financed by issuing bonds for sale after gaining taxpayer approval.

The director for community relations is the administrator who has the primary responsibility for coordinating tax-levy and bond-issue election campaigns. Major aspects that need to be addressed include: determining the proposal, establishing a campaign strategy, timing the campaigns, financing the campaign, adopting a theme and slogan, establishing a speakers' bureau, absentee ballots, canvassing the school district, and election-day plans.

Evaluating the Community-Relations Program

The final step in developing a community-relations program is to evaluate its effectiveness. As with all school programs, there are two aspects to this process. First, an evaluation must be made, especially in the initial stages of development, concerning the organization and implementation of the program. This will provide feedback about the weaknesses and strengths of the program, which can be used by the superintendent and director for community relations to modify or change the program structure to more effectively accomplish its goals and objectives. The most common method of evaluating this aspect of the community relations program is through checklists and rating scales similar to the one developed by Thomas Colgate, reproduced in Figure 6-4. This instrument contains thirty-three items, each followed by a maximum point value. Various staff and board members will have the broad-based understanding about the program necessary to use this type of instrument. If an individual believes that the program does not meet the item completely, a lesser value than the maximum is awarded. The total points are applied to the table provided with the rating scale, and judgment can then be rendered about the community-relations program.

A second aspect of program evaluation concerns the outcome of the program.

FIGURE 6-4: COMMUNITY RELATIONS EVALUATION SURVEY

Directions: Appraise your district's efforts in each of the listed criteria. Each statement is followed by a maximum point value that may be awarded if your school district meets the statement completely. A value less than maximum may be awarded according to the extent that the statement is met. Place the appraisal points in the **points credited** column at far right.

APPRAISAL STATEMENT	MAXIMUM POINT VALUES	POINTS CREDITED
1. There *is* a definite planned program of public relations.	5.5	_____
2. Purposes of our public relations program have been discussed and approved by all members of the school board, administration, and faculty.	5	_____
3. School district advisory committee is used to plan public relations program for our district.	5.5	_____
4. Public relations program is evaluated regularly.	6	_____
5. Public relations program is conducted with dignity and aggressiveness.	6	_____
6. Public relations program involves as many people as possible.	5.5	_____
7. All school board members, top level administrators, department heads, faculty, and nonacademic staff contribute to our public relations program.	6	_____
8. Superintendent or an appointed specialist is responsible for our public relations program.		
9. Board and superintendent provide leadership and gear district or school policy toward good public relations.	6	_____
10. Board and superintendent provide clear lines of authority and responsibility for public relations procedures.	5.5	_____
11. Duties related to public relations are delegated in terms of functions and jobs to be done.	6	_____
12. Board and superintendent understand clearly the purposes and organization of public relations program for the district.	6	_____
13. Board and superintendent utilize guidance and assistance of central public relations office.	5.5	_____
14. Board and superintendent cooperate with the central public relations director.	6	_____
15. Central public relations department determines administrative channels for public relations release.	5.5	_____
16. A written statement of public relations policies is given to each departmental faculty and nonacademic staff.	5	_____

17. Faculty and nonacademic staff understand their roles in the public relations program of the school district.   5.5   _____
18. Each departmental faculty member shares responsibility for public relations program of the school district.   6   _____
19. Faculty promotes good public relations.   5.5   _____
20. Faculty members are active in professional organizations.   5.5   _____
21. There are good faculty-pupil relationships.   6   _____
22. All available media are used.   5.5   _____
23. Topics are treated honestly and fairly; exaggeration is avoided.   6   _____
24. The publics served by the school district are identified.   6   _____
25. Specific information is directed toward each public.   5.5   _____
26. Surveys are conducted regularly to accumulate information for public relations releases.   4.5   _____
27. Topics of human interest value are used for public relations releases.   4.5   _____
28. All information gathered is utilized.   5   _____
29. Superintendent makes full use of his annual report as a public relations instrument.   6   _____
30. There is a close working relationship between departmental faculty and over-all district faculty.   6   _____
31. Value of a sound educational program as a foundation for public relations program is understood.   6   _____
32. There are regular attempts to improve the educational program.   6   _____
33. Students in the educational programs exhibit favorable attitudes toward their respective programs.   5.5   _____

Perfect Total: 185.5   Your Total: _____

Sum up the points credited to obtain the total. Apply this total score to the empirical table below to rate your school district's public relations program.

POINTS CREDITED	RATING
0.0–26.5	NONEXISTENT—No actual program of effort.
27.0–53.0	VERY POOR—Bare minimum, insufficient program.
53.5–79.5	POOR—A weak, loose program.
80.0–106.0	FAIR—A moderate, admissible program.
106.5–132.5	GOOD—A sufficient, satisfactory program.
133.0–159.0	VERY GOOD—A truly beneficial program.
159.5–185.5	EXCELLENT—The best or superior type of program.

SOURCE: Thomas P. Colgate, "How Good Is Your District's Public Relations Program? Take This Test," *American School Board Journal* (April 1970), 8-10.

In other words, has the school district improved relations with its respective publics as a result of the community-relations program? This question is best answered by asking community members about their knowledge and understanding of, and feelings concerning, the school district. Some of the most common methods of gathering such data include: telephone surveys, questionnaires, and panel discussions, in addition to analyzing complaints and asking key members of the staff to elucidate their personal observations about the effectiveness of the program.

JOB DESCRIPTION OF THE DIRECTOR
FOR COMMUNITY RELATIONS

Job Summary

The director for community relations is responsible for the school district's internal and external communications programs. This includes establishment and maintenance of effective two-way communication between the various organizational levels, and the formulation, recommendation, and administration of the school district's community-relations program.

Organizational Relationship

The director for community relations has a line relationship with the superintendent of schools and reports directly to him or her. He or she serves as the chief adviser on community-relations matters and has a staff relationship with other administrative personnel and a cooperative professional relationship with instructional and nonadministrative personnel. Of course, the director for community relations has a line relationship with his or her immediate staff.

Organizational Tasks

The director for community relations is responsible for the following tasks:

1. Making all contacts with members of the press, television, and radio stations
2. Writing press releases
3. Directing tax-levy and bond-issue election campaigns
4. Creating staff-development programs for district employees concerning community-relations techniques
5. Assessing the attitudes of the various publics about school-related issues and programs
6. Coordinating the school district's photographic needs
7. Writing, editing, and producing staff and community newsletters and publications
8. Representing the superintendent of schools, as he or she directs, as liaison with service and civic groups.

Job Requirements

In terms of educational requirements, the director for community relations should possess:

Bachelor's degree (minimum) in Journalism or a related field such as Communications, Public Relations, or English.

A minimum of two years' experience in community relations with a public institution or experience with public relations in the private business sector.

Good human relations skills, be sensitive to individual needs, work well with details, and must be a self-starter.

SUMMARY

Public school districts, by reason of their mission and very existence, have relations with various publics. Therefore, a school district's administration can either choose to develop a systematic community-relations program or to let its relationship with the community develop by chance. The consequences of the latter position can have a devastating effect upon the success of a district in fulfilling its mandate to educate children.

The basic principle upon which an effective community-relations program must rest is that the schools are brought into existence by the people, governed by the people, and financed by the people. Therefore, two-way communication between the school district and its various publics is the foundation of a community-relations program.

Community relations is quite different from public relations in private business and industry. Rather than a selling job or publicity program, community relations is a method of communicating.

There are five steps in developing a community-relations program. First, the board of education should create a policy that will give the administration direction in managing a community-relations program and establish its scope. Second, a central-office administrative position should be established, usually entitled Director for Community Relations. This should be a position on the superintendent's staff. The director's job involves planning and directing the school district's internal and external communications program. Third, the director for community relations should initiate a procedure for collecting data about the various publics that make up the school district. A sociological survey is the most appropriate vehicle for gathering these data. Fourth, from these data, the director of community relations can identify and implement techniques for communicating with the various publics. Using printed materials and working with and through the news media are significant methods of communicating. The final step is to evaluate the effectiveness of the program, in terms of its organization as well as its outcome.

IMPLICATIONS FOR EDUCATIONAL ADMINISTRATORS

Three implications for educational administrators emerge from this treatment of community relations.

First, administrators must become aware of the impact that good community relations has on carrying out the school district's mission.

Second, the superintendent of schools should work with the school board to create a community-relations policy and establish the central-office staff position of Director for Community Relations. This individual should be responsible for planning and implementing an ongoing, two-way communications program with the various publics in the school district. It is important for the school board and superintendent of schools to channel all official communications through the community-relations office.

Third, in addition to attending PTA/PTO meetings, school administrators should make themselves available to participate in community-relations activities such as speakers' bureaus, community forums, and service-club activities.

SELECTED BIBLIOGRAPHY

BAGIN, DON, FRANK GRAZIAN, and CHARLES H. HARRISON, *School Communications: Ideas That Work*. New York: McGraw-Hill Book Company, 1974.
——— , "PR for School Board Members," *AASA Executive Handbook Series*, Vol. VIII. Arlington, Va.: American Association of School Administrators, 1976.
CARITHERS, POLLY, *How to Conduct Low Cost Surveys: A Profile of School Survey and Polling Procedures*. Arlington, Va.: National School Public Relations Association, 1973.
KINDRED, LESLIE W., DON BAGIN, and DONALD R. GALLAGHER, *The School and Community Relations*. Englewood Cliffs, N.J.: Prentice-Hall, Inc., 1976.
SUMPTION, MERLE R., and YVONNE ENGSTROM, *School-Community Relations: A New Approach*. New York: McGraw-Hill Book Company, 1966.

NOTES

1. Don Bagin, Frank Grazian, and Charles Harrison, "PR for School Board Members," *AASA Executive Handbook Series* (Arlington, Va.: American Association of School Administrators, 1976), VIII, 13–14.
2. Leslie W. Kindred, Don Bagin, and Donald R. Gallagher, *The School and Community Relations* (Englewood Cliffs, N.J.: Prentice-Hall, Inc., 1976), p. 35.
3. Ibid., p. 36.
4. Ibid., p. 48.

7

Because school districts perform business functions common to private corporations, school districts should incorporate into their operations those business practices which have proven effective in the private sector.

The Role and Function of the Administrative Support Services Administrator

It may sound trite to say that everything has a price tag, but the truth of this statement is evident as school districts go through the painful process of cutting programs, activities, and personnel because of rising costs and shrinking balances and revenues. Thus, the importance of administrative operations and activities in school districts has been dramatically heightened over the last decade. Operational practices common to the business and industrial community have been adopted by school districts as they attempt to become more accountable to taxpayers. Such practices can help to demonstrate that the school board, along with the administration, is providing educational programs that are meeting the needs of the children and are still cost-effective.

The educational program is supported by two other programs that are usually managed from the business office, pupil transportation and food service. In addition, all the programs of the school district are enhanced by data processing. This chapter, therefore, deals with the operations of the administrative-services department as it manages the financial and auxiliary programs of the school system.

JOB DESCRIPTION FOR THE ASSISTANT SUPERINTENDENT FOR ADMINISTRATIVE SERVICES

Job Summary

The assistant superintendent for administrative services is responsible for the school district's administrative-support program. This includes the establishment and maintenance of effective two-way communication between the various organizational levels; and the formulation, recommendation, and management of the school district's administrative support-services policies.

Organizational Relationship

The assistant superintendent for administrative services has a line relationship with the superintendent of schools and reports directly to him or her. This individual serves as the chief advisor on administrative-services matters and has a staff relationship with other administrative personnel. The assistant superintendent for administrative services has a line relationship with and supervises his or her immediate staff, which includes the business manager, director of buildings and grounds, director of transportation, and director of food service.

Organizational Tasks

The assistant superintendent for administrative services is directly responsible for establishing and managing those processes, procedures, and techniques necessary to carry out the school district's administrative-support functions, which include:

Budgeting
Purchasing
Payroll Management
Investing School District Funds
Accounting
Auditing
Banking
Data Processing
Inventory Control
Warehousing and Distribution
Food Service
Transportation
Insurance Management
Facility Maintenance Management
Facility Custodial Services Management

**FIGURE 7-1: ORGANIZATIONAL CHART OF AN ADMINISTRATIVE SERVICES
DEPARTMENT**

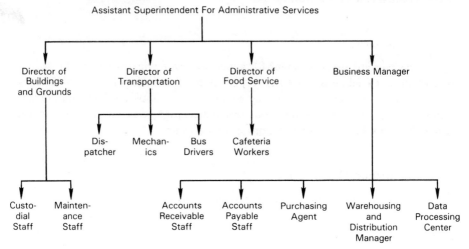

Job Requirements

In terms of education and experience, the assistant superintendent for administrative services should possess:

Appropriate state administrator certification

A doctorate in educational administration

Formal course work in the areas of school law, finance, accounting, facility management, school-district administration, and data processing.

Five years' experience in a central-office administrative position.

Many other job descriptions for administrators working in the administrative support-services department could have been included here. The assistant superintendent for administrative services is the executive administrator responsible for the overall management of the administrative-services department, which is the only job description included because of the nature of this presentation. Figure 7-1 presents an organizational chart for an administrative-services department, outlining a number of these other positions.

SCHOOL DISTRICT FINANCIAL MANAGEMENT

The financial management of school districts includes many interrelated functions, which ultimately demonstrate that the revenue and expenditures of the district support the best educational program possible, given the fiscal resources available.

The major components of financial management include: (1) budgeting procedures; (2) financial-accounting procedures; (3) purchasing, warehousing, and distribution procedures; (4) investing procedures; and (5) auditing procedures.

Constructing the School District's Budget

The school district's budget is a plan for delivering the educational program and for projecting the district's revenues and expenditures that will support this program. The last twenty years have seen many management innovations that addressed the budget construction process, including Program Planning Budgeting System (PPBS), Zero Based Budgeting, and Performance Budgeting. These and many other approaches to budgeting are seeking a process that can serve as a useful management tool while providing the school board with a method for prioritizing needs. No system of budgeting will satisfy all the needs of a school district. Modifications will, therefore, be introduced that address the particular character of the school district.

There are four basic steps to an effective budgeting process. First, the budget is not an entity unto itself but rather a vehicle for accomplishing a purpose. The purpose of a school district is to educate children. This purpose is further refined by establishing goals and objectives. The board of education is responsible for setting these goals after having received input from teachers, administrators, parents, students, and other school district patrons.

Second, these goals and objectives can then be translated into a curriculum and, finally, set forth in terms of educational requirements. The professional staff under the direction of the superintendent of schools can begin the process of attaching dollar amounts to educational requirements. For example, a school board may believe that a secondary-school remedial-reading program is needed. The superintendent, along with the building principals, teachers, and other central-office administrators, will be required to perform an assessment of needs for the purpose of identifying the number of secondary-school children who require remedial reading. The superintendent and staff should then proceed to calculate the personnel, supplies, material, and other costs that will be needed to introduce this program effectively.

Third, the business manager will be required to make a revenue projection, which will be combined into a budgetary document that also sets forth the proposed expenditures that operationalize the goals of the school district.

Finally, the board of education must approve the budget. The school board can certainly challenge the budget submitted by the assistant superintendent for administrative services before approving it. In fact, the school board may wish to make actual changes in the expenditures, based upon its perception of the district's needs.

Budgeting is a continual process, which will probably begin in January each year for the next fiscal year and will terminate with budget revisions' being approved by the school board in December. The fiscal year in most states begins on July 1 and ends on June 30.

The actual budget document may take various forms but should include the following: (1) a budget message by the assistant superintendent for administrative services describing the important features of the budget and major changes from last year's budget; (2) projected revenue from all local, state, and federal sources, with a comparison of revenue for the last two years listed by fund and source; (3) proposed expenditures for each program, with a comparison of expenditures from the last two years listed by fund, object, and function; (4) the amount needed to pay the principal and interest for the redemption of the school district's bonds maturing during the fiscal year; and (5) a budget summary.

FIGURE 7-2: STATEMENT OF GOALS FOR A SCHOOL DISTRICT BUDGET

Foreign Language Program for Elementary and Middle-School Students:

To work with each child to help him learn the basic intellectual skills of linguistic flexibility in thought and tongue through a foreign language.

To develop fluency in a foreign language to such a degree that an eighth-grade student could visit a foreign country and understand and converse with a native speaker on an elementary level, comprehend partially a publication in that language, and make himself understood in writing and language.

Objective Statement and Evaluative Criteria

At the End of Eighth Grade:

That 75% of the students be able to communicate in the language of instruction at an elementary level with a native speaker of that language as evaluated by the teacher.

That 50% of the students should be able to read a magazine or newspaper article in language of instruction and state briefly in that language a brief summary of the article as measured by the teacher.

That 80% of the students will be able to write with ease a dictation exercise in Spanish or French based on previously studied material from the text based on a teacher-prepared dictation test.

That 75% of the students will give a five-minute oral report in the language of instruction on a topic of the student's choice to the teacher's satisfaction.

That 70% of the students will pass the vocabulary test provided in the text with 85% accuracy.

Program Description

The foreign language program covers the four years of fifth, sixth, seventh, and eighth grades in the subjects of Spanish and French. There are six teachers in the program, three in each subject. The fifth and sixth grade students receive 150 minutes of instruction weekly, the seventh-grade students 135 minutes of instruction weekly, and the eighth-grade students 110 minutes of instruction weekly. Instruction is provided in a classroom environment using textbooks, and includes both written and oral work. Teachers may use other instructional materials such as songs, plays, magazines, newspapers, flashcards, etc. A language laboratory is available containing records, tape recorders, and filmstrips.

SOURCE: National School Public Relations Association, *PPBS and the School: New System Promotes Efficiency, Accountability* (Arlington, Va.: The Association, 1972), p. 21.

FIGURE 7-3: CATEGORIES OF EXPENDITURES FOR A SCHOOL DISTRICT BUDGET

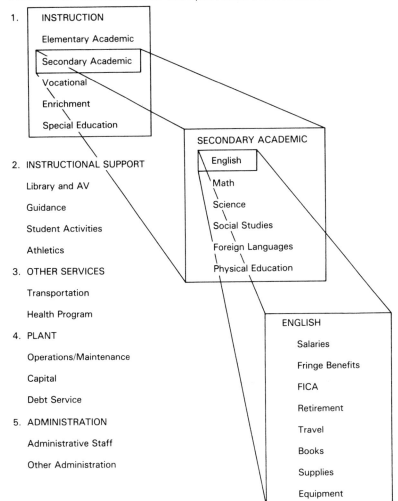

SOURCE: National School Public Relations Association, *PPBS and the School: New System Promotes Efficiency, Accountability* (Arlington, Va.: The Association, 1972), p. 18.

Figure 7-2 demonstrates program goals established by a school district, which could be used by the administration in constructing the budget. Figure 7-3 sets forth how programs are broken down to identify total costs.

Financial Accounting

Financial record keeping is an absolute necessity for the effective functioning of every school district. Such records set forth the financial transactions of the school district, which form the basis upon which sound financial decisions can be made by the board of education.

The systematic keeping of financial transactions also allows one to trace individual items transacted and identify what was expended, for what purpose, and by whom, in addition to supplying information about the source of the money used for the expenditure. Such data may be needed when unanticipated requests are made by the school board, the public, the superintendent, or another government agency.

While financial record keeping is usually referred to as bookkeeping, this is only one phase of a complete system, which involves the recording, classifying, summarizing, interpreting, and reporting of results of the school district's financial activities. This system is commonly known as *accounting.*

Because education is big business, it involves numerous financial transactions, which occur on a daily basis. Therefore, a sound accounting system must provide the school board and administration with the following services: (1) an accurate record of the details involved in business transactions; (2) safeguards assuring that the fiscal resources of the school district are used for their designated purpose; (3) data that can be used by the school board and administration in planning; (4) information to local, state, and national government agencies about the financial operations of the school district; it must also (5) facilitate an analysis of how the administration expended the school district's monies in relation to the educational goals inherent in the approved budget.

In addition, an adequate accounting system must meet certain minimal criteria commonly accepted by those in the profession. First, it must have a reasonable degree of internal controls that will continuously insure the accuracy of transactions recorded. Second, the accounting system should be consistent with generally accepted governmental accounting principles, incorporating uniformity of procedures and the use of standard terminology and definitions. Third, it should be simple and flexible, not only to accommodate new programs with minimal disruption but also to help the school's administration. Fourth, it should be a double-entry, accrual, and encumbrance system.[1] Fifth, as a governmental accounting system, transactions should be recorded in the following dimensions in order to answer certain critical questions: What was purchased? (object); from what financial source? (fund); for what purpose? (function); for which school? (operational unit); to provide what specific service? (program).

An accrual and encumbrance accounting system provides a school district with a truly realistic appraisal of its fiscal position. When the financial books are opened, the appropriated budget approved by the school board is recorded. When purchase orders are signed and contracts approved, the dollar amount is entered in an encumbrance column. When payments are made, the dollar amount is charged to a payment column and the original amount encumbered is credited to encumbrances. This procedure gives a continual analysis of the progress in expending the budget, because the budget balance is the difference between the appropriations minus expenditures and encumbrances.[2]

Not only can the accounting system thus provide the administration and school board with a summary of revenues and budget balances on a continual basis, but such data can also be formalized into a *budget operating summary* and presented to the board at its regular monthly business meeting.

Purchasing, Warehousing, and Distribution of Supplies and Materials

School districts are important buyers and consumers, because the supplies, materials, and services they need cost millions of dollars. Such large expenditures demand the creation of board policies and administrative procedures that will insure the proper purchase and use of these goods.

Central-office purchasing division. In a medium- to large-sized school district, purchasing will probably be made by a central-office division of the administrative services instead of by individual schools. The building principals should be charged with filling out purchase requisitions or supply lists. Administrative procedures should designate how items will be purchased. For example, items costing up to five hundred dollars may be purchased through catalogue pricing, those costing up to two thousand dollars by taking quotations from vendors, and anything over two thousand dollars by formal bidding after specifications have been made. A cooperative purchasing program is a method by which a number of school districts pool their supply, equipment, furniture, and other material needs in order to get lower prices because they are ordering so much. Copies of the purchase orders should be sent to the accounts payable and warehouse division.

Warehouse and distribution division. This division of the administrative-services department in a centralized system receives items from vendors. Smaller school districts may have items delivered directly to the schools. The employees in the warehouse and distribution division are usually charged with checking the shipping manifest against the items, affixing identification tags to them, preparing an asset inventory card, sending a copy of the purchase order marked "received" to the accounts payable division, and delivering the items to the schools or warehousing them for future distribution when requisitioned by memo.

Accounts payable division. When this division receives a copy of the purchase order from the warehouse and distribution division, it is coded per the chart of accounts. The purchase order is checked against the invoice, and entries are posted in the accounting books. Finally, disbursement checks are prepared and, after approval by the board of education at its next meeting, mailed to the vendor.

This process will insure that items are purchased in the most cost-effective manner and, further, that they are inventoried and used for their designated purpose.

Investing School District Funds

Most school districts can significantly increase their nontaxable revenue by developing an investment plan that places idle cash in interest-bearing money instruments. The budgeting process and accounting system can provide the assistant superintendent for administrative services with data concerning the cash-flow requirements of the school district. Comparing revenue receipts and expenditures on a monthly basis with previous years is especially helpful in projecting cash needs.

The following strategies can be used to increase the amount of cash available for investments: (1) depositing cash receipts on the day they are received, (2) deferring the payment of bills as late as possible under established terms, (3) deferring the payment of payroll withholdings as long as possible under the law, (4) using warrants instead of checks because funds are not needed until the warrant is presented back to the issuer for payment, (5) using bank floats, which is the difference between cash balances shown on the books and cash actually in the bank, (6) developing a program that spreads purchases over the entire year rather than making large ones once or twice annually.

Each investment transaction has three actions: purchasing the instrument, cashing in or selling the instrument, and receiving the interest. There are also three considerations when investing idle cash: the risk, yield, and liquidity of the instrument. Yield, of course, refers to the rate of return on the investment, and liquidity refers to when the instrument can be sold or cashed in without a penalty. Most states have statutes that limit the type of investments that can be made with public funds. Speculation in the stock market is usually prohibited, and most investments are limited to money instruments such as treasury bills, repurchase agreements, and certificates of deposit.

Balancing the risk, yield, and liquidity of investments is a judgment call, which requires a great deal of expertise on the part of the business manager. The banking and other financial institutions in our country have experienced consider-

FIGURE 7-4: RISK SCALE

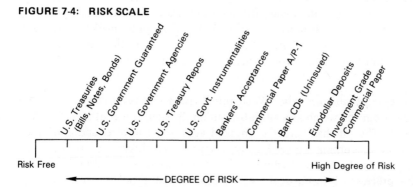

SOURCE: Municipal Finance Officers Association, *A Public Investor's Guide to Money Market Instruments* (Chicago: The Association, 1982), p. 78.

FIGURE 7-5: LIQUIDITY SCALE

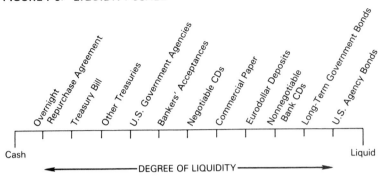

SOURCE: Municipal Finance Officers Association, *A Public Investor's Guide to Money Market Instruments* (Chicago: The Association, 1982), p. 79.

able regulatory changes over the past five years and may do so in the future, making the task of investing even more difficult.

Figures 7-4 and 7-5 exhibit the relationship between risk and liquidity, which should help to clarify these two concepts. The board of education must be informed on a regular basis—probably at its monthly business meeting—of details concerning the school district's investments.

Auditing School District Accounts and Programs

Auditing accounts and programs is a standard operating practice in private business and industry as well as in government agencies. Most large corporations and large school districts have *internal* auditing procedures, carried out by employees for the purpose of identifying ineffective and improper practices that could result in legal and/or financial problems. However, the emphasis here is on the *external* audit, which is usually conducted by an outside certified public accounting firm at the end of a fiscal year. It covers the scope of the school district's operations and attempts not only to analyze the accuracy of financial transactions recorded and verify the financial books, but also to understand the practices and procedures utilized in conducting the business activities of the school district.

In performing an audit, the certified public accountants must have access to certain records that will provide them with necessary data. The following is a list of those records that are usually examined: the minutes of school board meetings, the budget, accounting books such as ledgers and journals, revenue and nonrevenue receipt records, bank accounts, investment records, insurance policies, surety bonds, deeds to property, inventory lists, original documents relating to the authorization of expenditures and the making of payments.

While audit reports vary somewhat, they generally include the following: (1) a letter of transmittal, (2) a description of the scope and the limitations of the audit, (3) a summary of the examination findings, (4) financial statements and schedules, (5) recommendations for improving the accounting procedures and/or the business operations of the school district.

From time to time, the business manager will take bids from auditing firms to ascertain if the fee they are paying their auditors is competitive with that asked by other firms. It is important for the school district to employ a firm based not only on its fee but also on the experience and qualifications of its accountants. School districts are usually required to take the *lowest and best* bid, not merely the lowest. A multiple-year contract with an auditing firm will give it sufficient time to assess accurately and in detail the business operations of the school district.

The audit report is usually presented directly to the board of education, with copies sent to the superintendent and assistant superintendent for administrative services. A good auditing program provides the school board and the public with the assurance that the administration is conducting the business activities of the district in an honest and appropriate manner. Thus, the audit also becomes a method of protecting those charged with managing the fiscal resources of the district.

THE DATA-PROCESSING PROGRAM

It is a truism to say that we live in a computerized society. In fact, the instructional program must incorporate three separate components dealing with computers if the students of a school district are to meet the challenges facing them when they graduate from high school. Computer literacy, the first component, is usually taught in the elementary school; computer usage, the second component, is taught in middle or junior high school; computer programming, the final component, is taught in high school.

This discussion, however, deals with the administrative use of data processing as a vehicle that supports the instructional program. In most school districts, data processing can be applied to the following areas: budgetary accounting, payroll, personnel, scheduling, grade reporting, pupil accounting, attendance accounting, inventory, and enumeration census.

Data-processing services can operate from an in-house installation or computer time can be purchased from a private-service bureau. An alternative to these two approaches is for a number of school districts to form a cooperative, in which one district either purchases or merely houses the equipment and the cost is shared by the member school districts, or the districts buy time on the computer if the equipment is owned by a single district. Figure 7-6 is a checklist that can be used by the administration of a school district, first, to determine whether there is a need for data processing and, second, to determine the adequacy of a district's existing data-processing program. It also lists those components of a program that must be addressed if such a program is to be effective. These major areas are: goals and objectives, proper staffing, procedures for safeguarding the privacy and confidentiality of data, efficient operational procedures, and creative administration of the program.

FIGURE 7-6: CHECKLIST TO DETERMINE THE NEED FOR AND THE ADEQUACY OF A SCHOOL DISTRICT'S DATA PROCESSING PROGRAM

Indicate the degree to which the district conforms to the standards as follows: na = not applicable; 1 = unsatisfactory; 2 = fair; 3 = satisfactory; 4 = exceptional.

Part I—Need for D.P. Services for Districts Currently Without D.P. Services

1. The district has sufficient and timely accounting information.   na   1   2   3   4
2. The district has sufficient and timely payroll/personnel information.   na   1   2   3   4
3. Scheduling of students is accomplished using efficient and effective procedures.   na   1   2   3   4
4. Progress reporting of students is accomplished using efficient and effective procedures.   na   1   2   3   4
5. The district has sufficient and timely pupil information.   na   1   2   3   4
6. The district has adequate procedures available for meeting other informational needs.   na   1   2   3   4
7. The district has given consideration for the utilization of data processing services.   na   1   2   3   4

Part II—Descriptors for Districts Currently Utilizing D.P. Services

Indicate the Source(s) of D.P. Services:
(Check One) In-House Installation   _____
             Service Bureau/Cooperative Approach   _____

Data Processing Goals and Objectives

8. Goals and objectives are formulated by the total administrative staff.   na   1   2   3   4
9. Objectives are prioritized by the administrative staff.   na   1   2   3   4

Staff

10. The district has a written organizational chart for data processing.   na   1   2   3   4
11. The district has a written job description for each D.P. employee based on written performance standards.   na   1   2   3   4
12. The district has a formal education program that meets the needs of the D.P. staff.   na   1   2   3   4

Administration of D.P. Facilities

13. The district has a written multi-year D.P. plan consistent with both short- and long-range objectives.   na   1   2   3   4
14. The D.P. plan is evaluated and revised annually or more frequently.   na   1   2   3   4

Privacy, Security and Confidentiality

15. The district has written procedures governing the privacy and confidentiality of data.   na   1   2   3   4

16. The district has written procedures providing for the
security of software and data files.   na   1   2   3   4
17. The district has written procedures providing for the
security of the computer facility.   na   1   2   3   4

Systems and Programming

18. The district has developed written procedures for
requesting and developing D.P. services.   na   1   2   3   4
19. The district has developed procedures for monitoring
applications during the developmental process.   na   1   2   3   4
20. The district has written systems and programming
standards that are followed in all cases.   na   1   2   3   4
21. User manuals and/or instructions are provided for
each application.   na   1   2   3   4
22. The district has developed written procedures for
monitoring the effectiveness of existing applications.   na   1   2   3   4

Computer Operations

23. The district maintains a daily and weekly machine
processing schedule.   na   1   2   3   4
24. The district has job accounting procedures relative
to computer usage.   na   1   2   3   4
25. The district maintains operator manuals adequate
to schedule and process applications.   na   1   2   3   4
26. The district has a written procedure to monitor D.P.
supplies.   na   1   2   3   4

Data Input/Output

27. The district has procedures which control and secure
the processing of all incoming data.   na   1   2   3   4
28. The district maintains a daily and weekly data
preparation schedule.   na   1   2   3   4
29. The data entry section has complete instructions for
preparing all input data.   na   1   2   3   4
30. The district has procedures whereby new and revised forms
are reviewed and developed jointly by the users and the
D.P. department   na   1   2   3   4
31. The district has procedures for proper distribution
of all output.   na   1   2   3   4
32. The district has procedures for proper disposition of
test runs or other exceptional output.   na   1   2   3   4
33. The district has procedures for the verification and
accuracy of all output.   na   1   2   3   4

SOURCE: Missouri Department of Elementary and Secondary Education, *Checklist to Determine the Need For and the Adequacy Of a School District's Data Processing Program* (Jefferson City, Mo.: The Department, 1982).

The administration should be briefed from time to time on the effectiveness of the data-processing program by the manager of the center and its staff. This is particularly important because the operation of this program interfaces with a great many other school district activities.

THE PUPIL-TRANSPORTATION PROGRAM

School districts have an obligation not only to provide students with the opportunity to be taught by competent professionals at school, but also to help parents get their children to school, by establishing and maintaining a safe and effective pupil-transportation program. The significant increase in automobile traffic and the lack of sidewalks in suburban areas, along with inadequate public transportation in urban areas, have increased the importance of such programs.

Pupil transportation can also be considered an extension of curricular and extracurricular programs. Buses are needed not only to transport children from their homes to school and back again, but are also used for field trips, which certainly extend the educational horizons of the children beyond the classroom. In addition, it would be very difficult for children to participate in an interscholastic athletic program if the school district did not provide transportation.

Most states have statutes governing the pupil-transportation program. It is common for school districts to be required by law to provide some pupil transportation to the regular instructional program at no direct cost to parents. However, they are usually permitted to charge parents for transporting their children to athletic events and for field trips.

Figure 7-7 provides a list of descriptors that can be used by school district administrators as they evaluate the adequacy of their school districts' transportation program. Both the quality of service and the cost-effectiveness of the program are directly related to the policies created by the school board and the procedures used by the administration to manage the pupil-transportation program.

There is a major consideration with which most school districts will contend at one time or another: Is it better to contract pupil-transportation services with a private company or to have a district-operated program? The answer to this question will not be applicable to every situation. Basically, however, the administration must decide which option will provide the students of the district with the best and safest service at the most reasonable cost. The director of transportation and his or her staff can provide the assistant superintendent for administrative services with data about the cost of a district-operated program along with information about the safety of the operation and long-term concerns such as maintenance and vehicle-replacement costs in addition to revenue projections for the program. At that point, the assistant superintendent may have the director of transportation prepare specifications and take bids on contracting services. An analysis of the bids and a comparison of contracted services with a district-operated program can then be made in order to determine which of the two options is best for the school district.

**FIGURE 7-7:   GUIDELINES TO DETERMINE THE ADEQUACY
OF THE SCHOOL DISTRICT'S TRANSPORTATION PROGRAM**

1. The school board should adopt specific written policies covering the objectives of the school district's transportation program, which should include:
    a. A definition of what is considered a safe and reasonable walking distance for children.
    b. Transportation for all handicapped children regardless of the distance involved.
    c. A provision regarding the use of buses for noninstructional purposes.
2. The administration should develop a program to teach bus safety to students at all grade levels.
3. The administration should develop a detailed written contract of responsibilities when a school district elects to provide transportation services through a private contractor. Such a contract must be executed by the board of education. This contract should also contain clauses relating to the following:
    a. A performance bond to insure faithful fulfillment of the contract terms.
    b. The minimum amount of insurance to be carried by the private contractor.
    c. A schedule to inspect the school buses by a competent individual on a regular basis.
4. The administration should provide the school board with a cost analysis of the transportation services on an annual basis that should include the following:
    a. Original cost of equipment and the date of purchase.
    b. Total miles operated.
    c. Miles operated on a daily basis.
    d. Number of pupils transported daily and on a yearly basis by route.
    e. The cost for fuel and maintenance.
    f. Specific information on accidents involving school buses.
    g. Specific information on property damage and traffic violations.
    h. An inventory of repair parts.
5. The administration is responsible for developing and maintaining the following routing information:
    a. An up-to-date map of the district's boundaries and school attendance areas.
    b. The location of all roads and information relating the type and condition of roads.
    c. The distance between major intersections.
    d. The location of students that are transported and their grade level.
    e. The exact route for each school bus.
    f. The location, weight capacity, and condition of all bridges.
6. The administration is responsible for selecting pickup sites and routing buses in such a manner that:
    a. Bus stops are not on steep grades, blind curves, or near the crest of a hill.
    b. The walking distance, waiting times, and riding times are reasonable.
    c. Distances meet state guidelines.
    d. The time schedule is such that parents and children can be assured of a reasonably accurate pickup and discharge time.
7. The administration is responsible for establishing bus driver selection and training procedures that will insure the following:
    a. Previous driving experience is investigated.
    b. Consideration is given to the maturity and character of each applicant.
    c. Substitute drivers meet the general requirements of regular drivers.
    d. A driver's handbook is developed that includes procedures to be followed in pupil discipline cases and in emergency situations.

>   e. A training program is developed that includes classroom instruction and actual practice in driving a school bus.
>   f. Conferences are held with the bus drivers on a regular basis to discuss mutual problems and concerns.
> 8. It is the administration's responsibility to establish rules and regulations governing pupil behavior and safety that include the following:
>   a. Procedures for reporting student misconduct, complaints from pupils and parents, bus conditions, route conditions, accidents, injuries.
>   b. Designated personnel are present to supervise the unloading and loading of pupils at school.
>   c. Drivers are furnished with the names of pupils assigned to their routes.
>   d. Drivers are instructed that no child should be let off the bus for any reason except at the designated stop unless special instructions have been given by the proper authority.
>   e. Safe traffic patterns have been developed for approaching, parking on, and leaving the school grounds.

Two issues have arisen in the last five years that address school districts' concern with making the pupil-transportation program more cost-effective. First, the use of alternative methods of fueling school buses has received considerable attention, and experiments have been conducted using gasohol, propane, and diesel fuel. The assistant superintendent should require the director of transportation to provide data and a list of the current literature dealing with alternative fuels.

Secondly, computerized transportation programs have saved some districts a considerable amount of money, particularly in establishing routes and pupil pickup points, scheduling bus runs, and monitoring and reporting costs. Such computerized programs are available from private companies on a contract or fee basis, while medium-to-large districts may have their own computer hardware for developing such a system. The ultimate question that the director of transportation must ask is whether the capital outlay to convert vehicles to the use of alternative fuels and the capital investment to purchase or contract for computer capabilities in pupil transportation will pay the district back in a reasonable enough period of time to justify the expenditure.

THE SCHOOL FOOD-SERVICE PROGRAM

There are three reasons why a school district should provide a food-service program for children: (1) pupils should have the opportunity to obtain nutritional food during the school day, which is needed for physical, emotional, and intellectual development; (2) the school lunch program provides pupils with the opportunity to learn about the amount and kinds of food needed for good nutrition; (3) eating in the school cafeteria provides pupils with the opportunity to practice desirable social behavior.

The school food-service program includes much more than a hot-lunch program. Some school districts provide breakfast, especially in areas where family income severely limits the opportunity of a child to receive a nutritional breakfast at home. Many school districts have found that the food-service program can provide the school district with a cost-effective way of supplementing the extracurricular and school-sponsored clubs and associations. Every team and club member in the school district looks forward to culminating the season's activities with a banquet or dinner at which the team and individual members can be recognized for their accomplishments. The cost of a banquet served at school will be much less than at a private restaurant.

Like the pupil-transportation program, food service can be contracted for with a private company or district-operated. The guiding objective for the administration is the same as with pupil transportation: The best option is the one that provides the students in the district with the most nutritional meals at the most reasonable cost. In order to make this decision, the assistant superintendent for administrative services can use the checklist in Figure 7-8, which includes a set of descriptors to analyze the adequacy of a school district's food-service program. In addition, Figure 7-9 provides a "blueprint" for a food-service program. Developed

---

FIGURE 7-8:   DESCRIPTORS TO DETERMINE THE ADEQUACY OF A SCHOOL DISTRICT'S FOOD-SERVICE PROGRAM

A school district will have an effective and efficiently managed food service program if the following questions can be answered with a "yes":

1. Are the objectives of the food-service program defined in writing?
2. Is the school food-service program under the direction of a competent person who is considered an integral part of the administrative team?
3. Are the food-service policies, procedures, and regulations in written form and provided to all employees?
4. Are lines of authority and responsibility clearly defined in writing for the proper management of the program?
5. Does the school district have a policy regarding the sale of competitive food items such as packaged snacks, soft drinks, and candy?
6. Is the sale of all food items under the direct management of the director of food service and are all receipts deposited to the food-service account?
7. Has the school district developed a policy and procedure for providing meals to needy children?
8. Is the scheduling of lunch periods well planned, and does it allow the students sufficient time to eat their lunch?
9. Is nutrition education correlated with the school food-service program?
10. Is adequate supervision provided at lunchtime to students so that good food habits and social graces can be encouraged?
11. Does the administration evaluate the program's participation on a continual basis?
12. Are the cafeteria workers adequately supervised to insure that attractive and clean uniforms are worn by employees at all times?
13. Is there a staff-development program for cafeteria workers?
14. Are all personnel required to meet locally established health standards?

15. Is the community informed of federal and state program requirements in written publications?
16. Are menus planned on a monthly basis and published a week in advance?
17. Is maximum utilization made of all food items that are not sold?
18. Are students encouraged to participate in the planning of the food-service program?
19. Is the food prepared, handled, and served in a sanitary and safe manner?
20. Are inventory procedures effective in utilizing older shelf food items before they spoil?
21. Is there adequate security to protect against the possible theft of food items?
22. Is the storage space free from excessive temperature and humidity?
23. Is there a daily reading of thermostats in refrigerators and freezers to insure against spoilage?
24. Is the dining area clean, attractive, and well ventilated?
25. Are dishwashing facilities adequate and sanitary?
26. Are garbage and refuse disposed of in a sanitary manner?
27. Have rodent- and insect-extermination services been provided with regular applications?
28. Have procedures been established that allow for the proper handling of money?
29. Are monthly profit-and-loss statements prepared?
30. Are program costs calculated by using the full cost for labor, food, utilities, custodial services, capital outlay, and maintenance?

FIGURE 7-9: AMERICAN SCHOOL FOOD SERVICE ASSOCIATION'S BLUEPRINT FOR SCHOOL NUTRITION PROGRAMS

Reflecting the educational potential of proper school nutrition programs, it is hereby declared to be our philosophy that food service permitted in schools shall contribute to optimum learning ability through good nutrition, good example, and good instruction.

School nutrition programs should contribute to the education of the child in three ways: (1) to his physical well-being; (2) to his mental receptivity; and (3) to his knowledge of food and application of good eating habits.

I. Nutrition Offerings

The school, with the assistance of medical personnel, should determine the nutritional status of the individual child and his school-day nutritional needs.

School food service should be expanded to those children presently excluded because of a lack of facilities and/or funds.

Provision should be made for:

A. A meal that contains 1/3 of the child's recommended dietary allowances should be provided by the schools to all pupils without cost to the individual.
B. Two meals, each containing 1/3 of the recommended daily dietary allowances, should be available daily in all schools.

II. Nutrition Curriculum

A school nutrition program should provide:

A. A sequential curriculum plan of nutrition instruction for pupils from kindergarten through high school.

    B. Innovative curriculum materials.

    C. Nutrition counseling with parents and medical personnel.

    D. Continuing nutrition education for teachers through regional and local workshops and courses.

III. Professional Education and Training

    The state educational agency should:

    A. Establish qualifications for personnel responsible for directing, supervising, and implementing school food service and a nutrition program.

    B. Define criteria for preservice and in-service training programs.

    C. Cooperate with educational institutions and professional organizations in developing education programs.

IV. Staffing

    The local educational agency should provide:

    A. Direction and supervision by certificated personnel professionally trained in nutrition and/or administration and food services.

    B. Adequate staff, qualified through nutrition and food service training, to implement school food service programs.

V. Technology

    School nutrition program design should reflect the best technological research and development available to produce an optimum product at minimum cost.

VI. Research and Evaluation

    Continuing research and evaluation is essential to provide information which will enable school nutrition programs to define and apply practices of maximum effectiveness.

    Organizations, industry, and government should combine their resources toward this purpose as well as in defining means through which this information can be effectively disseminated.

VII. Expanded Use of Schools

    Reflecting the trend for schools to become community centers:

    A. School nutrition programs should be expanded to meet the needs of all ages at all times whenever they are using school facilities.

    B. Maximum use of school food service facilities and personnel may be anticipated in times of emergency.

    C. School food service facilities and staff should be used for vocational training of youth and adults.

VIII. Funding

    In fidelity to the premise that the school accept the responsibility for the child during the hours he is under its care, the school nutrition programs should meet the child's nutrition needs during the hours of the school's responsibility.

    Such nutrition programs should be funded as a public responsibility, and therefore at no cost to the individual.

    Taking cognizance that this goal far exceeds our present public commitment toward meeting school-day nutrition needs, a timetable is needed to reach the objective.

IX. Public Information

    An effective school nutrition program must be understood and supported by the public. All agencies with a concern for the nutrition of children should cooperate to develop and implement a public information program.

SOURCE: American School Food Service Association and Association of School Business Officials, *A Guide For Financing School Food and Nutrition Services* (Denver: The Associations, 1979), pp. 69-71.

by the American Food Service Association, it presents a set of objectives that will produce an effective program.

The director of food services can provide the assistant superintendent with data about the pupil participation in the program, state and federal reimbursements, menus and nutritional requirements, and direct costs such as salary information and maintenance and food costs. The assistant superintendent may wish to have the director of food services prepare specifications and take bids on a contracted service if there is any question about the effectiveness of the current program.

A major concern in many programs is the level of pupil participation. In some districts, a la carte and alternative menus have increased participation in the food-service program.

SUMMARY

The importance of administrative services and activities in school districts has been dramatically heightened over the last decade. Operational practices common to the business and industrial community have been adopted by school districts as they attempt to become more accountable to taxpayers. Such practices can help to demonstrate that the school board, along with the administration, is providing cost-effective educational programs that meet the needs of the children.

The financial management of school districts includes many interrelated functions that ultimately demonstrate that the revenue and expenditures of the district support the best educational program possible, given the fiscal resources available.

The major components of financial management include: (1) budgeting procedures, (2) financial-accounting procedures, (3) purchasing, warehousing, and distribution procedures, (4) investing procedures, and (5) auditing procedures.

The school district's budget is a plan for delivering the educational programs and projecting the revenue and expenditures that support it.

Financial accounting is a system that involves recording, classifying, summarizing, interpreting, and reporting the results of the school district's financial activities.

School districts are important buyers and consumers, because the supplies, materials, and services needed to conduct the educational enterprise cost millions of dollars. Such large expenditures demand the creation of board policies and administrative procedures that will insure the proper purchase and use of these goods.

Most school districts can significantly increase their nontaxable revenue by developing an investment plan that places idle cash in interest-bearing money instruments. The budgeting process and accounting system can provide the assistant superintendent for administrative services with data concerning the cash-flow requirements of the school district. Comparing revenue receipts and expenditures on a monthly basis with previous years is especially helpful in projecting cash needs.

Auditing accounts and programs is standard practice in private business and industry as well as in government agencies. The external audit is usually conducted by an outside certified public accounting firm at the end of a fiscal year. The audit covers the scope of the school district's operations and attempts to analyze the accuracy of recording financial transactions, verify the books, and determine the practices and procedures utilized in conducting the business activities of the school district.

The educational program is supported by two other programs that are usually managed by the administrative-services department—pupil transportation and food service. In addition, all the programs of the school district are enhanced by data processing. In most districts, data processing can be applied to the following areas: budgetary accounting, payroll, personnel, scheduling, grade reporting, pupil accounting, attendance accounting, inventory, and enumeration census.

A school district has an obligation not only to provide students with the opportunity to be taught by competent professionals at school but also by establishing and maintaining a safe and effective pupil-transportation program, to help parents get their children to school. The pupil-transportation program can enhance curricular and extracurricular programs by providing transportation for field trips and interscholastic athletic events.

A school district should provide a food-service program for three reasons: (1) pupils should have the opportunity to obtain nutritional food during the school day, (2) the school lunch program provides students with the opportunity to learn about good nutrition, and (3) eating in the school cafeteria provides pupils with the opportunity to practice desirable social behavior.

IMPLICATIONS FOR EDUCATIONAL ADMINISTRATORS

This discussion of administrative support services in a school district has three implications for educational administrators.

First, every building and district-level administrator must understand the importance of administrative-support services in determining the success of the educational program. Sound fiscal management will insure that district funds are available to pay for a high-quality education. Likewise, if children are unable to arrive safely at school or be properly nourished in order to be attentive during the learning-instructional process, their potential for failing at school will be significantly increased. Too often, building and even some central-office administrators are unfamiliar with and unappreciative of administrative-support services and tend to play down their relevance.

Second, the superintendent of schools, the assistant superintendent for administrative services, and other central-office administrators must help school-board members become completely familiar and comfortable with the administrative services of the school district. It will be impossible for the board of education to make realistic decisions concerning the educational program without this knowledge. A wide range of reports concerning administrative functions, particularly about the financial condition of the school district, should be presented to the school board on an ongoing basis, particularly at the monthly board meeting.

Third, through internal and external publications produced by the community-relations division, teachers, other school district employees, parents, other taxpayers, and students should be regularly informed about the operations of the district's administrative-support services. This will help all constituents to understand why the district is expending funds for administrative operations such as auditing services, new buses, computers, and cafeteria equipment.

SELECTED BIBLIOGRAPHY

AMERICAN SCHOOL FOOD SERVICE ASSOCIATION and ASSOCIATION OF SCHOOL BUSINESS OFFICIALS, *A Guide for Financing School Food and Nutrition Services.* Denver: The Associations, 1970.

BENSON, CHARLES S., *The Economics of Public Education* (2nd ed.). Boston: Houghton Mifflin Company, 1969.

BURRUP, PERCY E., *Financing Education in a Climate of Change* (2nd ed.). Boston: Allyn and Bacon, Inc., 1977.

CANDOLI, I. CARL and others, *School Business Administration: A Planning Approach.* Boston: Allyn and Bacon, Inc., 1978.

GONDER, PEGGY ODELL, *How Schools Can Save $$: Problems and Solutions.* Arlington, Va.: American Association of School Administrators, 1980.

JOHNS, ROE L. and EDGAR L. MORPHET, *The Economics and Financing of Education: A Systems Approach.* Englewood Cliffs, N.J.: Prentice-Hall, Inc., 1975.

JOHNS, ROE L., EDGAR L. MORPHET, and KEN ALEXANDER, *The Economics and Financing of Education* (4th ed.). Englewood Cliffs, N.J.: Prentice-Hall, Inc., 1983.

MUNICIPAL FINANCE OFFICERS ASSOCIATION OF THE UNITED STATES AND CANADA, *A Public Investor's Guide to Money Market Instruments.* Chicago: The Association, 1982.

NATIONAL SCHOOL PUBLIC RELATIONS ASSOCIATION, *PPBS and the School: New System Promotes Efficiency, Accountability.* Arlington, Va.: The Association, 1972.

NELSON, DEMPSEY FLOYD, and WILLIAM M. PURDY, *School Business Administration.* Lexington, Mass.: D. C. Heath Company, Lexington Books, 1971.

U.S. DEPARTMENT OF HEALTH, EDUCATION AND WELFARE, *Principles of Public School Accounting.* Washington, D.C.: U.S. Government Printing Office, 1967.

NOTES

1. U.S. Department of Health, Education and Welfare, *Principles of Public School Accounting* (Washington, D.C.: U.S. Government Printing Office, 1967), pp. 1–4.

2. Roe L. Johns and Edgar L. Morphet, *The Economics and Financing of Education: A Systems Approach,* 3rd ed. (Englewood Cliffs, N.J.: Prentice-Hall, Inc., 1975), p. 442.

8

The Role and Function of the Facilities- Management Administrator

The importance of school buildings and facilities is often overlooked by citizens, teachers, administrators, and even board members. Every school should be designed to support and strengthen the learning-instructional process. This cannot be accomplished unless the school district's administrators understand the integral relationship between educating children and the physical surroundings where this takes place.

Children have been the object of much research, which has provided us with a vast amount of data that must be taken into consideration when building, remodeling, and maintaining school facilities. For example, we know children have social needs that must be met via their educational experience if they are to be successful at school. A sense of belonging and companionship must, therefore, be developed at school. This cannot easily be accomplished if the school facilities lack a variety of spaces for group activities. In recent years the *commons* area, brightly decorated and furnished with comfortable chairs, has become one of many popular architectural methods for addressing the social needs of students.

How to build school facilities that meet the social, psychological, and educational needs of students is only one of the many issues that school administrators must address if they are to have a working knowledge of property management. This chapter, therefore, is divided into five sections, each dealing with an area that has a significant impact on school district property management.

JOB DESCRIPTION FOR THE DIRECTOR
OF BUILDINGS AND GROUNDS

Job Summary

The director of buildings and grounds is responsible for the school district's physical-plant program. This includes the establishment and maintenance of effective two-way communication between the various organizational divisions of the school district, and the formulation, recommendation, and administration of the school district's physical-plant policies.

Organizational Relationship

The director of buildings and grounds has a line relationship with the assistant superintendent for administrative services and reports directly to him or her. The director serves as the chief adviser on matters pertaining to the physical plant and has a staff relationship with other administrative personnel. The director's immediate staff includes the maintenance workers and custodial foremen.

Organizational Tasks

The director of buildings and grounds is directly responsible for establishing administrative processes, procedures, and techniques for school district construction and remodeling projects; for the district's risk-management program; the school district's compliance with Section 504 of Title V for the Rehabilitation Act of 1973; the energy-conservation program; the school district's maintenance and capital-improvement program; and the district's custodial program. Further, this individual is responsible for supervising the maintenance staff and custodial foremen.

Job Requirements

In terms of education and experience, the director of buildings and grounds should possess:

A bachelor's degree in architecture or one of the engineering sciences.
Experience in supervising skilled and unskilled workers. (Note: It may be possible and advantageous for a school district to hire an educational administrator, such as a building principal, who was an industrial-arts teacher, or an individual whose advanced degree from a school of education is in the management and administration of the physical plant.)

Others are also employed to perform supervisory functions in the buildings and grounds division of the administration department. These administrators will have titles that exemplify their specific function, such as Lead Custodian, Grounds Keeper, and Maintenance Supervisor. This discussion does not include job descriptions for all of the supervisory personnel in a district, but rather considers the executive administrators charged with the overall management of a department or division, as outlined in Chapter 1. Many, if not all, of these supervising administrators will be classified personnel with skill qualifications rather than academic credentials.

ARCHITECTURAL PRINCIPLES
AND THE LEARNING ENVIRONMENT

There were no recognizable schoolhouse structures in the United States until the seventeenth century. At that time, they were neither attractive nor comfortable, consisting primarily of one room, with long tables for the pupils and a raised podium for the teacher. Until the 1850s, the basic philosophy was that schoolhouses were shelters in which pupils and teachers came together. Through the efforts of eminent educators such as Horace Mann and Henry Barnard, free public education became an accepted American institution and so the design of schools began to attract the attention of architects.

Shortly after the acceptance of public education, another, unrelated event occurred, which has had a significant effect not only on the design of schools but also on the entire field of architecture. In 1880, Louis Sullivan, an eminent American architect, enunciated the principle, "Form follows function." In fact, the planning of *functional* school buildings has been of primary concern to both architects and educators since the 1940s. Until then, American architecture was more concerned with imitating what was in vogue in Europe, and particularly in England.

The function of educational institutions is to educate children and young people. Consequently, the design of school facilities began to be viewed within the context of educational concepts. Today, all school construction and remodeling projects must be part of the process whereby fundamental educational concepts are formulated, developed, expressed, evaluated, and incorporated into the design of the school.[1] Hence, the need to use educational specifications when designing a building. Such specifications should clearly describe the various learning activities to take place, their spatial requirements, and any special features of the curriculum.

Four principles of operation mirror the human condition and must be considered when planning an educational facility today. First, the principle of gradualism dictates that the teachers, administrators, students, and parents are ready for curricular changes that are also reflected in architectural design. The "open-space" classroom is a case in point. Without proper preparation, in a newly constructed school utilizing this concept, gradually partitions will be made with bookcases and other movable objects.

Secondly, the principle of reversibility dictates that new dimensions in the design of school facilities that support a specific curricular approach can be changed without extensive structural modification. Soundproof sliding partitions can be used to convert an open area into a more confined space for small-group instruction or for that teacher who is more effective in a traditional classroom setting.

Third, considering our high mobility, decreased population, and the tremendous cost of construction, school facilities should be designed for more than one use. Many school districts across the United States are closing school buildings because of decreasing enrollments. A building constructed only to be a school would require considerable structural modifications in order to convert it, for example, into an office building. A more universal design would give the school district the opportunity to recoup its investment, which in turn could be put into other educational areas.

Finally, schools should be designed for people. Every child has physical, social, intellectual, and psychological needs, all of which may or may not be enhanced by the design of the school building. For example, mental fatigue will certainly retard a student's ability to learn. Thus, the physical conditions that cause fatigue can be minimized if a building is well ventilated, has functional heating and air-conditioning systems, and is decorated with bright colors.

STEPS IN A SCHOOL CONSTRUCTION OR REMODELING PROGRAM

There are four steps involved in a school construction and/or remodeling program, each of which has a number of components that are implemented by various staff members. Each component contains a number of procedures and subprocesses that are very complex. However, every administrator should be familiar with the overall process, which will provide one with a frame of reference when interacting with the director of buildings and grounds about construction and/or remodeling.

Step 1: Establishing Educational Goals and Objectives

It is absolutely imperative that the board of education and administration establish a five-year plan consisting of educational goals and objectives, any of which may be altered from year to year. The administration needs the input of citizens, students, teachers, staff members, and administrators before deciding on district-wide goals.

These goals and objectives are subsequently converted into a curricular plan. The curriculum is the responsibility of the superintendent of schools and his or her staff. Certainly, teachers, building-level administrators, and curriculum specialists will be engaged in the curricular-planning process.

The curriculum is then translated into educational specifications, which present in great detail the kinds of spatial, equipment, and building requirements needed to operationalize the curriculum. For example, the teaching of high-school-level chemistry will require a laboratory with specialized equipment. It is also the responsibility of the superintendent and director of buildings and grounds to formulate these educational specifications. Teachers and building-level administrators have on-the-line experience, which will be invaluable to them.

Step 2: Developing Architectural Plans

The first concern in operationalizing the second step is the selection of an architect. Because architects are professionals who provide a service, one of the most successful ways to select architects is to advertise that the board of education is accepting credentials and proposals. The credentials should include documentation of the successful school projects completed by the architect, and the proposal should include the method of payment. Traditionally, there are two: a flat fee or a percentage of the project cost. The American Institute of Architects has established guidelines for members to decide on compensation for professional services. Based on the recommendation of the superintendent, the school board selects the architect.

The architect is responsible for taking the educational specifications and developing preliminary sketches and cost estimates for the project. Once these sketches are reviewed by the superintendent, teachers, curriculum specialists, and the building principal who helped develop the specifications, the board of education should approve or reject the sketches.

Next, the architect should select a site for a new school project and develop working drawings and architectural specifications. The architect will require the services of other professionals, such as electrical and mechanical engineers, in developing these plans. Of course, the school board exercises final approval of the school site and plans.

Step 3: Developing the Financial Plan

The superintendent and director of buildings and grounds are responsible for developing preliminary plans for a bond-issue election. The campaign should be organized and coordinated by the director of community relations. If the bond issue passes, the board of education must select an attorney who specializes in bonding. The process used in selecting an architect also applies to a bonding attorney. The various aspects of bond flotation are outlined later in the chapter.

Step 4: Implementing the Construction and/or Remodeling

The architect is responsible for advertising and taking bids for a general contractor, who will actually construct or remodel the building. It is more effective for the general contractor to handle the subcontracting with electrical contractors and all other construction specialists. The board of education approves the contract with the general contractor but should have it executed by the school district's attorney.

The business manager, in conjunction with the building principal, who will administer the new school, should prepare an equipment list. In many cases, the architect will be responsible for taking bids on furniture and large equipment that will be used in the building.

The building should be inspected on a regular basis by the architect and the director of buildings and grounds. Upon certification of the architect, monthly payments can be made to the general contractor from the money generated through the sale of the bonds. Final payment should be withheld until the board of education can make a final inspection of the new or remodeled facility.

PUBLIC BORROWING FOR CAPITAL PROJECTS

In recent years, almost 80 percent of new U.S. corporation financing has been accomplished through the issuing of bonds. In the public sector, however, bonds are sold for limited purposes. State statutes closely regulate the process of flotation, debt limits, and all aspects of public borrowing. A distinctive characteristic of public borrowing is its voluntary nature. If the citizens of a school district do not wish to bind themselves and future generations to paying taxes for the retirement of the district's bonded indebtedness, they simply vote "no" in the bond-issue election.

Bonds are formal IOUs. Most state statutes permit boards of education to ask the citizens of a school district for approval (via a bond-issue election) to borrow money by selling bonds to raise funds for capital projects. *Capital projects* usually refer to building schools, furnishing schools, remodeling programs, replacing roofs, buying boilers, and the purchasing of large, expensive equipment such as school buses. The critical aspect is voter approval, because without it, a school district cannot engage in public borrowing. When a bond issue is passed, the taxpayers have in essence said that, until the entire debt is repaid, they will make annual payments, through a special tax, on the principal and interest for the bonds that the school district sells.

Traditionally, capital projects have been financed through public borrowing for three major reasons. First, such projects are usually nonreoccurring expenditures that should not be financed with funds generated through the operating tax levy. The operating levy is meant for paying salaries, fringe benefits, utilities, routine maintenance, and other ongoing expenses. Secondly, the large dollar outlay for capital projects would seriously affect the monies available for continuing daily operations if the funding were taken from the operating levy. Finally, the burden for financing capital projects should be spread out over many generations, because they, too, will benefit from them. Most municipal bonds are repaid over a twenty-year period.

The Process of Bond Flotation

The first step is for a board of education and administration to determine what capital projects are and will be needed by the present and future generations of the school district. This must be accomplished by the superintendent and his or her administrative team. Enrollment projections are essential. Most capital projects are predicated on the number of students who will be occupying a place in the schools. If the student population is increasing, additional buildings will be needed. As a school district matures and the student population decreases or stabilizes, there remains a need to remodel or refurbish existing buildings. Energy-conservation modifications of older facilities have become essential in recent years. A number of existing techniques, such as the Cohort-Survival method of enrollment projecting, can provide the school board with adequate data about pupil population trends.

The second step in floating a bond is to review the state statutes that pertain to municipal bonds and bond-issue elections. For example, there is a significant statutory limitation in most states that could prevent a school district from even considering a bond-issue election. A debt ceiling expressed as a certain percentage of the school district's assessed valuation can limit the bonding capability of the district. For example, if a school district has an assessed valuation of $100 million and the state statutes limit a district to a bonding capacity of 10 percent of this assessed valuation, the school district can borrow only $10 million. If the district has already issued bonds worth $9 million and has retired $1 million of this debt, the bonded indebtedness of the school district is $8 million, which leaves a bonding capacity for an additional capital project of only $2 million, which does not buy a very elaborate school building today. Such restrictions are placed on school districts to prevent them from incurring a debt that their tax base will not support.

The third step is to initiate a bond-issue election campaign headed by the director of community relations, if the board of education decides that a capital project is needed.

If the bond issue passes, the fourth step is to initiate those procedures that are necessary to insure the legality of the bonds. Because school district bonds are purchased and traded under the *bearer* form, legality is of primary importance. The administration should always recommend that the board of education hire an attorney who specializes in bonds to review and handle the entire process of flotation.

The following steps should be taken by the board of education to minimize confusion and maximize the potential for selling the bonds.

1. Pass a resolution approving the results of the bond-issue election.
2. Obtain a certification from the appropriate authority concerning the assessed valuation of the school district.
3. Have the treasurer of the school board certify the outstanding indebtedness of the district.
4. Prepare a bond maturity schedule.
5. Pass a resolution directing the sale of the bonds.
6. Prepare a notice that the bonds are for sale and advertise in the appropriate publications.
7. Notify Moody's Investors Service and/or Standard & Poor's Corporation about the bond sale.

8. Solicit bids for the printing of the bonds.
9. Accept the bids for the sale of the bonds and for printing the bonds.
10. Pass a resolution directing the issuance of the bonds.
11. Once the bonds are delivered to the school district, they should be signed by the secretary and treasurer of the board.
12. The bonds should then be registered with the appropriate state authority.
13. The bonds should then be delivered to the purchaser.
    a. A nonlitigation certificate must be signed by the clerk of the circuit court.
    b. A receipt for the funds obtained through the bond sale must be signed by the treasurer of the board.
    c. A verification of the president's and secretary's signature should be prepared and attested to by an official of the bank handling the school district's money.

Facts about Bonds

It is impossible to talk about municipal bonds of the type issued by public bodies in isolation from the bonds issued by corporations, because both have similar characteristics. It is also important for educational administrators to have at least a rudimentary understanding of bonds. The following facts constitute the essential data necessary to that understanding.

1. The amount to be repaid by the school district is the *principal amount, face value,* or *par value,* which is printed on the face of the bond.
2. The repayment date is the *maturity date.*
3. The interest rate paid by the school district to the person who owns the bond is the *coupon rate.*
4. The period of time that the bond is outstanding is the *term.* Municipal bonds usually have a term from one through twenty years.
5. Bond certificates either come with coupons which are *clipped* from the bond and presented for interest payments; or the bonds are *registered* with the issuing agent who mails the interest payments directly to the bond holder.
6. The *bearer* form is used with most municipal bonds, by which the person who holds the bond is presumed to be the owner.
7. When the bonds are backed up by the collateral of a corporation, such as property, the bonds are referred to as *mortgage bonds.*
8. When the bond is issued on the full faith of the borrower, it is called a *debenture.*
9. *Municipal bonds* are issued by cities, states, and political subdivisions.
10. Municipal bonds differ from corporate bonds in the following ways:
    a. Municipal bonds are *tax exempt,* which means that the interest is exempt from federal income taxes, and, if the investor lives in the state of issue, the interest is also exempt from state and local taxes.
    b. Municipal bonds are issued in *serial* maturities rather than on a term basis. Therefore, a portion of the total issue matures annually, with each year in the series having its own interest rate. While the overall net interest might be 10 percent, the 1983 issue could yield 7.703, with the 1984 issue yielding 7.90, and the 1985 issue yielding 8.10, etc.
    c. Municipal bonds are generally issued in $5000 principal amounts and traded in the Over-the-Counter (OTC) market.

    d. There are three basic types of municipal bonds:
      (1) *General obligation bonds,* which are backed by the faith and taxing authority of the issuer.
      (2) *Revenue bonds,* which are backed by the earning power of the facility constructed. (A stadium would generate gate receipts which would be used to retire the bonds.)
      (3) *Special tax bonds,* which are backed by a special tax levied yearly to pay the principal and interest of a maturing series. This is the type generally issued by school districts.

11. Bonds are rated by the following two independent agencies, which measure the probability of a bond issuer being capable of repaying the principal amount at maturity and the interest schedule.
    a. Standard & Poor's Corporation uses the first four letters of the alphabet—AAA, AA, A; BBB, BB, B; CCC, CC, C; through D (default)—in rating bonds, with AAA being the most secure. At times a plus or minus may be added to a rating in order to more finely delineate the rating.
    b. Moody's Investor Service Incorporated also uses the alphabet but stops with C.

12. Bonds which carry the greatest risk also demand the highest interest.

13. New bonds are issued at interest rates dictated by the economy. Therefore, the following explanation of yield is very important.
    a. Bonds are negotiable and are often traded among investors.
    b. Because the *interest is fixed,* adjustments in profit or loss are made through the price of the bond.
    c. *Current yield* is calculated through dividing the annual interest by the price of the bond.
    d. If a $1000 bond is *bought at par* and pays $90 interest, the yield is 9 percent ($90/$1000 = 9.00%).
    e. If a $1000 bond is *bought at a discount* of 10 percent and pays $90 interest, the yield is 10 percent ($90/$900 = 10.00%).
    f. If a $1000 bond is *bought at a premium* of 10 percent and pays $90 interest, the yield is 8.18 percent ($90/$1100 = 8.18%).[2]

RISK MANAGEMENT AND INSURING SCHOOL PROPERTY

The 1950s saw a significant advance in the commercial-insurance industry. By drawing together all of a business's property and casualty insurance coverage into one package, a business could have a convenient, improved, and cost-effective insurance program. However, insurance is only one aspect of a total risk-management program. With the rising cost of all services, it is important for the superintendent of schools to require that the director of buildings and grounds develop an approach to school property management that incorporates the tenets of risk management.

Principles of Risk Management

The very act of living is a risk. No matter what you do or how careful you are, there is always the possibility that an accident will cause injury to you or damage to your property. There are, however, certain principles for handling risks that have been proven by experience and operationalized for some time by large corporations.

First, identify and evaluate the school district's exposure to risks. It might be necessary to ask the insurance agent/broker or the underwriter for the district's insurance coverage to help the director of buildings and grounds in conducting an audit of the school district's facilities to ascertain potential risks. If such services are not available from the underwriter and the district's agent or broker, it may be necessary to contract with a management-consulting firm that employs *safety engineers*, who can advise the administration about hazards. For example, steps may not have slip-retarding strips or adequate handrails to protect the students as they move from one floor to the next. Custodial and maintenance areas may need additional ventilation to prevent the accumulation of fumes that may be sparked into an explosion. Driver's-education cars should have dual steering mechanisms to prevent an accident if a student driver loses control of the vehicle. While numerous additional examples could be given, the following question explains how to identify the school district's potential exposure to accidents: What are the sources, causes, and kinds of potential losses, and how significant are these losses likely to be?

The second step in managing risks should be an attempt to eliminate or minimize them. Repairing defective handrails and installing slip-retarding strips on steps are easy and relatively inexpensive ways of minimizing potentials risks; those that require a major building modification will be more costly. However, the expense of installing a new and more effective fire-alarm system is much more cost-effective than rebuilding a facility significantly damaged by fire. The coinsuring of buildings is an added incentive to the administration in developing and implementing a risk-management program.

Finally, if it is impossible to eliminate or significantly minimize a risk, it is common practice to transfer that risk to another party. Purchasing insurance is the most common method of doing so. There are other circumstances, however, when a school district should transfer a risk to another party through a contractual agreement. Many school districts in metropolitan areas have seen enrollments decrease, which has eventuated in the closing of schools. Many of these facilities have been leased to private firms and other public institutions. The lease agreement should contain a provision requiring the lessee to protect the property and the school district from liability through insurance. A second example of transferring risk through a contractual agreement involves the usual requirement of a performance bond from a contractor who is building or remodeling a school facility.

The Value of Deductibles

In purchasing insurance, the premium paid by the school district is a measure of the transferred risk. The greater the risk, the more it will cost the district in premiums. If the risk assumed by the insurance company is reduced, not only will the premium be reduced, but the competition for the premium will be increased.

There are many reasons besides reduced premiums for using deductibles. It is good management for a business or institution to retain some portion of a risk, because it encourages a continual concern over safety. In addition, deductibles eliminate nuisance claims, preserve a market for the district's coverage, broaden that coverage, and reduce internal administrative costs.

Although there is no magic formula for determining the appropriate size of a deductible, there are a few guidelines that can be used to analyze a school district's situation in order to settle on one. Determine (1) the district's loss expectancy from past history, (2) how much loss can be absorbed by the district per location and occurrence or in the aggregate, and (3) how much money can be saved in reduced premium costs if the district assumes a portion of the loss.

There are many different types of deductible, ranging from a *straight* dollar amount to *percentage, disappearing, franchise,* and *time* deductibles. It is most important for the director of buildings and grounds to review the school district's deductible approach from time to time and especially when the current insurance contract is up for rebidding.

Commercial Package Insurance Policies

Before 1960, packaged commercial-insurance policies were nothing more than separate property and liability exposures brought together under one cover. The true commercial package, which combines both property and liability coverage, has three distinct advantages for school districts: lower premiums, convenience, and broader-based protection.

Property insurance. This is, of course, the most extensive aspect of the school district's exposure. Direct damage to property and building contents can be disastrous. The basic property coverage will insure both buildings and contents against damage caused by fire, lightning, windstorm, hail, smoke, vandalism, riot, explosion, vehicles, and aircraft. Through endorsements, this coverage can be extended to include such additional perils as glass breakage, ice and snow, water damage, and even earthquakes. A more common approach today in providing property coverage is, however, the *all-risk* policy, which is broader than the most inclusive *named-peril* policy. All-risk protection means that a loss is covered unless it is clearly excluded in the policy.

Most property-insurance policies limit the amount of recovery on losses to *actual cash value,* which is commonly defined as the current replacement cost minus actual physical depreciation. It is possible, however, to have property insurance endorsed to provide coverage for *replacement cost* instead. A school district will probably be required to carry insurance equal to 80 percent of replacement value with such an endorsement. Most insurance companies will also cover furniture, machinery, and equipment on a replacement-cost basis.

Liability insurance. The liability portion of a package policy should be written on a *comprehensive* basis, which provides automatic coverage for newly acquired or rented premises. The standard liability protection covers proven claims of bodily injury or property damage arising out of the facility. For example, if a student slips on a loose floor tile and breaks an arm and/or damages a wristwatch, the hospital bills, physician's fees, and a new watch should be covered under the liability portion of the property-insurance coverage. The limits of coverage are determined by the history of claims, but protection under $1 million in the aggregated claim is very risky for a school district.

Additional types of coverage. Many different kinds of insurance coverage can be included in a package. Some of the more common types in a school-district package are: (1) crime coverage for loss of money occurring inside or outside the premises; (2) boiler and machinery insurance for losses and injuries sustained in a boiler explosion or because of failure of major machinery such as a high-voltage electrical panel; (3) automobile and vehicle insurance coverage for driver's-education cars and district-owned vehicles; (4) inland marine insurance on such items as musical instruments.

Selecting an Agent or Broker

Insurance constitutes a legal contract between the insurance company and the insured person or organization. This contract is facilitated through a third party, the insurance agent or broker. A majority of insurance companies operate under the American Agency System, by which the company contracts with an individual who is authorized to issue policies, collect premiums, and solicit renewals within a given territory. *Independent* agents may represent several companies, while *exclusive* agents usually limit their practice to a single company's products. In either case, the agent is a legal representative of the insurance company and can act for the school district on the company's behalf.

Brokers are not tied to a specific insurance company by contract and act on a free-lance basis to buy coverage for clients. The broker may place business through an agent or go directly to an insurance company. The significant difference between an agent and a broker lies in the *legal* character of the agent. As the legal representative of an insurance company, if the agent says that the school district is covered, it is. The broker must first obtain verification from the insurance company.

Selecting an Insurance Company

There are literally thousands of insurance companies selling property and casualty insurance in the United States. These companies differ significantly in their capacity to handle risks. A good reference about the ability of an insurance company to cover the possible losses of a school district is the rating service A. M. Best Company, Incorporated.[3] Because insurance companies are competitive in establishing premiums, it is imperative that the administration recommend that the board of education select the insurance package through a public bidding process initiated by the director of buildings and grounds. The directory published by A. M. Best can be used by school district administrators and school-board members when they analyze the bids from various insurance companies before awarding a contract.

It will be necessary for a school district to have an up-to-date appraisal of the school buildings and their contents before initiating the bidding process. A land appraisal is, of course, not necessary for insurance purposes but could be necessary for those districts wishing to sell schools abandoned because of decreasing enrollment. The services of a professional appraiser are easily obtained, but the director of buildings and grounds should thoroughly understand the procedures and criteria the appraiser will use to establish values. This will have a significant effect on a school district if a catastrophe occurs and the district needs to replace a building. The coinsurance provisions in most insurance packages, by which a school district is required to retain 10 to 20 percent of the property and content value, make it imperative for a district to keep its appraisal values consistent with replacement value. Otherwise, a school district may be underinsured.

There are certain questions that the director of buildings and grounds should ask the insurance companies that submit bids. First, does the insurance company write all the forms of coverage needed by the school district? Second, is the insurance package flexible enough to include optional coverages that are not available in conventional packages? Third, does the insurance company have nearby offices staffed by professionals who can handle all lines? Fourth, are the company's adjusters qualified to deal with all types of claims? Fifth, is the company's underwriting philosophy progressive enough to consider new types of insurance risks?

Figure 8-1 represents an instrument developed by the Missouri Department of Elementary and Secondary Education. It has been modified for this presentation and is meant to be used by the administration as it evaluates its district's insurance program. Each descriptor is a criterion for evaluating the management of the program. The degree to which the school district's management procedures conform to each descriptor is evaluated by a yes or a no.

FIGURE 8-1:   CHECKLIST TO DETERMINE THE ADEQUACY OF A SCHOOL DISTRICT'S INSURANCE PROGRAM

	YES	NO
Legal Requirements		
The school district has developed policies and procedures which comply with common understandings of the state statutes as they apply to school insurance.	_____	_____
The school district utilizes open competition to determine who carries their insurance; also the board accepts the lowest responsible bid.	_____	_____
The school district's total insurance program is open for inspection.	_____	_____

Organization and Administration

RESPONSIBILITY

The school district has developed a policy which places

the responsibility for managing the insurance program with
the central office administration.   ____ ____

The school district maintains adequate records on the
total insurance program.   ____ ____

The school district utilizes professional assistance as
needed in evaluating the total insurance program.   ____ ____

The school district reviews the total insurance program
annually.   ____ ____

PROCEDURES

The school district has developed a standard operating
procedure utilizing a definite set of written criteria for
awarding insurance on the basis of competition.   ____ ____

The school district recognizes that the continuity of the
insurance program is important and changes in the program
or carriers are made on the basis of substantial improvement
of coverage or cost reduction.   ____ ____

The school district utilizes acceptable business principles
in developing its risk management program.   ____ ____

The school district has developed procedures to follow on
insurance losses.   ____ ____

The school community in general and interested local
insurance agents and brokers in particular are well aware of
the objectives of the program.   ____ ____

The school district's policy on insurance matters neither
favors nor discriminates against local insurance representatives.   ____ ____

Risk Management

IDENTIFICATION

The school district has a clearly defined, written and legally
defensible policy on liability coverage.   ____ ____

The school district has developed a clearly defined, written
policy on providing for adequate protection for all school
properties.   ____ ____

The school district's policy provides for a definite procedure for periodically appraising replacement cost and the
insurable value of buildings and contents.   ____ ____

The school district keeps a current listing of all buildings
and/or additions for insurance purposes, including such details
as dates of construction, condition, and square footage.   ____ ____

The school district, for insurance purposes, classifies as
building-fixed equipment laboratory tables, built-in cabinets,
and other items that are attached to the building.   ____ ____

The school district keeps a current inventory of all school
supplies and equipment classified as contents for insurance
purposes, including such details as current market value, date
of purchase, and condition.   ____ ____

The school district keeps a current listing of all school
vehicles for insurance purposes, including details such as
model, purchase price, and current value.   ____ ____

The school district has a standard procedure to account for
depreciation on the various types of property.   ____ ____

The school district's vehicle coverage includes comprehensive, liability, personal injury, property damage, fire, theft, collision, and uninsured motorist types where applicable.   _____ _____

The school district provides a bond on the treasurer.   _____ _____

The school district provides burglary insurance.   _____ _____

The school district provides broad form coverage on money and securities.   _____ _____

The school district carries broad form boiler insurance.   _____ _____

The school district's boiler insurance includes a provision for regular inspection and reports.   _____ _____

The school district reports crimes and vandalism to the proper police authorities.   _____ _____

Employees and supervisors are familiar with reporting procedures in the event of accidents.   _____ _____

The school district is prepared to cover all of the risks which have been determined as responsibilities of the school system, i.e., fire, and extended floater, boiler, liability, Workmen's Compensation, vehicle, crime, athletics, honesty bond, health and medical for employees, student, builder's risk, sprinkler.   _____ _____

REDUCTION

The school district has cooperated with outside agencies such as the insurance carriers, fire department, police department, and others in developing policy and procedures to eliminate hazards to human life and property and for possible reductions in insurance premiums.   _____ _____

ASSUMPTION

The school district is aware of all coverage which is not transferable and also of limitations on insurance coverage.   _____ _____

The school district utilizes coinsurance coverage on property.   _____ _____

The school district includes a deductible clause in its insurance policy or policies where the premium difference is favorable.   _____ _____

TRANSFER

The school district has considered the possibility of transferring some risks to contractors or lessors. Transportation is an area where this might be considered.   _____ _____

The school district's policy statement on insurance outlines an approach which provides effective coverage at a minimum cost for those risks which have been classified as responsibilities to be transferred from the district.   _____ _____

The school district schedules premium payments in such manner that approximately equal amounts are paid each year and insures that policies are written for a specified period of time.   _____ _____

The school district has insured property on the basis of insurable value and/or replacement cost.   _____ _____

The school district includes an agreed amount clause in the carrier's written policy or policies if coinsurance is utilized.   ____ ____

The school district has considered a package plan which combines coverages.   ____ ____

The school district utilizes blanket coverage, schedule coverage, and/or specific coverage plan in its insurance program.   ____ ____

The school district endeavors to engage a minimum number of agencies and companies in its insurance program.   ____ ____

The school district uses services such as Best's Rating Guide to determine the managerial and financial status of the insurance companies with which it deals.   ____ ____

SOURCE: Missouri Department of Elementary and Secondary Education, *Checklist to Determine the Adequacy of a School District's Insurance Program* (Jefferson City, Mo.: The Department, 1982).

SELECTED ISSUES IN PROPERTY MANAGEMENT

There are three significant issues currently facing public school districts that will persist into the next two decades and present the director of buildings and grounds with major challenges: adapting school facilities to meet the needs of handicapped students and employees; designing school buildings that are energy-efficient or modifying them so that they are; closing, selling, and/or leasing school buildings because of decreased enrollments.

Title V of the Rehabilitation Act of 1973 contains five sections. Section 504, Subpart C, applies to school facilities, requiring that they be accessible to the handicapped. All new construction is to be barrier-free, and all programs were to be accessible within three years of the bill's passage. School districts are not obliged to make each school accessible to the handicapped, but the district must make such accommodations as allow the programs "as a whole" to be accessible. All non-structural accommodations were to be completed within sixty days after these regulations went into effect. Outside ramps, however, were to be immediately built after June 1, 1977, and all structural changes completed no later than three years later.

From a very practical perspective, every school district must be energy-conscious; energy costs the district a large amount of money, a portion of which could be redirected into other areas if savings could be realized through an energy-conservation program. A skilled director of buildings and grounds, with help from other central-office administrators in the Administrative Services Department, can analyze the district's energy efficiency by examining utility bills, lighting systems, major energy loads, walls, doors, windows, roofs, and other outer shell features, and the heating, ventilating, and air-conditioning systems. Such an audit will point out areas of immediate concern. However, an organized energy-conservation program is the only long-term solution to escalating costs. Such a program will be successful only if it is people-centered. Figure 8-2 presents an outline of how all members of the school community can be part of an energy-conservation program.

One of the most highly charged issues that a district may be faced with is the closing of a school. Parents, students, and teachers usually have very strong emotional ties to individual schools and will not immediately see the wisdom in closing "their school." While there is no "right" way to proceed, the central-office administration can minimize the potential disruption. First, it can form a committee composed of teachers, administrators, parents, citizens, and students charged with formulating criteria to be used in deciding which schools will be closed and which will remain open. It is important for the school board to ask the various components of the school community to designate who will serve on the committee. For example, the teacher unions (NEA, AFT, and so on) should appoint the teacher representatives, and the PTA/PTO organizations can choose the parent representatives. The criteria should include such descriptors as the age of the schools, maintenance and janitorial costs, classroom size, location of the schools, repair requirements, energy costs, and the quality of education.

Once the criteria are established, it is the task of the administrative staff to apply them to the schools under consideration. Before the board of education makes a final decision, a public hearing should be conducted, during which the criteria and administrative staff analysis are presented to those in attendance. The public should then be allowed to provide further input. The board of education is advised to consider all of these data and make a final decision at an official board meeting held after the public hearing.

**FIGURE 8-2:   STAFF INVOLVEMENT IN AN ENERGY
                CONSERVATION PROGRAM**

  I. District Level
      A. School Board
          1. Commit school district to energy conservation ethic
          2. Establish basic energy usage policy for school district
          3. Authorize energy audit
          4. Set goals for energy savings
          5. Evaluate energy conservation efforts and results
      B. Superintendent
          1. Initiate and lead commitment to energy conservation ethic
             a. Provide philosophy and rationale
             b. Be aware of applicable funding and compliance legislation
             c. Demonstrate impact of energy dollars exported from school district
             d. Develop district-wide, long-range energy conservation in-service educational program
             e. Visibly reward persons and programs that meet or exceed energy conservation objectives
             f. Set personal example of energy conservation
          2. Establish persuasive district-wide energy conservation task force or committee

        a. Solicit energy policy suggestions
        b. Help establish energy conservation priorities
        c. Provide data on energy conservation performance of district
        d. Utilize members in public information efforts
    3. Assign specific energy conservation responsibilities to specific district individuals
        a. Monitor their performance
        b. Examples: building level energy manager, district public information officer
    4. Realize energy consumption is a political and an economic matter

C. Assistant Superintendent for Business Affairs
    1. Prepare technical reports for school board, superintendent, energy conservation task force, principals, physical plant staff
    2. Monitor and report on applicable energy conservation funding and compliance legislation
    3. Evaluate energy usage and provide factual record
        a. Identify source, quantity, and cost of each district energy source
        b. Inspect facilities, equipment, and supplies usage
        c. Present data in comparable forms
        d. Establish tough yet realistic and measurable energy objectives to support district goals and priorities
        e. Assess progress toward meeting objectives
    4. Purchase and construct with energy savings in mind
    5. Identify and recommend expert consultant help
    6. Demonstrate cost effectiveness of any energy measures
    7. Work with building engineers in scheduling operations, maintenance, and repairs to reduce energy consumption
    8. Convey energy usage progress to school publics by:
        a. district and by individual school buildings
        b. monthly, weekly, or daily energy consumption charts for principals, teachers, and pupils
        c. less complex charts and graphs for mass media
    9. Attend conferences and workshops on energy conservation

II. Building Level
  A. Principals
    1. Program and schedule to conserve energy
    2. Participate in district-wide energy conservation conferences and workshops
    3. Establish building energy audit and operations over-sight committee
    4. Survey teachers and staff regarding their suggestions for energy conservation in their rooms and/or building areas
    5. Compare and compete with similar school concerning energy conservation
    6. Report in meetings and in bulletins at least monthly about comparative energy conservation effectiveness
    7. Prepare individual classroom energy checklists
    8. Encourage teachers to attend conferences on energy usage
    9. Demonstrate commitment to energy conservation ethic by setting a personal example
  B. Teachers
    1. Heighten pupil awareness of energy topics in imaginative ways
    2. Put energy conservation in appropriate course materials
    3. Program and schedule to conserve energy

4. Follow operational guidelines for building and district energy conservation
C. Physical Plant Staff
1. Lead or assist in collecting energy audit data
   a. Keep accurate records
   b. Analyze bus routes and field trip requests
   c. Assess food services energy usage
2. Read and follow operational and maintenance manuals
3. Read and follow school district guidelines for energy conservation
4. Monitor and report compliance with district energy reduction objectives
5. Investigate alternative energy sources—especially solar—that may be used to conserve conventional sources
6. Suggest both short-term and long-term operational and maintenance guidelines modifications which promise energy conservation
7. Monitor trade journals and catalogs for energy saving tips, supplies, and equipment
8. Help all fellow personnel to be familiar with equipment, installations, and distribution systems.
9. Assist in developing energy efficient purchase specifications
10. Participate in hands-on training opportunities
D. Pupils
1. Form committees for energy conservation awareness
2. Act through Student Council projects
3. Plan competition between classes, buildings
4. Present student forums
5. Instill awareness through curriculum projects

SOURCE: Dale E. Kaiser and James C. Parker, "Staff Involvement in Energy Programs," *School Business Affairs,* 47, no. 7 (June 1981), 10, 11, 23.

SUMMARY

The importance of school buildings and facilities in the success of the instructional program is often overlooked by citizens, teachers, administrators, and even board members. The function of educational institutions is to educate children and young people. Consequently, the design of school facilities must be viewed within the context of educational concepts.

Historically, schoolhouses as such did not appear until the seventeenth century, and consisted primarily of one room, with long tables for the pupils and a raised podium for the teacher. In 1880, Louis Sullivan, an eminent American architect, enunciated the principle, "Form follows function." The planning of functional school buildings has been the continual concern not only of architects but also of educators.

There are four principles of operation that mirror the human condition and must be considered when planning an educational facility: (1) gradualism, (2) reversibility, (3) dual-purpose design, (4) people-centered design.

In addition, there are four steps in the process of carrying out a school construction and/or remodeling program. First, establish educational goals and objectives; second, develop architectural plans; third, develop a financial plan; fourth, implement the construction and/or remodeling project. Each of these steps has a number of components, which are implemented by various staff members. Each component involves, in turn, a number of procedures and subprocesses.

In the public sector, capital projects are usually financed through public borrowing, bond issues. Bonds may be sold to build, furnish, or remodel schools, replace roofs, and purchase large, expensive equipment. Voter approval through a bond-issue election is necessary for a board to be authorized to sell bonds. State statutes closely regulate the process of flotation, debt limits, and all aspects of public borrowing.

Capital projects have traditionally been financed through public borrowing because such projects are nonreoccurring expenses that should not be financed from the operating-fund levy. In addition, the burden of financing capital projects should be spread out over many generations, because they will also benefit from them.

The process of bond flotation involves four steps. First, the board of education and administration must determine what capital projects are and will be needed by the present and future generations of the school district. Next, the administration must become familiar with the state statutes that pertain to municipal bonds and bond-issue elections. Third, the administration needs to initiate a bond-issue election campaign. Finally, if the bond issue passes, the school board and administration must initiate those procedures that will insure the legality of the bonds.

The 1950s saw a significant advance in the commercial-insurance industry, the packaging of multiple coverages, although insurance is only one aspect of a total management program. There are three principles of operation in risk management that should be implemented by the director of buildings and grounds: Identify and evaluate the school district's exposure to risk, attempt to eliminate or minimize it, and, if that is impossible, transfer the risk to another party.

In purchasing insurance, the premium paid by the school district is a measure of the transferred risk. If the risk assumed by the insurance company is reduced by the use of deductibles, the competition for the premium will be increased. Deductibles also encourage a continual concern for safety, eliminate nuisance claims, and reduce internal administrative costs.

The commercial package that combines property and liability coverages usually will provide the district with a lower premium, convenience, and broader-based protection. Property coverage should be "all risk," which is broader than the most inclusive named-peril policy; in it, a loss is covered unless it is clearly excluded in the policy.

Insurance constitutes a legal contract between the insurance company and the insured party or organization. This contract is facilitated through a third party, the insurance agent or broker. A majority of insurance companies operate under the

American Agency System, by which the company contracts with an individual agent who is authorized to issue policies, collect premiums, and solicit renewals within a given territory. Brokers, on the other hand, are not tied to a specific company by contract, and act on a free-lance basis to buy coverage for clients.

There are literally thousands of insurance companies selling property and casualty insurance in the United States. A good reference about the ability of an insurance company to cover the possible losses of a school district is the rating service A. M. Best Company, Incorporated.

A district must have an up-to-date appraisal of the school buildings and their contents made before initiating the bidding process.

There are three significant issues currently facing public-school districts that will continue into the next two decades: (1) adapting school facilities to meet the needs of handicapped students and employees, (2) designing and modifying school buildings to be energy-efficient, (3) closing, selling, and/or leasing school buildings because of decreased enrollments.

IMPLICATIONS FOR EDUCATIONAL ADMINISTRATORS

This presentation of school district property management has three implications for educational administrators.

First, all administrators should be concerned with maintaining school facilities that are safe, healthy, pleasant, and stimulating, because such an environment has a significant effect upon the quality of the learning-instructional process.

Second, the director of buildings and grounds occupies a position of considerable importance in the effective education of children and should be recognized as an integral part of the school district's management team.

Third, while some administrators have a narrow focus, which usually centers only on the instructional program, issues such as energy conservation and accessibility of facilities to the handicapped should be viewed by the superintendent of schools and other administrators as priorities.

SELECTED BIBLIOGRAPHY

CASTALDI, BASIL, *Creative Planning of Educational Facilities.* Chicago: Rand McNally & Company, 1969.

COUNCIL OF EDUCATIONAL FACILITY PLANNERS, *Guide for Planning Educational Facilities* (rev. ed.). Columbus, Ohio: The Council, 1982.

——— , *Surplus School Space: The Problem and the Possibilities.* Columbus, Ohio: The Council, 1978.

RESEARCH CORPORATION OF THE ASSOCIATION OF SCHOOL BUSINESS OFFICIALS, *Energy Conservation and Management.* Park Ridge, Ill.: The Association, 1981.

——— , *School Facilities Maintenance and Operations.* Park Ridge, Ill.: The Association, 1981.

——— , *Schoolhouse Planning.* Park Ridge, Ill.: The Association, 1980.

NOTES

1. Basil Castaldi, *Creative Planning of Educational Facilities* (Chicago: Rand McNally & Company, 1969), p. 143.

2. Jeffrey B. Little and Lucien Rhodes, *Understanding Wall Street* (Cockeysville, Md.: Liberty Publishing Company, 1978), pp. 126–128.

3. A. M. Best Company, Inc., *Condensed Version of Ratings* (Old Wick, N.J.: The Company, 1983).

As a service-rendering institution, a school district will be capable of reaching its goals in direct proportion to the effectiveness of its policies and administrative procedures for recruiting and retaining high-quality employees and staff members.

The Role and Function of the Personnel-Management Administrator

In every school district, people must be recruited, selected, placed, appraised, and compensated. These functions may be performed by a central-office unit or assigned to various administrators within the district.

The goals of administrators charged with personnel responsibilities are basically the same in all school systems—to hire, retain, develop, and motivate personnel in order to achieve the objectives of the school district, assist individual members of the staff to reach the highest possible level of achievement, and maximize the career development of personnel.

These goals must be implemented through the following dimensions:

1. *Manpower Planning.* Establishing a master plan of long- and short-range personnel requirements is a necessary ingredient in the school system's program-, curricular-, and fiscal-planning processes.
2. *Recruitment of Personnel.* High-quality personnel are, of course, essential for the delivery of effective educational services to children, youth, and adults.
3. *Selection of Personnel.* The long- and short-range manpower requirements are implemented through selection techniques and processes.

4. *Placement and Induction of Personnel.* Through appropriate planning, new personnel and the school system accommodate to one another.
5. *Staff Development.* Development programs help personnel meet school district objectives and also provide individuals with the opportunity for personal and professional growth.
6. *Appraisal of Personnel.* Processes and techniques for appraisal help the individual grow professionally and the school district attain its objectives.
7. *Compensation of Personnel.* Establishing programs that reward high-quality performance helps to motivate personnel.
8. *Collective Negotiations.* The negotiating process gives personnel an opportunity to participate in matters that affect their professional and personal welfare.

Unfortunately, many school systems still see personnel management only as the hiring of competent teachers. These eight dimensions of personnel management are not discrete, isolated entities, but, rather, integral aspects of the same function.

PERSONNEL ADMINISTRATORS

Recently, many school districts have seen the need to delegate a major share of the personnel function to a specialized central-office unit. In this type of organization, an assistant superintendent (personnel director) administers personnel functions and aids the superintendent in solving personnel problems. "Personnel administrator" is usually a staff position that services line administrators. Line positions include the assistant superintendents for secondary education and elementary education, administrators of certain support services, and building principals. These administrators have been granted authority to make decisions in the supervisory process as it relates to staff, faculty, and students.

A major question facing school districts with increasing enrollments is: When does it become necessary to establish a central-office personnel administrator? William Castetter suggests a formula:

> One way of examining the problem of whether or not to include a central staff position for personnel in a school system is through the staff adequacy assumption. Simply stated, this assumes that for every 1,000 pupils enrolled, there should be a *minimum* of fifty professional personnel. Thus, a hypothetical school district with an enrollment of 4,000 pupils should have at least 200 professional employees. When classified personnel are taken into consideration, this district would have close to 300 members. If one considers the ramifications of performing, without proper organization all of the personnel processes . . . for this number of school employees, the conclusion is inescapable that the function will be inefficiently handled.[1]

Not only does personnel management have an impact on the continual staffing of positions, which in turn directly affects the quality of educational programs, but it also has a significant effect on the budget. Approximately 80 percent of all school district expenditures are for personnel salaries and benefits. Inefficiency in personnel management can, potentially, cost the taxpayer unnecessarily large sums of money.

Boards of education and administrators are seldom fully aware of the pervasive effect their personnel decisions have on the planning process. Every position within a school system generates a series of decisions regarding the type of work to be performed, the qualities needed for its proper performance, and its economic value. A variety of actions are required for the proper recruiting, selecting, inducting, developing, and appraising of personnel. Policies and procedures must also be established regarding academic freedom, tenure, health, grievances, leaves of absence, and retirement. In all but the very smallest districts, the movement of personnel into and out of a school system requires the attention of personnel specialists.

The number of strikes by public-school teachers has increased dramatically over the last ten years. Salaries, fringe benefits, and working conditions constitute the major issues that may lead to an impasse at the bargaining table and result in a strike. Education, however, is a relative newcomer to the negotiating process.

Collective negotiation is traditionally a function of the personnel department, and correctly belongs under the jursidiction of the assistant superintendent for personnel. Because of the magnitude of the issues involved in this process, most school districts should consider establishing the position, "employee relations." The American Association of School Administrators sponsored the publication of a monograph in 1974 entitled, "Helping Administrators Negotiate," with the prophetic subtitle, "A Profile of the Emerging Management Position of Director of Employee Relations in the Administrative Structure of a School System."[2]

The knowledge explosion and the constantly changing social milieu have also had a major impact on personnel administration. In the past, staff development was viewed primarily in terms of the in-service training model, which concentrated on providing a few workshops on instructional materials. In the last quarter of a century, however, federal legislation and litigation have more clearly defined the rights of racial minorities, women, students, and the handicapped. Along with a battery of new instructional technologies, different attitudes of those entering the teaching profession, and the changing values of our society as manifested by parents and students, these have created a need for an ongoing staff-development program for administrators and teachers alike. Staff development is so specialized that, like collective bargaining, it requires the attention of a new personnel specialist, the director of staff development.

The avalanche of federal legislation and litigation on minority rights has made it necessary to establish a central-office administrative position, usually entitled "director of affirmative action." Most federal legislation contains an equal-opportunity clause, which, in turn, dictates the organization of a detailed program for carrying out the intent of the law in all phases of personnel management. This organized program is more commonly called *affirmative action*. The fact that the director of affirmative action reports directly to the superintendent of schools is unique within the organizational structure. This provides the school district with integrity in complying with civil rights legislation, because the director is independent of influence by other administrators.

If a school district of 4,000 students justifies creating the position of assistant superintendent for personnel, a school system of over 5,000 pupils certainly justifies hiring additional personnel administrators.

JOB DESCRIPTION FOR THE ASSISTANT SUPERINTENDENT FOR PERSONNEL

Job Summary

The assistant superintendent for personnel is responsible for the school district's human-resource program. This includes the establishment and maintenance of effective two-way communication between the various organizational levels, and the formulation, recommendation, and administration of the school district's human-resources policies.

Organizational Relationship

The assistant superintendent has a line relationship with the superintendent of schools and reports directly to him or her. Serving as the chief adviser on human-resource matters, this individual has a staff relationship with other administrative personnel. The assistant superintendent for personnel has a line relationship with his or her immediate staff, which includes the directors of staff development and employee relations, both of whom report directly to him or her.

Organizational Tasks

The assistant superintendent for personnel is directly responsible for establishing administrative processes, procedures, and techniques for human resource planning and recruitment, selection, placement, and induction of personnel, staff-appraisal techniques, and compensation programs. He or she is further responsible for supervising the directors of staff development and employee relations.

Job Requirements

In terms of education and experience, the assistant superintendent for personnel should possess:

Appropriate state administrator certification
A doctorate in educational administration
Formal course work in the areas of curriculum, finance, school law, personnel administration, and collective bargaining
Classroom teaching experience and five years as a building-level administrator

JOB DESCRIPTION FOR THE DIRECTOR
OF STAFF DEVELOPMENT

Job Summary

The director of staff development is responsible for the establishment and maintenance of effective two-way communication between the various organizational levels, and for the formulation, recommendation, and administration of the school district's staff-development policies.

Organizational Relationship

The director of staff development has a line relationship with the assistant superintendent for personnel and reports directly to that individual. He or she serves as the chief adviser on staff relationships with other administrative personnel and has a cooperative professional relationship with nonadministrative personnel with whom he or she works. The director has a line relationship with his or her immediate staff, which reports directly to him or her.

Organizational Tasks

In planning and implementing a staff-development program, the director shall:

Establish and implement ongoing needs-assessment techniques with all personnel

Analyze and evaluate assessment instruments

Secure input from administrative personnel concerning the most desirable time and place for program presentation

Evaluate program presentations

Job Requirements

In terms of educational requirements, the director of staff development should possess:

A master's degree (minimum)

Formal course work in the areas of testing and measurement, statistics, curriculum, and supervision

A minimum of two years' professional experience as a teacher or building administrator

JOB DESCRIPTION FOR THE DIRECTOR
OF AFFIRMATIVE ACTION

Job Summary

The director of affirmative action is responsible for administering the school district's affirmative-action program. This includes establishing and maintaining effective two-way communication between organizational levels and formulating, recommending, and administering the school district's affirmative-action program.

Organizational Relationship

The director of affirmative action has a line relationship with the superintendent of schools, to whom he or she reports directly and serves as the chief adviser on affirmative-action matters. The director of affirmative action has a staff relationship with other administrative personnel and a cooperative professional one with nonadministrative personnel with whom he or she works. Of course, the director has a line relationship with his or her immediate staff, which reports directly to him or her.

Organizational Tasks

The director of affirmative action is responsible for the following tasks:

Studies affirmative-action problems and suggests solutions to the superintendent, if possible

Uses school district data in reviewing the qualifications of all employees, with particular emphasis on minorities and women, as they relate to fair employment practices

Develops and updates goals and timetables for correcting identifiable deficiencies

Advises the superintendent about the recruitment of minorities and women for those classified and certified positions that may be falling short of the district's affirmative-action goals

Assumes the role of compliance officer and makes all contacts with state and federal agencies

Reviews all job announcements, job descriptions, and selection criteria to ensure compliance with all affirmative-action requirements

Advises the superintendent regarding the nature, purpose, and intent of all laws, executive orders, policies, regulations, and reports of external agencies for the implementation of the school district's affirmative-action program

Helps district administrators investigate formal complaints of alleged discrimination relating to fair employment practices and recommends corrective measures to the superintendent

Maintains liaison with local, state, and federal agencies and with organizations concerned with promoting fair employment practices

Represents the school district at meetings, conferences, and other gatherings pertaining to affirmative-action programs, as approved by the superintendent

Works with appropriate individuals and agencies in ascertaining correct population-characteristic data for the district

Compiles an annual report to the superintendent on the progress of the school district's affirmative-action program

Job Requirements

In terms of educational requirements, the director of affirmative action should possess:

A master's degree (minimum)

Formal course work in the area of educational administration, with exposure to school law, collective bargaining, and personnel administration

A minimum of two years of teaching experience, two years as a building principal, and two years as a central-office administrator

Personal abilities and characteristics are universal for all administrators. The superintendent, assistant superintendents, directors, and building principals must have good human-relation skills, be sensitive to individual needs, possess good writing skills, work well with details, and, to borrow a term from the business community, be self-starters.

MANPOWER PLANNING

Planning is a common human experience. Before embarking on a journey, we must understand where we are, know where we want to go, and decide how best to get there. Even in such an elementary form, this process applies to educational organizations.

Through manpower planning, a school district ensures that it has the right number of people, with the right skills, in the right place, at the right time, and that these people are capable of effectively carrying out those tasks that will aid the organization to achieve its objectives. If a school district is to do so, it needs financial and physical resources and people. Too often, the people are taken for granted, yet they are the force that directly effects the main objective of a school district— to educate children. Manpower planning thus translates the organization's objectives into human-resource terms.

In some school districts, long- and short-range objectives are couched in ambiguous language and are often known only by central-office administrators. This makes it difficult to involve building principles in the hiring process when unexpected vacancies occur, when replacements are needed because of natural attrition, or when new programs must be staffed.

Manpower planning, as a process, ensures the smooth development of an organization. "We assess where we are; we assess where we are going; we consider the implications of these objectives on future demands and future supply of human resources; and we attempt to match demand and supply so as to make them compatible with the achievement of the organization's future needs."[3]

Assessing Manpower Needs

The process of assessing human resources needs has four aspects. First, manpower inventories must be developed to analyze the various tasks necessary to meet the school district's objectives; these tasks are then matched against the skills of current employees. Second, five-year enrollment projections must be developed. The extreme mobility of the American population has made this increasingly important over the past ten years. Third, the overall objectives of the school district must be reviewed within the context of changing needs. At a time of high inflation and shrinking revenue, all but the wealthiest districts must establish priorities in meeting objectives. Fourth, manpower inventories, enrollment projections, and a school district's objectives must be organized into a manpower forecast, which becomes the mandate of the personnel administrator.

Implementing the manpower mandate becomes more involved, however, when viewed in the light of compliance with federal legislation and litigation and the staff reductions brought on by decreasing enrollments. Because both issues have had such a tremendous impact on personnel management, they have been given particular emphasis in this chapter.

Manpower planning is sometimes understood only within the confines of the instructional program. However, for every teacher, there is usually a support employee. The contemporary school district employs not only teachers and administrators, but also cooks, custodians, maintenance personnel, secretaries, computer programmers, telephone switchboard operators, warehouse personnel, distribution truck drivers, and other specialists whom the average citizen often thinks are employed only in the private business sector.

The future objectives of a school district determine future manpower needs. The number and mix of human resources is determined by the types of services called for by these organizational objectives. Establishing objectives is the prerogative of the board of education. The board, however must rely on the experience and expertise of the school administrators to formulate objectives that will best meet the educational needs of the community.

The review of current objectives in light of future educational needs is a cooperative task. In a district working under the organizational structure presented in Chapter 2, the assistant superintendents for secondary education, elementary education, and instructional services would have the primary responsibility for determining future objectives. The assistant superintendent for personnel would develop a manpower forecast to meet the projected objectives developed by the three curriculum-related assistant superintendents. The assistant superintendent for administrative services would then translate the objectives and manpower needs into fiscal-resource data. The superintendent of schools, finally, is charged with prioritizing objectives for school-board approval.

This review of objectives is not a one-time task, but a continual process. The objectives, however, should be established for at least five years; if the need occurs, they can be revised into a new five-year plan. Thus, a set of objectives is always in effect for a set period of time.

Manpower forecasting.   Once the objectives have been reviewed and an overall manpower forecast established, a more explicit projection of future manpower needs must be developed. There are five commonly accepted methods for computing future needs.[4]

1. *Expert Estimate.* Those staff members in the school district most familiar with employment requirements use their experience to estimate future needs.
2. *Historical Comparison.* By this method, past trends are projected into the future.

3. *Task Analysis.* Each person in each type of position is reviewed to determine demand. This method is sometimes effective in uncovering specific quality shortages within a school system.
4. *Correlation.* Manpower requirements fluctuate in relation to such variables as decreasing enrollment, fiscal resources, and new programs. A correlation of these variables can be statistically formulated.
5. *Modeling.* This usually refers to decision-making models. However, it may be broadened to include reviewing the programs and how they are organized in other school systems, which in turn may serve as a model for staffing.

Whatever method or combination of methods is used, the manpower inventories on current human resources will be used to provide data about the age, sex, education, certification, and positions held by the employees in the district.

The supply of human resources. An increase in a school system's supply of human resources can come from two sources, newly hired employees and individuals returning from leaves, such as maternity, military, and sabbatical leaves. Both types of increases are relatively easy to incorporate into a manpower forecast because hiring is controlled and leaves are usually for set periods of time.

Decreases in a school system's supply of human resources, however, are more difficult to predict. Deaths, voluntary resignations, and dismissals are unpredictable except in the broadest sense, as through statistical averaging. Some decreases, such as sabbatical leaves, can be controlled; others, such as retirement, are easier to predict when the school district has a mandatory retirement age.

The available labor force has a significant effect on manpower forecasting. Graduates from high schools, colleges, and universities continually replenish the supply of labor necessary to carry out the mandate of public education. In recent years, however, educational organizations have experienced a decrease in the number of applicants for mathematics and science teaching positions because of the higher wages and employment opportunities available in private business and industry.

Those entering the work force other than recent graduates include women seeking full-time or part-time employment either to supplement or to provide the primary family income. Divorce rates and high inflation are key factors contributing to the number of women reentering the labor force.

Matching needs with supply. A final activity in manpower forecasting is to match the school district's future human-resource needs with supply. This will pinpoint shortages, highlight areas of potential overstaffing, and identify the number of individuals who must be recruited from the labor force to satisfy current and future needs.

In the final analysis, human-resource planning ensures that we have the right number and mixture of human resources to meet the school district's future needs as determined by its future objectives.

Reduction in Force

A pressing problem facing metropolitan areas is decreasing pupil enrollments, which has led to a surplus of teachers. Declining enrollments have particular significance in the manpower-planning process and have caused the initiation of a procedure commonly referred to as a reduction in force, or RIF. Excess employees are usually placed on involuntary leave according to the seniority system, which follows the principle of "last in, first out." Retained employees may be transferred within the school system to balance a particular staff or faculty. Such changes are certain to create anxiety among individuals who have become accustomed to the atmosphere and procedures of a particular school. Because many school districts have only recently attempted to properly represent minority groups in their work force, the use of seniority-based reduction procedures usually means that minority employees are among the first to go. Court-mandated desegretation in hiring practices and the legislative demand for affirmative action calls for the introduction of alternatives to RIF whenever possible.

Two of the most successful alternatives to RIF have been early-retirement incentive programs and retraining individuals for positions that will become vacant through attrition or be created because of program development.

Teacher negotiations have, in recent years, centered on the job-security issue, and many contracts now call for teachers in excess areas to be transferred to other positions, hired as permanent substitutes, or retrained for new assignments at school district expense.

The Role of the Principal

A key person in manpower planning is, of course, the building principal. He or she is usually the first to spot dwindling enrollments. The principal can provide the central-office staff with up-to-date and projected enrollment figures, projected maintenance and capital-improvement costs, and projected staffing needs.

The principal also has front-line contact with staff members, students, and parents, and therefore will be responsible for preparing teachers for possible job loss and easing the concerns of parents and students. To perform these tasks effectively, the principal must become an integral part of the manpower-planning process, being relied on for data and input. Likewise, he or she must constantly be kept informed of central-office decisions before they are announced to the staff and public.

FEDERAL INFLUENCES ON MANPOWER PLANNING

A hallmark of contemporary American society is the avalanche of federal legislation and court decisions delineating and more clearly defining civil rights. The term *civil rights* is somewhat misunderstood and is most often applied to the constitutional rights of racial minorities. However, it correctly refers to those constitutional and legislative rights that are inalienable and applicable to all citizens. In manpower planning, the master plan should provide direction for the recruitment and selection processes. In so doing, the plan must not violate the civil rights of job applicants or lead the school district into an indefensible position.

What follows is an explanation of major federal legislation, executive orders, and court decisions that should help to develop a manpower plan. It is not meant to be exhaustive, because the legislative and judicial processes are organic in nature; therefore, modifications will undoubtedly occur. The underlying concept of equality, however, has universal application.

First, the important concept of affirmative action must be clearly understood because it is a requirement incorporated or implied in civil-rights legislation and executive orders.

Affirmative Action

Definition. The notion that there can be justice for none if there is not justice for all, captures the intent of civil-rights legislation, while the motto of many women, "in business we must all be like our fathers," highlights affirmative-action programs.

Affirmative-action programs are detailed, result-oriented procedures, which, when carried out in good faith, result in compliance with the equal-opportunity clauses found in most legislation and executive orders. Affirmative action, therefore, is not a law within itself but rather a set of guidelines that organizations may use to insure compliance with legislation and executive orders. Thus, an organization does not "violate" affirmative action; it violates the law.

Brief history of affirmative action. Although the term *affirmative action* is of recent origin, the concept of an employer's taking specific steps to hire and treat minority groups equally can be traced to President Franklin D. Roosevelt's Executive Order 8802, issued in June 1941. This order, which has the force of law, established a policy of equal employment opportunity in defense contracts. President Roosevelt issued a new order in 1943, extending the order to all government contractors and mandating for the first time that all contracts contain a clause specifically forbidding discrimination.

In 1953, President Dwight D. Eisenhower issued Executive Order 10479, which established the Government Contract Compliance Committee. This committee received complaints of discrimination by government contractors but had no power to enforce its guidelines.

The period of voluntary compliance ended in 1961, when President John F. Kennedy issued Executive Order 10925. This order established the President's Committee on Equal Employment Opportunity and gave it the authority to make and enforce its own rules by imposing sanctions and penalities against noncomplying contractors. Government contractors were required to have nondiscrimination clauses covering race, color, creed, and national origin.

In September 1965, President Lyndon B. Johnson issued a very important executive order, giving the secretary of labor jurisdiction over contract compliance and creating the Office of Federal Contract Compliance, which replaced the Committee on Equal Employment Opportunity. Every federal contractor was required to include a seven-point equal-opportunity clause, agreeing not to discriminate against anyone in hiring and during employment on the basis of race, color, creed, or national origin. Further, the contractor also had to agree in writing to take affirmative-action measures in hiring. President Johnson's Executive Order 11375, in 1967, amended Executive Order 11246, by adding sex and religion to the list of discriminators.

The Secretary of Labor issued Chapter 60 of Title 41 of the Code of Federal Regulations for the purpose of implementing Executive Order 11375. The secretary delegated enforcement authority to the Office of Federal Contract Compliance (OFCC), which reports to the assistant secretary of the Employment Standards Administration.

The Office of Federal Contract Compliance provides leadership in the area of nondiscrimination by government contractors and also cooperates with the Equal Employment Opportunity Commission (EEOC) and the Department of Justice on matters relating to Title VII of the 1964 Civil Rights Act as amended.

The EEOC was established by Title VII of the Civil Rights Act to investigate alleged discrimination based on race, color, religion, sex, or national origin. The EEOC was greatly strengthened in 1972 by the passage of the Equal Employment Opportunity Act, extending coverage to all private employers of fifteen or more persons, all educational institutions, all state and local governments, public and private employment agencies, labor unions with fifteen or more members, and joint labor-management committees for apprenticeships and training. This act also gave the Commission the power to bring litigation against an organization that engages in discriminatory practice.

Equal Employment Opportunity Commission. A major failing of many school administrators is their lack of understanding about the EEOC and its influence on human-resource administration. This five-member commission has, from time to time, established affirmative-action guidelines that, if adopted by school districts, can minimize liability for claims of discrimination. To further aid employers, on December 11, 1978, the EEOC adopted additional guidelines that can be used to avoid liability from claims of "reverse discrimination" resulting from affirmative action providing employment opportunities for women and racial and ethnic minorities. The following, compiled from several sources, will provide a framework for affirmative-action compliance.

Eight steps should be followed to conform to federal guidelines:

First, a district's board of education must issue a written equal-employment-opportunity policy to be enforced by the superintendent. Such a policy would constitute a determination to recruit, hire, and promote for all job classifications without regard to race, creed, national origin, sex, or age (except where sex or age is a bona fide occupation qualification); to base decisions concerning employment solely on individual qualifications as related to the requirements of the position for which the applicant is being considered; and to insure that all personnel actions such as compensation, benefits, transfers, layoffs, and continuing education will be administered without discrimination.

Second, the superintendent must appoint a top official directly responsible to him or her who has the responsibility and authority to implement the program. The affirmative-action officer should develop policy statements, write affirmative-action programs, initiate internal and external communications, assist other administrators in the identification of problem areas, design and implement audit and reporting systems, serve as a liaison between district and enforcement agencies, and keep the superintendent informed of the latest developments in the area of equal opportunities.

Third, a school district should disseminate its affirmative-action program both internally and externally. The board policy should be publicized through all internal media channels, such as at meetings and on bulletin boards. External dissemination might take the form of brochures advertising the district; written notification to recruitment sources; clauses in purchase orders, leases, contracts; and written notification to minority organizations, community agencies, and community leaders.

Step four begins with a survey and analysis of minority and female employees by school and job classification. The percentage and number of minority and female employees currently employed in each major job classification should be compared to their presence in the relevant labor market—that is, the area in which one can reasonably expect to recruit. This will determine "underutilization," defined as having fewer minorities or women in a particular job category or school than could be reasonably expected; and "concentration," defined as more of a particular group in a job category than would reasonably be expected. A survey should also be conducted of transferable females and minorities who have the credentials to handle other positions.

With this information, the school district administration should proceed to step five, developing a timetable containing measurable and remedial goals. Once long-range goals have been established, specific and numerical targets can be developed for the hiring, training, transferring, and promoting of personnel to reach goals within the established time frame. During this step, the causes of underutilization should be identified.

Step six calls for developing and implementing specific programs to eliminate discriminatory barriers and achieve goals. This is the heart of an affirmative action program, and, since it is quite complicated, will be discussed in more detail in subsequent sections. All those involved in every aspect of the hiring process must be trained to use objective standards that support affirmative-action goals. Recruitment procedures must be analyzed and reviewed for each job category, to identify and eliminate discriminatory barriers. Recruitment procedures might include contacting educational institutions and community-action organizations that represent minorities.

Reviewing the selection process to insure that job requirements and hiring contribute to affirmative-action goals is a vital part of step six. This includes being certain that job qualifications and selection standards do not screen out minorities unless the qualifications can be significantly related to job performance and no alternate nondiscriminatory standards can be developed.

Upward-mobility systems such as assignments, promotions, transfers, seniority, and continuing education plays an important role in step six. Through careful record-keeping, existing barriers may be identified and specific remedial programs initiated. These programs might include targeting members of minorities and women by identifying those currently qualified for upward mobility and providing training for those who are not.

Wage and salary structures, benefits, and conditions of employment are other areas to be investigated. Title VII of the 1964 Civil Rights Act and the Equal Pay Act require fiscal parity for jobs of equal skill and responsibility. All fringe benefits such as medical, hospital, and life insurance must be equally applied to personnel performing similar functions. Even in instances where states have "protective laws" barring women from hard and dangerous work, the courts have generally found that the equal-employment requirements of Title VII supersede state law. Courts have also barred "compulsory maternity leave," or discharge of pregnant teachers.

Under affirmative-action programs, the criteria for deciding when employees shall be terminated, demoted, disciplined, laid off, or recalled should be the same for all. Seemingly neutral practices should also be reexamined to see if they have a negative effect on minority groups. Special considerations, such as job transfers or career counseling, should be given to minorities laid off because of legitimate seniority systems.

Step seven is to establish internal auditing and reporting systems to monitor and evaluate progress in each aspect of the affirmative-action program. Quarterly reports based on the data already outlined should be available to all administrators, enabling them to see how the program is working and where improvement is needed. The issue of keeping records on employees and potential employees by sex, race, or national origin is a very sensitive one. Such record-keeping has been used in the past as a discriminatory device, and some states have outlawed the practice. In certain litigation, it has even been used as evidence of discriminatory practices. On the other hand, these data will be demanded by enforcement agencies, and they are necessary for affirmative-action record-keeping. The EEOC suggests that such information be coded and kept separate from personnel files.

Developing supportive district and community programs is the last step in an affirmative-action program. This may include developing support services for recruiting minority and female employees and encouraging employees to further their education to qualify for promotion.

Bona fide occupational qualification. Discrimination by sex, religion, or national origin is allowed by the Equal Employment Opportunity Act on one condition, referred to in the law as follows:

Notwithstanding any other provision of this title, (1) it shall not be an unlawful employment practice for an employer to hire and employ employees, for an employment agency to classify, or refer for employment any individual, for a labor organization to classify its membership or to classify or refer for employment any individual, or for an employer, labor organization, or joint labor management committee controlling apprenticeship or other training, or retraining programs to admit or employ any individual in any such program, on the basis of his religion, sex, or national origin in those certain instances where religion, sex, or national origin is a bona fide occupational qualification reasonably necessary to the normal operation of that particular business or enterprise and (2) it shall not be an unlawful employment practice for a school, college, university, or other educational institution or institution of learning to hire and employ employees of a particular religion if such school, college, university, or other educational institution or institution of learning is, in whole or in substantial part, owned, supported, controlled, or managed by a particular religion or by a particular religious corporation, association, or society, or if the curriculum of such school, college, university, or other educational institution or institution of learning is directed toward the propagation of a particular religion.[5]

Therefore, a school district's personnel administrator has the right to specify a female for the position of swimming instructor when part of the job description includes supervising the locker room used by female students. In like manner, a Lutheran school official may hire only those applicants who profess the Lutheran creed because the mission of the school is to propagate that particular faith.

In certain school districts the national origin of teachers is extremely important. One out of every twenty persons in the United States is now of Spanish-speaking origin, making this group the nation's second largest minority, after blacks.[6] If, in a particular school district, over 30 percent of its student population have Spanish surnames, being of Latin origin would be a bona fide job qualification for certain teaching positions in that school system.

Judicial review of affirmative action.   Court decisions have further modified affirmative-action laws and regulations. Although the courts will continue to refine the interpretation of the Civil Rights Act and the Equal Employment Opportunity Act, certain basic conclusions have emerged and provide direction to school districts in their efforts to construct and implement an affirmative-action program.

First, discrimination has been broadly defined, in most cases including a class of individuals rather than a single person. Where discrimination has been found by the courts to exist, remediation must be applied to all members of the class to which the individual complainant belongs.

Second, it is not the intent but rather the consequences of the employment practice that determine if discrimination exists and dictate the remedy.

Third, even when an employment practice is neutral and impartially administered, if it has a disparate effect upon members of a protected class (those groups covered by a law), or if it perpetuates the effects of prior discriminatory practices, it constitutes unlawful discrimination.

Fourth, statistics that show a disproportionate number of minorities or females in a job classification relative to their presence in the work force constitute evidence of discriminatory practices. Where such statistics exist, the employer must show that this is not the result of overt or institutional discrimination.

Fifth, for an employer to justify any practice or policy that has a negative effect on a protected class, a "compelling business necessity" must be demonstrated. The courts have interpreted this in a very narrow sense, to mean that no alternative nondiscriminatory practice can achieve the required result.

Finally, court-ordered remedies not only open the doors to equal employment but also require employers to "make whole" and "restore the rightful economic status" of all those in the affected class. In practice, courts have ordered fundamental changes in all aspects of employment systems.

Equality for the Handicapped

Title V of the Rehabilitation Act of 1973 contains five sections, four of which relate to affirmative action for handicapped individuals and one of which deals with voluntary actions, remedial actions, and evaluation criteria for compliance with the law. The congressional intent of the Rehabilitation Act is identical to other civil-rights legislation, such as the Civil Rights Act (covering discrimination based on race, sex, religion, or national origin) and Title IX of the Educational Amendments (discrimination based on sex). However, the U.S. Department of Health, Education and Welfare (HEW) emphasized in the Federal Register promulgating the law that it also contains a fundamental difference:

The premise of both Title VI (Civil Rights Act) and Title IX (Educational Amendments) is that there is no inherent difference of inequalities between the general public and the persons protected by these statutes and, therefore, there should be no differential treatment in the administration of federal programs. Section 504 (Rehabilitiation Act), on the other hand, is far more complex. Handicapped persons may require different treatment in order to be afforded equal access, and identical treatment may, in fact, constitute discrimination. The problem of establishing general rules as to when different treatment is prohibited or required is compounded by the diversity of existing handicaps and the differing degree to which particular persons may be affected.[7]

Subpart B of Section 504 specifically refers to employment practices. It prohibits recipients of federal financial assistance from discriminating against qualified handicapped individuals in terms of recruitment, hiring, compensation, job assignment/classification, and fringe benefits. Employers are further required to provide reasonable work-environment accommodations for qualified handicapped applicants or employees unless they can demonstrate that such accommodations would impose an undue hardship on the employer. The law applies to all state, intermediate, and local educational agencies. Finally, any agency that receives assistance under the Education of the Handicapped Act must take positive steps to employ and promote qualified handicapped persons in programs assisted under that act.

Equality for Women

The French writer Stendhal believed that granting women equality would be the surest sign of civilization and would double the intellectual power of the human race. Although he wrote over 100 years ago, equality for women continues to be a significant issue.

In educational organizations, the question of equal employment opportunity for women traditionally applies to a specific job classification—administration. It is obvious to all observers that women are well represented in teaching, custodial, food-service, and bus-driving positions. Skilled trade jobs, such as carpenters, electricians, or plumbers (all of whom may be part of a school district maintenance staff), however, are frequently dominated by males, as are industrial-arts teaching positions. In such cases, the norms of affirmative action previously outlined in this chapter would become applicable. The critical issue, however, is the need to have women better represented in administrative ranks.

The legal mandate of equal employment opportunity for women emanates primarily from two federal laws: Title IX of the Educational Amendments of 1972, which prohibits sex discrimination in educational programs or activities including employment when the school district is receiving federal financial assistance; and, of course, Title VII of the Civil Rights Act of 1964, as amended in 1972, which prohibits discrimination on the basis of sex as well as religion, national origin, race, or color.

Potential areas of employment discrimination concerning women. As a general rule, school districts—and all employers—are prohibited from establishing job qualifications that are derived from female stereotyping. The courts have uniformly required employers to prove that any restrictions are indeed bona fide occupational qualifications.

Some of the most common forms of discrimination against females in the business-industrial community are even less defensible in educational organizations. Females have been denied employment because of height and weight limitations. In such situations, a woman who is capable of performing the job-related tasks has clearly established case-law precedents to bring the employer to court. However, it still occurs that an exceptionally talented woman may not be hired for an administrative position because she is "nice and petite" and does not measure up to the image of a strong leader held by those in a position to hire her. Discrimination is much harder to prove in the latter situation.

The Equal Employment Opportunity Commission prohibits discriminating against women because they are married, pregnant, not the principal wage earner in a family, or have preschool-aged children.

The preferences of customers and clientele are also not bona fide occupational qualifications. Thus, the preference of parents, teachers, and even students for male principals and administrators in a given school district does not permit the district to discriminate against females for these positions.

Maternity as a particular form of discrimination. On October 31, 1978, President Carter signed into law a pregnancy-disability amendment (PL95-555) to Title VII of the Civil Rights Act of 1964. The law had the effect of eliminating unequal treatment for pregnant women in all employment-related situations. The EEOC issued guidelines for implementing this law, indicating that it is discriminatory for an employer: to refuse to hire, train, assign, or promote a woman solely because she is pregnant; to require maternity leave for a predetermined time period; to dismiss a pregnant woman; to deny reemployment to a woman on maternity leave; to deny seniority credit to a woman on maternity leave; and to deny disability or medical benefits to a woman for disabilities unrelated to but occurring during pregnancy, childbirth, or recovery from childbirth.

Equality by Age

Peter Drucker, the nationally recognized expert in management theory and practice, predicts that "flexible retirement is going to be the central social issue in the U.S. during the next decade. It is going to play the role that minority employment played in the 1960's and women's rights played in the seventies."[8] Drucker's prediction is, however, only one aspect of an even larger issue: we are rapidly becoming a nation whose population is by percentage mostly middle-aged.

The Age Discrimination in Employment Act of 1967, as amended, is taking on ever-increasing importance for personnel administrators. This act was passed by Congress to promote the employment of the older worker based on ability rather than age, by prohibiting arbitrary discrimination. Also, under this act the Department of Labor has consistently sponsored informational and educational programs on the needs and abilities of the older worker. The "Statement of Findings and Purpose" in the Age Discrimination in Employment Act sets forth a rationale for its passage that is a true reflection of current societal attitudes toward older workers:

> Sec. 2.(a) The Congress hereby finds and declares that:
> (1) in the face of rising productivity and affluence, older workers find themselves disadvantaged in their efforts to retain employment, and especially to regain employment when displaced from jobs;
> (2) the setting of arbitrary age limits regardless of potential for job performance has become a common practice, and certain otherwise desirable practices may work to the disadvantage of older persons;
> (3) the incidence of unemployment, especially long-term unemployment, with resultant deterioration of skill, morale, and employer acceptability is, relative to the younger ages, high among older workers; their numbers are great and growing; and their employment problems grave;
> (4) the existence in industries affecting commerce of arbitrary discrimination in employment burdens commerce and the free flow of goods in commerce.[9]

This section has dealt with four major federal influences on the manpower-planning process. Although affirmative action and the legislation on equality for the handicapped, women, and individuals by age represent basic issues in personnel administration, they are by no means the only federal considerations that affect personnel processes.

BOARD OF EDUCATION POLICY
ON EQUAL EMPLOYMENT OPPORTUNITY
AND AFFIRMATIVE ACTION

The following sample policy has been developed to illustrate more clearly how school districts can comply with the intent and practices of federal legislation and litigation set forth in this chapter:

The board of education recognizes that implementation of its policy to provide an effective educational program depends on the full and effective utilization of qualified employees regardless of race, age, sex, color, religion, national origin, creed, or ancestry.

The board of education initiates an affirmative-action program that will be in compliance with Title VII of the Civil Rights Act of 1964 and the Equal Employment Opportunity Act of 1972. This program shall insure: proportional minority and female representation and participation in all employment opportunities; that civil rights will not be violated, abridged, or denied; that recruitment and selection criteria will be unbiased; that information relative to employment and promotional opportunities will be disseminated on an equal basis; and, finally, that every employee has a right to file an internal or external complaint of discrimination and to obtain redress therefrom, based on the finding of facts that substantiate the complaint.

The following school district administrators are responsible for the effective implementation of the affirmative-action program:

Superintendent of Schools. As the chief executive officer of the school system, the superintendent is directly responsible for exercising leadership in formulating and implementing procedures that are in keeping with this policy.

Director of Affirmative Action. Under the supervision of the superintendent, the director is responsible for the formulation and administration of the affirmative-action program.

RECRUITMENT OF PERSONNEL

After the manpower-planning process identifies current and future staffing needs, qualified personnel must be recruited. However, certain constraints on recruitment must be taken into consideration in program development. Affirmative-action requirements, the reputation and policies of a school district, the enormous responsibilities of certain positions in education, the salary and fringe benefits offered in particular school districts—all have an influence on how a district will implement the recruitment process.

To carry out a recruitment program effectively, personnel administrators must have a good understanding of vocational-development theory. The following principles are common to many theories and can be used to formulate recruitment strategies. First, people have different interests, abilities, and personalities, which will qualify them for a number of occupations. Second, people's occupational preferences and competencies, as well as self-image, will change with time and experience, making personal adjustment a continuous process. Third, both life and work satisfaction depend on how well individuals can utilize their abilities and find outlets that satisfy their interests, personalities, and sense of values. Fourth, the process of occupational choice is influenced by employment variables such as salary, fringe benefits, location, the opportunity for advancement, and the nature of the work to be performed. Finally, vocational development is essentially a compromise between personal characteristics, such as interests and abilities, and external factors, such as the type of work to be performed.

Experience shows that certain recruiting methods produce the best candidates for a particular job vacancy. Therefore, before initiating the recruitment process, each job vacancy should be analyzed to ascertain what method will be most effective. The most common methods include: internal search, referrals, contacting employment agencies, advertising vacancies with college and university placement services, advertising in newspapers and professional publications, following up unsolicited applications, and contacting community organizations that promote the interests of minority groups.

When a school district wishes to communicate that it has a vacancy, it usually relies on a formal advertisement. The content of an advertisement is dictated by the job description and criteria to be used in selecting the most qualified candidate for the position. An effective advertisement must accurately reflect the major responsibilities of the position and the minimum qualifications needed to become a candidate for the job.

In terms of content and style, the most effective advertisement will include the title of the position, information about the school district, information on how to apply, and qualifications for candidates. It is generally not appropriate to list subjective qualifications and use "blind ads." It is also more effective, when possible, for a school district to advertise each position by itself, or to list only a few vacancies in a given advertisement.

A special type of advertisement is the recruitment brochure. Its purpose is to provide potential candidates with enough information to determine if they wish to apply for the job and possess the minimum requirements. The brochure should include the announcement of the vacancy, the procedure for applying, a description of the qualifications that the successful candidate must possess, information about the community served by the school or school district, and financial, personnel, and curricular data about the school and/or school district.

A general-information brochure containing data about the community and school district could be used when recruiting teachers and support personnel. A more extensive one is usually limited to use in executive positions, because the cost of printing such a brochure for each vacancy would be prohibitive.

SELECTION OF PERSONNEL

The objective of the selection process is to hire individuals who will be successful in the job. This process is a major expenditure for most school districts. It includes advertising the position, printing and mailing applications, interviewing candidates, and checking references. It should be implemented through a series of activities that will minimize the chances of hiring individuals who are inadequate performers. The following steps constitute the selection process.

1. *Writing the Job Description.* The job description is the end product of a process known as the *job analysis.* Information about each job is gathered by observations, interviews, questionnaires, consulting, and diary/keeping. The job description outlines specific details of a position and establishes its minimal qualifications.

2. *Establishing the Selection Criteria.* Criteria instruments delineate those ideal characteristics that would ensure the successful performance of the job. Selection criteria can also be used to quantify the expert opinion of those who will be interviewing candidates.

3. *Writing the Job-Vacancy Announcement and Advertising the Position.* The advertisement is based on the job description and provides interested individuals with sufficient information to decide whether to apply for the position. The advertisement must clearly identify the job title, major responsibilities, name and location of the school district, application procedure, and minimal job qualifications.

4. *Receiving Applications.* A central-office staff member should be assigned to receive all applications for a given vacancy. As the applications are received, they should be dated and filed together. This will provide integrity to the process and establish a method of monitoring progress toward filling the vacancy.

5. *Selecting the Candidates to be Interviewed.* The application form should contain a statement requesting the applicants to have their placement papers, transcripts, and letters of reference sent to the personnel department. The form should provide sufficient information to evaluate each person against the selection criteria and minimal requirements for the job. A selected group of applicants is then interviewed for the position.

6. *Interviewing the Candidates.* Interviewing candidates is a responsibility shared by the personnel department and other school district employees. It is important to include not only those who will supervise the new employee but also those who have the most knowledge about the duties to be performed. An interview is essentially a conversation between two or more individuals conducted to generate information about the respondent. Interviewing is a learned skill; it also has profound legal implications.

7. *Checking References and Credentials. Credentials* refers to such items as a college or university transcript, teaching certification, and a physician's

verification of health. These credentials, along with letters of reference, should, whenever possible, be sent directly to the personnel department by the issuing source.

8. *Selecting the Best Candidate.* The personnel administrator who is responsible for implementing the selection process for a particular vacancy must organize all relevant data in such a manner that a choice can be made by the superintendent of schools.

9. *Implementing the Job Offer and Acceptance.* For professional positions, a contract must be approved by the board of education and signed by the finalist. For classified positions, once the candidate affirms that he or she will accept the offer, employment may commence at a mutually acceptable time.

10. *Notifying the Unsuccessful Candidates.* This step is taken only after the offer of employment has been accepted, because it may be necessary to offer the position to another individual if the preferred candidate refuses it.

The first formal task in applying for a position is to fill out the application form, which may consist of two basic formats. The first emphasizes detailed factual information; the second, the applicant's attitudes, opinions, and values.

The basic principle in constructing such a form is "Only ask for information you need to know." The information requested on most applications falls under one of the following headings: personal data, education and/or professional preparation, experience, and references. The form should leave sufficient space to answer questions and provide the requested information.

As part of the selection process, the business and industrial community employs two techniques that are seldom used by school districts: employment tests and assessment centers. Aptitude and ability tests can be used successfully as part of the selection process for most classified jobs in school districts, and are even necessary for some positions. At assessment centers, supervisors have an opportunity to observe candidates for a particular job. They are given a series of simulated administrative problems that will probably be encountered on the job. Large metropolitan school districts could find this technique beneficial in selecting and promoting teachers to the principalship and other administrative positions.

PLACEMENT AND INDUCTION OF PERSONNEL

The last phase in procuring a new employee for the school district is the individual's assignment and orientation to the school community.

The placement of employees within the system is the responsibility of the superintendent of schools. The planning required in making assignments is very complicated, demanding the full-time attention of at least one personnel administrator in most metropolitan-area school districts. It is to the advantage of the school district to make assignments that are in harmony with the wishes of the employees. A staffing survey is one method of systematically gathering information on the placement preferences of employees.

Other variables that the personnel department must take into consideration in making assignments include staff balancing, certification requirements, experience, and work relationships. The welfare of students and implementation of the school district's instructional program is the primary consideration. When there are a number of requests for reassignment, seniority is a defensible criterion after other variables have been considered. Due process should be established to give employees the opportunity to have an assignment reviewed by the appropriate administrator.

Induction is the process designed to acquaint newly employed individuals with the school system and the relationships they must develop to be successful. An effective induction program must have well-defined objectives that will help the employee to feel welcome and secure, become a member of the "team," be inspired to excel, adjust to the work environment, and become familiar with the school community.

Induction programs may be informational or oriented toward personal adjustment. Informational programs are concerned with either initial material or updating information. Initial data consist primarily of information about the school system, the community it serves, and the school where a new employee will work. Updating information is geared to the employee who is reassigned; it concentrates on a particular school and community. Personal-adjustment programs are designed to help newly hired or reassigned employees interact with the other people for whom and with whom they will work.

In effectively orienting new employees to the school district, policies and services must be thoroughly explained and system-wide personnel identified. Orientation must convey a knowledge and understanding of the social, cultural, ethnic, and religious makeup of the community. How people make a living, customs, clubs and organizations, church denominations, museums, libraries, colleges and universities, and social services are all within the scope of this program.

Orienting new employees to a particular school and program is begun by introducing them to their colleagues. A tour of the facility and an explanation of administrative procedures and the instructional program are also important aspects of this induction.

Personal-adjustment orientation includes encouraging new employees to establish working relationships with their colleagues. Organized activities, such as faculty meetings with time for socialization, Christmas parties or dinners, serving on faculty and district committees, and membership in professional organizations, are effective methods of establishing desired relationships among members of the professional staff.

Evaluating the effectiveness of the induction process is extremely important in order to develop data for improving the program. An area of special concern in the induction process centers around first-year teachers. Many potentially excellent teachers are lost to the education profession because they are not properly inducted. A number of suggestions and models have been developed, all of which recognize the importance of giving first-year teachers time to consult with colleagues and feedback concerning their performance.

STAFF DEVELOPMENT

Change occurs constantly, and improved communications alert students and educators to advances in politics, economics, and science almost as soon as they happen.

School districts have a mandate to educate our youth. To do so successfully, schools need qualified teachers, administrators, and support personnel. No employee will remain qualified in the face of accelerating change without some form of ongoing education and training. This is the impetus behind the recent emphasis on staff-development programs.

Adult learning usually consists of two processes, training and education. Training is designed to teach a sequence of programmed behaviors; education seeks to impart understanding and an ability to interpret knowledge. Both types of learning occur through a staff-development program based on particular objectives. In all learning environments, four basic components must be present to ensure success: stimulus, response, reinforcement, and motivation.

Creating a staff-development program consists of six separate but sequential processes: (1) establishing school district goals and objectives, which become the foundation of the program; (2) assessing the needs of the school district employees to determine if there is a discrepancy between the competencies of the staff and the requirements of the organization; (3) establishing staff-development goals and objectives; (4) designing a program that will meet the developmental requirements; (5) implementing the plan in such a way that learning may be effective; and (6) evaluating the program to ascertain if it is meeting its objectives, which in turn will affect future program designs.

A staff-development program for the instructional staff will focus on updating subject-area skills and knowledge, outlining societal demands and changes, presenting the findings of research on teaching methods and practices, and keeping teachers up-to-date about advances in instructional materials and equipment.

In assessing the needs of teachers, four sources of information may be helpful: (1) the teacher-needs assessment survey, (2) community surveys, (3) certification information coupled with the manpower master plan, and (4) research and curriculum studies.

In the last decade, school principals have experienced multiple challenges resulting from such trends as cultural pluralism, community involvement, special education, student rights, and collective bargaining. A recent study conducted in California identified the following areas as appropriate for principal-development programs: instructional skills, management skills, and self-understanding.

Besides the traditional model of staff development for principals, which includes workshops and seminars, many school districts are taking a more personalized approach, directed at helping principals acquire skills that relate to their job and their personal development.

Staff-development programs have been limited to the professional staff in many school districts. However, all employees can profit from development programs, and classified employees should have the opportunity to increase their skills and participate in personal-growth activities. Newly hired and promoted classified employees are usually informed of their responsibilities through a staff-development program. The three most commonly used methods are on-the-job, off-the-job, and apprenticeship training.

APPRAISAL OF PERSONNEL

During this century, the evaluation of teachers has gone through three historical stages. In the 1920s, the concern was primarily whether a given teaching style correlated with the philosophy and psychology of William James and John Dewey. In the 1940s and 1950s, certain personality traits were related to excellence in teaching. The 1960s saw the development of the final stage, which emphasized teaching behaviors.

The last five years have ushered in a dramatic change in evaluation procedures. The traditional concept of teacher evaluation has been replaced by the broader concept of appraisal management, in which the employee is evaluated in terms of how much certain preestablished objectives have been achieved. A significant aspect of this process is measuring an employee's performance against job responsibilities as outlined in a job description.

The reasons for establishing and implementing an appraisal process for all school district employees include: to foster self-development, identify a variety of tasks that an employee is capable of performing, identify staff-development needs, improve employee performance, determine if an employee should be retained and what his or her salary increase should be, and help in the proper placement or promotion of an employee.

In developing an appraisal process, a board of education should establish a policy on employee appraisal that will give direction to the various divisions within a school district. These divisions are responsible for developing objectives aimed at implementing the goals of the school board. Each employee is then responsible for developing personal objectives that further the divisional objectives. Consequently, employee performance is measured against the degree to which each individual has attained his or her objectives. Feedback data are then available to analyze if divisional objectives have been reached. The actual appraisal procedures for implementing this process are best developed by involving representatives of the employees who will be evaluated.

As with the development of appraisal procedures, evaluation instruments are most appropriately constructed by a committee. There are two basic categories of evaluation instruments: trait forms and result forms. The first rates an employee against a predetermined list of traits to ascertain overall performance. The second compares an employee's performance against objectives that were developed by the employee and agreed to by the supervisor. Using both types of instruments helps to identify areas where improvement is needed.

Developing Termination Procedures

A universal reason for evaluating performance is to determine whether the employee should be retained. A decision to dismiss an employee, of course, is extremely difficult to make because of the importance of employment to the individual and his or her dependents.

Employment counselors have seen the devastating financial and psychological effects that getting fired has on a person's life. In fact, the trauma usually centers on the individual's self-concept. Feelings of inadequacy, failure, self-contempt, and anger are common to people who have had their employment terminated. Although most individuals are able to cope with such an experience, others never fully recover from it. Consequently, both good personnel management and a sense of responsibility toward others mandate that school district administrators develop termination procedures that are objective, fair, and incorporate a due-process procedure that gives an employee the opportunity to modify or defend his or her behavior.

The following presentation discusses the nuances of due process, which can be used as a guide in establishing grounds for terminating employment. It is based upon court decisions and a compilation of state statutes. School administrators should consult the statutes of their particular state in creating procedures for their school system. While this presentation refers to teachers, the concepts elucidated are applicable to all other categories of employees.

Grounds for terminating the employment of tenured teachers. A tenured teacher may have employment terminated for one or more of the following causes: physical or mental condition making the individual unfit to instruct or associate with children; immoral conduct; insubordination, inefficiency, or incompetency in the line of duty; willful or persistent violation of the published policies and procedures of the school board; excessive or unreasonable absence from work; conviction of a felony or crime involving moral turpitude.

The first cause listed must be understood within the context of the Rehabilitation Act of 1973. A handicap does not constitute a physical condition that may in any way be construed as making an individual unfit to associate with children or students. In fact, the prevalent interpretation of the law is that an aide must be hired to assist an employee if the employee's handicap interferes with instruction or supervision. The only physical condition that could prevent an employee from associating with children is contracting a contagious disease. This would be a potential cause for dismissal only if the individual refused to get medical treatment and insisted on working. Emotional illness that produces dangerous or bizarre behavior is also a potential cause for dismissal if the employee refuses to receive medical treatment and insists on working. In both cases, the documentation of a physician is necessary to proceed with the termination process. The school district is, of course, responsible for all expenses incurred in securing the expert opinion of the physician.

Immoral conduct must be judged within the context of local standards but also must be reasonable and consistent with recent court decisions. A number of significant court cases form the foundation for the following principles, which should be used in judging employee conduct. First, the health of the pupil-teacher relationship is the criterion for judging employee behavior. A teacher or other employee who has established a relationship with a student that goes beyond friendship and involves some form of "dating" is unacceptable. Second, illegal sexual acts are cause for immediate suspension. If one is convicted of such an act, employment with the district must be terminated. Suspension is a justifiable practice while investigating allegations of sexual misconduct if the employee receives his or her salary during this period. Third, private nonconventional sexual life-styles are not a cause for employee dismissal. Such practices as wife-swapping, homosexuality, and living together outside of matrimony may be unacceptable to the majority of people in the community, but they do not inherently affect an individual's performance in the workplace. These and other life-styles are depicted on television and described in other media; to a certain extent, this has nullified their impact on students. Fourth, if an employee advocates nonconventional sexual life-styles to students, that individual has placed his or her position in jeopardy, because such life-styles are in direct conflict with local standards.

Insubordination in the line of duty is always a cause for dismissal. Although the interpretation of what constitutes insubordination may appear to be self-evident, in fact it has restricted application. Employees can be insubordinate only if they refuse to comply with a directive of their supervisor that is clearly within their field of expertise. If a principal asks a teacher to supervise the children on the playground during the teacher's preparation time and is refused, the teacher is insubordinate because his or her job responsibility includes supervising children. On the other hand, if the principal were to direct a custodian to do so, that individual would not be guilty of insubordination because his or her expertise would not include such supervision. Nor would it be insubordination if a teacher refused to fill in for the principal's secretary, who was absent from work because of illness. The teacher was not hired to perform secretarial functions and may refuse this directive. The manner in which an employee responds to a directive does not usually constitute insubordination if the employee performs the task. Thus, if a teacher responds in a sharp tone to the principal when assigned to playground duty but obeys the directive, the teacher is not guilty of insubordination.

Inefficiency is relatively easy to document. It usually refers to the inability of an individual to manage those tasks that are integral to a job. A teacher who never takes class attendance or cannot account for the equipment, books, or materials assigned to his or her class is obviously inefficient. A principal who is always late turning in building budgets or other reports also falls into this category.

Incompetency is perhaps the most difficult reason to document in terminating an employee. It also is related directly to the formal evaluation process. If a tenured teacher is performing in an incompetent manner, it means that he or she is hindering the instructional-learning process. The evaluations made by the principal must clearly indicate that major deficiencies have been identified and objectives to remediate them have not been met.

Claiming willful or persistent violation of state school laws or board of education policies and procedures as a cause for termination presupposes that school district employees have been informed of these. An effective method of notifying employees about these laws, policies, and procedures is through the publication and distribution of a handbook or manual that clearly outlines employees' responsibilities.

Excessive or unreasonable absence from work is a relative term that can be explained only if there is a policy definding what is meant by "excessive" or "unreasonable." Local school boards will probably rely on patterns of absences in making their determination. Five consecutive days per month over a year's span, for example, could be considered excessive if the employee is not suffering from a chronic physical condition that interferes with attendance at work.

Conviction of a felony is obviously a reason to terminate employment. Being convicted of a crime involving moral turpitude, however, requires some explanation. For instance, prostitution is usually classified as a misdemeanor, but, because it involves morally offensive conduct according to most community standards, it is a reason to terminate a tenured teacher. The selling of pornography or a conviction for the use or sale of drugs also falls within the definition of moral turpitude.

Notification of charges against a tenured teacher. After a behavior that could result in termination has been identified, the next step in a due-process procedure is notification. This is a formal process, which involves serving the employee with written charges specifying the alleged grounds that, if not corrected, will eventuate in dismissal. It must be kept in mind that notification with an opportunity to correct behavior is applicable only to charges arising out of incompetency, inefficiency, or insubordination in the line of duty. Physical or mental conditions as described above, immoral conduct, violation of school laws or board of education policies and procedures, excessive absences, and conviction of a felony or crime involving moral turpitude require a hearing before termination of employment, but obviously not a period of time to correct the behavior. The behavior has already gone beyond what is rectifiable in an educational setting. A hearing is required, however, to determine if the facts substantiate the allegation.

Notification of charges, an extremely formal process, must not be confused with evaluation procedures that permit an employee the right to disagree with a written evaluation. As a normal course of action, employees may attach a written rebuttal to the evaluation instrument, setting forth points of disagreement and including any documentation to support their position.

Time periods are specified in state statutes. For example, a thirty-day period may be specified, during which time the employee has an opportunity to modify his or her behavior; a twenty-day period may be required before a hearing is held, which allows the employee time to gather evidence supporting his or her position; and a ten-day period may be allowed after being informed that a hearing has been scheduled, during which time the teacher must respond that he or she wishes to have the hearing. If the employee does not wish to have a hearing on the charges, the board of education may terminate his or her employment with the school district by a majority vote of the board members.

The teacher may be suspended with pay after being notified of a hearing, until the board of education makes a determination concerning that person's employment.

Termination hearing on charges against a tenured teacher. This procedure must be followed in conducting a hearing that might eventuate in the dismissal of a tenured teacher. This section presents a model that is applicable to all termination proceedings, and includes the following provisions:

1. The hearing shall be held in a public forum. There is a distinction between a public hearing and a hearing held in public: at a public hearing, those in attendance are usually allowed to address those conducting the hearing, according to preestablished procedures; at a hearing held in public, only those representing the party making the allegation and those representing the party against whom the allegation is made are allowed to speak at and participate in the hearing.

2. Both parties may be represented by an attorney, who may cross-examine witnesses.

3. The testimony given at a hearing shall be under oath. Government agencies such as school districts are usually allowed the privilege of administering oaths in official proceedings. The president or secretary of the board of education is normally the official so empowered.

4. The board of education may subpoena witnesses and documentary evidence requested by the teacher. As with the power to administer oaths, school districts usually have subpoena rights and may limit the number of witnesses called on behalf of the teacher or school district administrators.

5. The proceedings at the hearing should be recorded by a stenographer employed by the school district. A tape recording of the hearing is usually acceptable in lieu of a stenographer. A transcript of the proceedings must be made available not only to the school board but also to the teacher. The transcript of a hearing held in public should be open to public inspection.

6. Except for the fee paid to the attorney representing the teacher, all expenses for conducting the hearing should be paid by the school district.

7. The decision by the board of education should be reached within a preestablished time period, to ensure fair treatment of the employee.

The board of education is exercising judicial authority in conducting the hearing and reaching a decision about the dismissal of a tenured teacher. This is a unique circumstance because the school board acts in two capacities: as prosecutor, in the sense that the charges are brought against the employee in the name of the school board; and as judge, because the school board renders the decision. In this respect, the board of education is reviewing its own action in alleging charges. Consequently, as much as possible, it is extremely important to give an impartial structure to the hearing. The evidence should be presented by an attorney representing the building principal and other line administrators up to the superintendent of schools, because these administrators have the responsibility for evaluating and reviewing employee evaluations.

The hearing room should also be set up so as to delineate clearly the roles of those in attendance. Seated at a table, the members of the board of education will occupy a central place in the room. A second table could be set up, perhaps ten to fifteen feet in front of and facing the board members, where witnesses will give testimony. On either side of the board table and facing each other should be two tables: seated at one, the teacher and his or her attorney, and at the other, the appropriate administrator with the school district's attorney. Those in attendance should be seated in a manner that clearly indicates they must not interfere with the proceedings.

Another mechanism sometimes used in lieu of a formal hearing when discussing the possible termination of any employee is an executive session of the school board. Most state statutes permit a government body to hold private meetings from which the public is excluded when personnel matters are discussed. If a teacher or any employee is confronted with documentation that could result in termination and given notice that his or her behavior must be modified, it may be possible to invite the employee to discuss a lack of improvement at an executive session of the school board. If the employee resigns in the face of this documentation, the expense and potential embarrassment of a public hearing are avoided.

Appeal by a tenured teacher of a termination decision issued by the board of education.   Because school districts are state government agencies, an appeal regarding the decision of a school board is made to the state circuit court, which is the court of original jurisdiction in state civil and criminal matters. In most states, this appeal must usually be made within a specific period of time. All evidence, documentation, records, and a transcript of the hearing will probably be requested by the court. Of course, the employee has the right to appeal the decision of the circuit court, as in any civil action, up to the court of appeals and Supreme Court, if there is justifiable reason.

Termination procedures for probationary teachers.   A distinction must be made from the very beginning between terminating the employment of a probationary teacher and not renewing such a teacher's contract. In the latter situation, no formal due process is necessary; the employer-employee obligation simply ceases to exist with the expiration of the contract. This may occur if a probationary teacher is not performing at a level acceptable to the administration. A probationary teacher may have difficulty interacting with the students, staff, and parents in the school district or may be teaching at a minimally acceptable level. It benefits not only the district, but also the teacher, if the contract is not renewed, since the instructor might be more successful in another district. Not renewing a contract presupposes that evaluations have been made by the supervisor, deficiencies have been pointed out, and advice and help have been offered on how to improve performance or remove the stated deficiencies. If such a process has occurred, non-renewal of the teacher's contract is justified.

Terminating the employment of a probationary teacher before contract expiration is a different matter. In this situation, as with all other school district employees, the employee must be given a written statement setting forth the allegations, along with a reasonable time period to remove deficiencies or improve performance. If such corrections or improvements are not made within the specified time, the employee may be dismissed by action of the board of education.

Grounds and procedure for revocation of a license to teach.   One final formal procedure must be briefly alluded to when discussing termination procedures. A teacher's license to teach may be revoked if it can be proven that he or she has exhibited incompetency, cruelty, immorality, drunkenness, or has neglected duties or has broken a written contract with the board of education. As with terminating a tenured teacher, these reasons have a very narrow application.

Incompetency means that the teacher seriously hinders the instructional-learning process. A chronic mental illness or sociopathic behavior that has been diagnosed by a psychiatrist is an example of incompetency that could result in revocation of a teacher's license.

Cruelty refers not only to physical but also to mental or emotional abuse of children. The conditions that constitute cruelty may be summarized as follows: any act that is meant to injure or bring serious ridicule and embarrassment to a child.

Immorality is, of course, an extremely sensitive issue. For practical considerations, this cause is commonly interpreted to mean that an individual has been convicted of an illegal sexual offense or a crime involving moral turpitude. The examples provided earlier in this chapter are applicable to immorality as a cause for a revocation of a teacher's license.

Drunkenness as a cause for revocation of a license is usually interpreted to mean that the employee either is intoxicated or drinks alcoholic beverages while working. Imbibing alcoholic beverages in a government building such as a school is a misdemeanor in most states. To further complicate the situation is the question of how drunkenness relates to alcoholism. Because alcoholism is considered a disease by the medical profession, the same consideration should be afforded the alcoholic as is given other employees with a medical problem. This usually involves granting sick leave to an employee receiving medical treatment or reassigning the employee to a position with limited responsibilities during treatment. If an employee is not a diagnosed alcoholic and persists in drinking alcoholic beverages at work or arrives at school intoxicated, license revocation is in the best interest of a school district's clientele, the children.

Neglect of duty presupposes that an employee has been informed about the responsibilities that are integral to his or her position with the school district. This is usually accomplished by a written job description or in a policy manual and handbook specifying these responsibilities. Neglect of duty as a cause for revoking a teacher's license requires that the teacher be given an opportunity to rectify his or her behavior. Thus, evaluations that set forth the employee's deficiencies are necessary. It must also be remembered that the revocation of a license is extremely serious; likewise, the neglect of duty must be extremely serious and chronic. A teacher who leaves young children unattended on a field trip—behavior that could result in an injury to a child—and who continues such irresponsible behavior after being informed of the danger by the principal—has exhibited a lack of understanding that seriously affects his or her ability to supervise children. This is a reason not only to terminate employment but also to safeguard against this teacher's potential employment at another school by proceeding to have his or her license revoked.

The breaking of a written contract with the board of education is a potential cause for license revocation. This should not be confused with annulment, which means that both parties have agreed to the dissolution of the contract and the governing board has formally approved the dissolution. Sometimes a teacher or other employee is offered a position with another school district or in private business or industry. If that teacher neglects to request a contract annulment from the school board and assumes another position, the board of education may proceed to have his or her license revoked. Most school boards are not resistant to annulling a contract except in those cases when the education of the students would be seriously affected. A teacher who tenders a resignation the day before the opening of school in September may not receive a contract annulment until a suitable replacement is obtained.

It should be clearly understood that the board of education does not have the authority to revoke a license; rather, it may follow a statutory procedure that could eventuate in the revocation of a teacher's license. Only the state board of education, which issues teaching licenses, has the authority to revoke them.

Finally, revocation of a teacher's license is usually irreversible unless the statutory procedures were neglected or the evidence was faulty. It is, therefore, a very serious matter that should be initiated only if the education or health and safety of children would be significantly jeopardized now and in the future. Terminating an individual's employment obviously prevents the injury of children presently in his or her care. Revocation of a license prevents the teacher from injuring children because he or she cannot be employed in another school district. A classic example involves the teacher who is convicted of child molestation and subsequently fired but manages to get hired in another school district and commits a similar crime because the teaching license was not revoked.

Humane considerations in the termination process. The procedures described in this section may appear to overemphasize the legal and negative side of the appraisal process. Termination is, however, an aspect of appraisal that is seldom addressed and is extremely important. Confusion over appropriate and fair termination procedures could result in a school district's being saddled with an employee who hinders the instructional-learning process or who, in fact, may place children in an unsafe situation.

The educational welfare of children is the primary mandate of a school district. The hiring, retaining, development, and termination of personnel should be guided by this mandate. However, employees also have rights that must be taken into consideration when developing appraisal procedures and dealing with employee evaluation. Due process is one right that has long been a fundamental principle of English common law and is basic to the American legal process.

REWARDING PERFORMANCE

Psychologists have long recognized that satisfaction of needs is the primary motivation for all human actions. In satisfying their needs, individuals will act in ways that they perceive to be in their own best interest. A manager who understands human motivation and what employees believe to be in their best interest is able to develop a unique rewards system.

School district administrators should attempt to utilize an "expectancy model" as the vehicle for developing a rewards system. With this model, rewards are linked to employee behavior that both meets the objectives of the school district and satisfies the needs of the employees.

Five variables must be taken into consideration in a rewards program: employee performance, effort, skills, seniority, and job requirements. The rewarding of performance, however, must be the primary objective of a rewards program.

An effective program must include both intrinsic and extrinsic rewards. Intrinsic rewards are those that pertain to the quality of the job situation; they may include participation in the decision-making process, increased responsibility, and more discretion in how a job is to be performed. Extrinsic rewards include compensation that is direct, indirect, and nonfinancial. Direct compensation is commonly referred to as salary or wages; indirect compensation is frequently referred to as fringe benefits. Nonfinancial rewards are limited only by the imagination of the administration and are tailored to meet the needs of individual employees. For example, a status-conscious employee might consider the services of a private secretary and a reserved parking place a reward for exceptional performance.

Direct compensation, salary or wages, can be administered effectively only if the following principles are incorporated into the pay policy: skills required in various positions must be recognized; salaries must be competitive; the primary focus of salary increases must be improved performance; and salary schedules must be reviewed annually.

An important question central to any pay policy is: "Does money motivate?" A reasonable conclusion, supported by experience and research, is that money does affect performance if it is clear that performance is rewarded by a salary increase.

There are a number of other issues in salary and wage management that must command the attention of personnel administrators. They will have an effect on pay-policy development, and include: public disclosure of salaries, compensation packaging, equity of pay with performance, techniques for collecting community wage data, methods of making salary recommendations to the school board, payroll deductions, employee reactions to salary decisions, appropriate pay periods, annual wage review, and salary schedule construction.

Indirect compensation, or fringe benefits, may be defined as benefits available to all employees that help a school district to attract and retain good employees. Certain fringe benefits are required by law; these include social security, state retirement programs, unemployment insurance, and workmen's compensation.

Voluntary fringe benefits may be divided into insurance programs, time away from the job, and services. Group insurance programs are available for almost every human need, including medical and hospitalization, dental, term-life, errors and omissions, and optical.

A fringe benefit often taken for granted by employees is time away from the job, including sick leave, vacation time, paid holidays, and sabbaticals. In like manner, certain services offered by school districts are in reality fringe benefits. These include expenses paid for attendance at workshops, professional meetings, and conventions; tuition reimbursement; and free lunches and coffee. Central-office administrators are usually given the use of a school district automobile or receive mileage compensation. With decreasing enrollments, many school districts are offering career-counseling services to teachers who will be looking for a job outside the field of education.

Fringe benefits will continue to play a significant role in compensating employees as an alternative to large salary and wage increases.

CONTRACT MANAGEMENT

Teachers and administrators usually work under the provisions of an individual contract; classified personnel such as secretaries, bus drivers, and custodians are employed at an hourly rate or for an annual salary. In school districts where a master contract has been negotiated by a union, teachers and administrators belonging to the bargaining units do not have individual contracts but rather work under the provisions of the master agreement. There are exceptions to this; however, for all practical purposes, these are the alternative methods by which employees are hired to work in a school system.

The question may legitimately be asked, "What is the purpose of issuing individual contracts to teachers and administrators?" The most accurate response is, "Tradition." As professionals, teachers and administrators are employed to perform a service for which they receive a certain amount of financial compensation. Performing the service may require a teacher to take student projects home to be graded or stay late to talk with the parents of a student having problems in school. The time it takes to perform the service or the amount of work involved is not a consideration under the contract method of employment.

Classified employees are also paid to perform a service, but the time and work involved does make a difference in the amount of money received. When such employees are required to work after the regular eight-hour day, they receive overtime pay. If they are required to perform a task not specified by the categories outlined in the job description, they receive additional compensation.

Those professional employees who are covered by the terms of a master agreement are more closely identified with classified employees than with teachers and administrators who have individual contracts. Their working conditions are spelled out in the master agreement.

Board of education policies sometimes address working conditions, but these policies are usually not as specific as the terms of a master agreement. Teacher and administrator handbooks may also contain references to working conditions, but these are more concerned with internal procedures.

Using individual contracts for teachers and administrators is, therefore, a matter of tradition and is mandated by statutes in some states. Individual contracts also distinguish an individual's working conditions from those termed *classified.* A teacher's or administrator's contract must meet the requirements of general contract law. Because school districts are legal entities with a corporate character, they may sue and be sued; purchase, receive, or sell real and personal property; make contracts and be contracted with. The contracts entered into by a school district must conform not only to contract law but also to state statutes governing contracts and to the precedents established through case law.

A contract is an agreement between two or more competent persons for consideration on a legal subject matter in the form required by law. Every valid contract, therefore, has five basic components: offer and acceptance, competent persons, consideration, legal subject matter, and proper form. Each of these components will be discussed individually.

Offer and Acceptance

A valid contract must contain an offer and an acceptance. In the selection process, therefore, it is improper to notify unsuccessful candidates that the job has been filled until the prospective employee has accepted the offer of employment. If the board of education approves a contract for a specific person to teach high school English, there is no agreement until the contract is executed, which constitutes acceptance.

A few other facts about the legal nature of an agreement must be kept in mind. First, an offer can be accepted only by the person to whom it was made. The husband of a candidate for a teaching position, for example, cannot accept the offer for his wife. Second, an offer must be accepted within a reasonable time. If an individual does not sign and return a contract within a few weeks, in the hope that another job offer will be made by a different school district, the board of education may offer the contract to another candidate. Finally, a newspaper advertisement is not an offer of a position, but rather an invitation to become a candidate.

Competent Persons

A contract is not valid unless it is entered into by two or more competent persons. This means that the persons have the legal capacity to enter into a contract. As a corporate entity, the school district has the power, through the legal action of the school board, to enter into a contract. The most commonly identified classes of incompetents include minors and those who are mentally ill or intoxicated.

If a person was so mentally ill or intoxicated at the time of entering into a contract that he or she did not understand the significance of the action, that individual may have the contract set aside because there was no agreement, which is essential to the validity of every contract.

Consideration

For a contract to be valid, it must be supported by a consideration, which is usually defined as something of value. The type of consideration found in an employment contract is referred to as "a promise for an act." For example, in a teacher's contract, the board of education promises to pay an individual $15,000 to teach third grade for one year. The teacher fulfills the act by teaching during the designated time period.

Legal Subject Matter

In all fifty states, an individual may teach only if he or she possesses a license to teach issued by the state department of education. Consequently, if a board of education enters into a teaching contract with a person who does not possess a license, such a contract would involve illegal subject matter and would be invalid.

Proper Form

For a contract to be enforceable, it must be in the form required by law. The courts recognize both oral and written contracts. However, most states have statutory provisions that require teachers' and administrators' contracts to be in writing, and even specify the proper wording for the contract.

SUMMARY

Personnel management is a function carried out by every school district, either by a central-office division or by administrators throughout the district. The goals of administrators charged with personnel responsibilities are to achieve the objectives of the school system while helping individual staff members maximize their potential and develop their professional careers. These goals are achieved through manpower planning, recruitment, selection, placement and induction, staff development, appraisal, compensation, and collective negotiations.

All but the very smallest school districts should delegate the personnel function to an assistant superintendent. The complexity of this function in our schools and the great impact it has on total school operations necessitate the hiring of a personnel specialist.

Collective bargaining has also created a need in most school districts for another specialist, the director of employee relations, who reports to the assistant superintendent for personnel and is charged with managing the negotiations process.

The knowledge explosion, increased litigation and federal legislation, and the changing attitudes of parents, students, and educators have necessitated an ongoing staff-development program for administrators and teachers. Like collective bargaining, this area is so specialized that most districts should consider establishing the position of director of staff development, who also reports to the assistant superintendent for personnel.

This avalanche of litigation and federal legislation has also mandated the creation of a central-office administrative position, director of affirmative action. Most federal legislation requires that a detailed compliance program be established under the direction of an administrator who will be free from the influence of other administrators. Thus, the director of affirmative action reports directly to the superintendent of schools.

Planning is a part of all human experience. It encompasses an understanding of the present, future objectives, and methods for achieving them. Manpower planning as a process in personnel management is undertaken to ensure that a school district has the right number of people, with the right skills, in the right place, and at the right time. The first step in manpower planning is to assess human-resource needs, which includes developing (1) manpower inventories, (2) a five-year enrollment projection, (3) school district objectives, and (4) a manpower forecast.

One of the most pressing problems facing metropolitan areas, and with a particular significance in manpower planning, is declining pupil enrollments. Two of the most successful alternatives to reducing the work force have been early-retirement incentive programs and the retraining of individuals for positions that will become vacant through attrition or be created through program development.

A hallmark of our society is the avalanche of federal legislation and court decisions, which in turn have had a definite influence on the manpower-planning process. Incorporated or implied in all civil-rights legislation is the important concept of affirmative action. Affirmative action is not a law within itself but rather a set of guidelines that organizations may use to comply with legislation and executive orders.

The Equal Employment Opportunity Commission was established by Title VII of the Civil Rights Act to investigate alleged discrimination in employment practices based on race, color, religion, sex, or national origin. The five-member commission has also, from time to time, established affirmative-action guidelines. Discrimination charges can be filed with any of EEOC's regional or district offices. The administrative process includes an individual's filing a charge, the investigation and determination of that charge, and the process of conciliation.

Limited discrimination is allowed by the Equal Employment Opportunity Act under one condition: when there is a bona fide occupational qualification mandating the employing of an individual of a particular sex, religious affiliation, or national origin. Therefore, a school district personnel administrator has the right to

employ a female rather than a male as a swimming instructor when part of the job includes supervising the girls' locker room.

The Rehabilitation Act of 1973 prohibits recipients of federal financial assistance from discriminating against qualified handicapped individuals in recruitment, hiring, compensation, job assignment/classification, and fringe benefits. Employers are further required to provide reasonable accommodations for qualified handicapped applicants or employees.

Equality in employment opportunities for women is a central issue of the 1980s. The legal mandate of equal opportunity for women emanates primarily from two federal laws: Title IX of the Educational Amendments of 1972, which prohibits sex discrimination in educational programs or activities, including employment, when the school district is receiving federal financial assistance; and, of course, Title VII of the Civil Rights Act of 1964, as amended in 1972. In addition, President Carter in 1978 signed into law a pregnancy-disability amendment to the latter, which law had the effect of eliminating unequal treatment of pregnant women in all employment-related situations.

The Age Discrimination in Employment Act of 1967, as amended, promotes the employment of the older worker based on ability rather than age, by prohibiting arbitrary discrimination.

Because of their importance, four major federal influences in the manpower-planning process have been presented in detail. However, personnel administrators must also become familiar with all legislation that protects employment-opportunity rights.

Termination is an aspect of the appraisal process that is extremely important. Because getting fired has such a devastating effect on the financial and emotional welfare of an individual, termination procedures must be fair and objective. Most states have statutory provisions outlining the due process that must be afforded teachers before termination. Such legislation, while applying to the professional staff, provides a model for boards of education in establishing similar procedures for all employees. The education and welfare of students is the primary concern of a school district, but employees also have rights that must be taken into consideration when developing appraisal procedures and dealing with employee dismissal.

Teachers and administrators usually have individual contracts; classified personnel are employed at an hourly rate or for an annual salary. Using individual contracts for teachers and administrators is a matter of tradition, which is also mandated by law in some states and distinguishes professional employees' working conditions from those of classified employees.

Teachers' and administrators' contracts must meet the requirements of general contract law, state statutes, and the precedents established through case law. A contract is an agreement between two or more competent persons for legal consideration of a legal subject matter. The five basic components of every valid contract are: offer and acceptance, competent persons, a consideration, legal subject matter, and proper form.

IMPLICATIONS FOR EDUCATIONAL ADMINISTRATORS

Personnel management as described in this chapter has three implications for school administrators.

First, administrators must remain informed about new state and federal legislation and court decisions dealing with personnel issues such as affirmative action, equal employment opportunity, employment termination, and tenure.

Second, administrators must continually review and update their policies and procedures concerning personnel management. Policies and procedures regarding manpower planning, recruitment, selection, placement and induction, staff development, appraisal, compensation, and collective bargaining are necessary to give direction and guidance in personnel management.

Third, most states have statutes setting forth the due process required in the termination of professional personnel. However, school administrators have some latitude in establishing procedures to implement these statutes. It is imperative that these procedures be objective, defensible, and humane.

SELECTED BIBLIOGRAPHY

CASTETTER, WILLIAM B., *The Personnel Function in Educational Administration* (3rd ed.). New York: Macmillan Publishing Co., Inc., 1981.

HARRIS, BEN M., KENNETH E. McINTYRE, VANCE C. LITTLETON, and DANIEL F. LONG, *Personnel Administration in Education: Leadership for Improvement.* Boston: Allyn & Bacon, Inc., 1979.

MATHIS, ROBERT L., and JOHN H. JACKSON, *Personnel: Contemporary Perspectives and Applications* (2nd ed.). St. Paul: West Publishing Co., 1979.

REBORE, RONALD W., *Personnel Administration in Education: A Management Approach.* Englewood Cliffs, N.J.: Prentice-Hall, Inc., 1982.

STOCKARD, JAMES G., *Rethinking People Management: A New Look at the Human Resources Function.* New York: American Management Association, 1980.

NOTES

1. William B. Castetter, *The Personnel Function in Educational Administration,* 2nd ed. (New York: Macmillan Publishing Co., Inc., 1976), p. 41.

2. American Association of School Administrators, *Helping Administrators Negotiate* (Arlington, Va.: The Association, 1974).

3. Stephen P. Robbins, *Personnel: The Management of Human Resources* (Englewood Cliffs, N.J.: Prentice-Hall, Inc., 1978), p. 53.

4. Bruce Coleman, "An Integrated System for Manpower Planning," *Business Horizons,* October 1970, pp. 89–95.

5. The Equal Employment Opportunity Act of 1972 (Washington, D.C.: U.S. Government Printing Office, 1972), p. 4.

6. Carlos J. Orvando, "School Implications of the Peaceful Latino Invasion," *Phi Delta Kappan,* 59 (December 1977), 230, 231.

7. Department of Health, Education and Welfare, "Nondiscrimination on the Basis of Handicap," *Federal Register,* 41, no. 96 (May 17, 1976).

8. Peter F. Drucker, "Flexible-Age Retirement: Social Issue of the Decade," *Industry Week,* May 15, 1978, p. 66.

9. *The Age Discrimination in Employment Act of 1967* (Washington, D.C.: U.S. Government Printing Office, 1967), p. 7.

10

The Role and Function of the Employee-Relations Administrator

Collective bargaining has become a way of life in American education. The first significant collective-bargaining agreement in the field was negotiated in 1962, with New York City teachers. Since that time, over half of all state legislatures have enacted collective-bargaining laws relating to public-school teachers.[1] Personnel considerations such as salaries, fringe benefits, and working conditions constitute the major negotiable issues. Membership in teacher organizations has also increased, and consequently, because of dues, so have the fiscal resources of these organizations, amounting to millions of dollars annually. Because personnel expenditures constitute approximately 80 percent of school budgets, virtually every aspect of education has been influenced by the phenomenon of negotiations.

The now-famous Air Traffic Controllers strike has been misunderstood by many people who have a casual knowledge of collective bargaining in the public sector. Collective bargaining has not been abrogated by the fact that many PATCO members were fired because they refused to return to work. It is, therefore, here to stay. The form and style are still subject to alteration, but the basic process is irreplaceable.

Experience dictates that the underlying consideration in collective bargaining is participation in the decision-making process. Teachers and administrators want to have significant input into the priorities that are established by boards of education when these affect their salaries, benefits, and working conditions. It is a natural development in our democratic life-style to look continually for more significant ways to participate in governance, whether in the political sphere or in our employing institutions. Furthermore, as a process, collective bargaining successfully works in the private sector and certainly has application to the public sector. This chapter deals with the major components of the collective-negotiations process as it operates in education.

The terms *collective bargaining, collective negotiations,* and *professional negotiations* have all been used, with some changes in meaning, when referring to this process in public education. To avoid confusion and because the "process" is universal in scope, these terms will be used interchangeably in this chapter.

Also, there has been much discussion as to whether the National Education Association and the American Federation of Teachers are labor unions or professional organizations. This distinction appears to be functional in nature. If representatives of an organized group bargain collectively with management over salaries, fringe benefits, and working conditions for their members, they are in essence a labor union. The terms *labor union* and *professional organization,* therefore, will be used interchangeably in this chapter when referring to their involvement in the negotiations process. This same definition holds true for administrator organizations when they collectively negotiate. This interchange of definitions appears to be a trend in public education.

HISTORICAL PERSPECTIVE

Collective Bargaining in the Private Sector

Collective actions by employees have a long history, going back to the medieval guilds. These actions have always been influenced by current economic, political, and social conditions. Such influences are even stronger today, because the media keep the public up-to-date on political, social, and economic trends.

Four major congressional acts provide legal guidelines for collective bargaining in the private sector: The Norris-LaGuardia Act of 1932, the National Labor Relations Act of 1935 (Wagner Act), The Labor-Management Relations Act of 1947 (Taft-Hartley Act), and the Labor-Management Reporting and Disclosure Act of 1959 (Landrum-Griffin Act).

The Norris-LaGuardia Act was the first general public policy position on labor unionization. The act supported the concept that workers have a right to organize, if they so desire, into unions. In particular, the act restricted the courts from issuing injunctions that would restrict labor activities. It also outlawed the yellow-dog contract, an agreement employers required employees to sign as a condition of employment, in which employees stated that they were not members of a union and would not join one as long as they worked for that company.

The Wagner Act is perhaps the most important piece of labor legislation. It guaranteed workers the right to organize and join labor unions for the purpose of collective bargaining with their employers. The Wagner Act also prohibited employers from engaging in the following unfair labor practices: (1) interfering with or coercing employees in exercising their rights to join labor unions and bargain collectively, (2) interfering with the formation or administration of any labor union, (3) discriminating against an employee because of union activity, (4) discharging or discriminating against an employee because he or she filed charges or gave testimony under this act, (5) refusing to bargain with the representatives chosen by the employees. The National Labor Relations Board (NLRB) was established and given the responsibility for conducting elections to determine union representation and for applying this law to designated unfair labor practices.

The Taft-Hartley Act was passed to amend the Wagner Act and prevent unfair labor practices by unions. It sought to protect a worker's right not to join a union and employers from mistreatment by unions. The Taft-Hartley Act specifically outlawed the closed shop, allowed the federal government to seek an injunction preventing work stoppages for eighty days in a strike defined as injurious to the national welfare, prohibited the use of union funds in connection with national elections, required union officers to swear that they were not members of the Communist Party, required unions to file financial statements with their membership and the U.S. Department of Labor, allowed the states to pass right-to-work laws, and made it illegal for any collective agreement to contain a clause requiring compulsory union membership.

The Taft-Hartley Act also prohibits unions from engaging in the following unfair labor practices:

1. Refusing to bargain collectively with an employer
2. Causing an employer to discriminate against an employee who was refused membership in or expelled from a union
3. Engaging in secondary boycotts, an act that exerts pressure on an employer not directly involved in a dispute
4. Causing an employer to pay for services that were not rendered
5. Engaging in a conflict between two or more unions over the rights to perform certain types of work
6. Charging excessive or discriminatory initiation fees

The Landrum-Griffin Act resulted from internal corruption in some unions. This act contains a bill of rights for union members, which includes freedom of speech at union meetings, a secret ballot on proposed dues increases, and protection against improper disciplinary action. It also established the conditions to be observed in electing union officers.

The Landrum-Griffin Act, in addition, contained the following amendments to the Taft-Hartley Act:

1. Repealed the requirement for union officials to take a non-Communist oath
2. Gave states authority over cases outside the jurisdiction of the NLRB
3. Prohibited picketing by a union when a rival union was recognized or an NLRB election had taken place within twelve months
4. Guaranteed the right of a striker to vote in union representative elections for twelve months
5. Prohibited agreements by which employees seek to bring economic pressure on another employer by refusing to handle, sell, use, or transport his products
6. Authorized union shops in the construction industry and required membership after seven days of employment rather than the traditional thirty days

Collective Negotiations in the Federal Government

In 1962, President Kennedy issued Executive Order (E.O.) 10988, which affirmed the right of federal employees to join labor unions and bargin collectively. It required federal agency heads to bargain in good faith, defined unfair labor practices, and established a code of conduct for labor organizations. However, it also prohibited the union shop and banned strikes by federal employees.

In 1968, a presidential committee reviewed employee-management relations in the federal service and recommended improvement in the provisions of E.O. 10988. As a consequence, President Nixon issued E.O. 11491 in 1969, to supersede the previous directive.

The objectives of E.O. 11491 are to standardize procedures among federal agencies and to bring federal labor relations more closely in line with those in the private sector. It gave the assistant secretary of labor the authority to determine appropriate bargaining units, to oversee recognition procedures, to rule on unfair labor practices, and to enforce the standards of conduct on labor organizations. E.O. 11491 also established the Federal Labor Relations Council, which is responsible for supervising the implementation of this executive order, handling appeals about the decision of the assistant secretary of labor, and ruling on questionable issues.

Collective Negotiations in Local and State Governments

Although some professional organizations, including the National Education Association, support passage of a federal teacher collective-bargaining law, most educators see this as a state issue. Public-school employees are, in fact, working for a state agency operating in a local unit, the school district.

Over half the states have permissive or mandatory statutes governing the right of public-school employees to organize, negotiate, exercise sanctions, or strike. There are, of course, substantial differences in these laws from state to state. In a number of states, legislation covers all public employees, while in others, there is a specific law covering school employees. Because the acts of legislative bodies are organic in nature and subject to amendment, repeal, and judicial interpretation, these laws will certainly undergo some modifications in the future. Appendix A is an attempt to analyze and categorize present state collective-bargaining laws. It is included to exemplify the various components of state laws, but it is not intended to defend the status of future collective-bargaining legislation.

JOB DESCRIPTION FOR THE DIRECTOR
OF EMPLOYEE RELATIONS

In keeping with the model established in Chapter 2, medium to large school districts should have a director of employee relations, who has the responsibility for managing the entire process of collective negotiations and acts as the chief negotiator on the school board's team.

Job Summary

The director of employee relations is responsible for the administration of the school district's management-employee–relations program. This includes the establishment and maintenance of effective two-way communication between the various organizational levels; the formulation, recommendation, and administration of school district management-employee–relations policies; and the administration of the collective-negotiations process.

Organizational Relationship

The director of employee relations has a line relationship with the assistant superintendent for personnel, to whom he or she reports directly, serving as the chief adviser concerning employee relations. He or she has a staff relationship with other administrative personnel, and a cooperative-professional one with nonadministrative personnel with whom he or she negotiates. The members of the immediate staff have a line relationship with the director, to whom they report directly.

Organizational Tasks

In preparing for negotiations, the director of employee relations shall:

Develop a negotiating strategy for school district management
Prepare proposals and counterproposals for school district management
Analyze and evaluate employee proposals, and advise the school district management accordingly
Know state laws, court decisions, and other litigation relevant to professional negotiations
Secure input from all administrative personnel prior to developing school district management proposals

In at-the-table negotiations, the director of employee relations shall:

Serve as the chief negotiator for the school district
Direct the school district's negotiations team

Keep administrative personnel informed during negotiations

Draft negotiated agreements reached with employees

Maintain records of proposals or counterproposals presented by all parties during negotiations

In administering the negotiated agreement, the director of employee relations shall:

Serve as the school district's chief adviser in the interpretation of adopted agreements

Serve as the school district's chief adviser in all grievance matters

Consult with principals and other supervisors concerning their understanding of and compliance with the adopted agreement

Initiate school district management's grievance and mediation activities

Job Requirements

In terms of educational requirements, the director of employee relations should possess:

Appropriate state administrator certification

A master's degree (minimum)

Formal course work in the areas of educational administration, with exposure to curriculum, finance, school law, collective negotiations, and personnel administration

Classroom teaching experience and at least two years as a building principal[2]

MODEL BOARD OF EDUCATION POLICY
ON COLLECTIVE NEGOTIATIONS

The board of education finds that joint decision-making is the most effective way of governing the school system. If school district employees have the right to share in decisions regarding salaries, fringe benefits, and working conditions, they become more responsive and better disposed to exchanging ideas and information concerning operations with administrators. Accordingly, management becomes more efficient.

The board of education further declares that harmonious and cooperative relations between itself and school district employees protect the patrons and children of the school district by assuring the orderly operation of the schools.

This position of the board is to be effectuated by:

1. Recognizing the right of all school district employees to organize for the purpose of collective negotiations
2. Authorizing the director of employee relations to negotiate with the duly elected employee representatives on matters relating to salaries, fringe benefits, and working conditions

3. Requiring the director of employee relations to establish administrative policies and procedures for the effective implementation of the negotiations process. This is to be accomplished under the supervision of the assistant superintendent for personnel, who, in turn, is directly responsible to the superintendent of schools

Upon successful completion of the negotiations process, the board of education will enter into written agreements with the employee organizations.

From this board of education policy, a definition for negotiations may be established as follows: Collective bargaining is the process by which representatives of the school board meet with representatives of the school district employees to make proposals and counterproposals for the purpose of mutually agreeing on salaries, fringe benefits, and working conditions for a specific period of time. Both parties are required either by a state statute or by a renegotiations provision of the current master contract to bargain in "good faith." This refers to the intention by both teams to enter the bargaining process for the purpose of reaching an agreement. Any attempt to hinder this is considered "bad faith" bargaining, and the other party usually has to turn to a public employees relations board or the state court system. The court may issue an injunction requiring the two teams to return to the bargaining table.

RECOGNITION AND BARGAINING-UNIT DETERMINATION

This section is concerned with answering a basic question: "Who represents whom?" In labor history, most of the violence that occurred in the private sector centered around this query. Unions fought one another for the right to represent workers against management. The prize was power. In education, the prize is still the same, but the contest is usually nonviolent.

Recognition is defined as the acceptance of the authorized representative of two or more employees for the purpose of collective negotiations. Without recognition, each teacher is left to make his or her own arrangements with the school board, an approach that is the antithesis of collective bargaining.

There are two basic types of recognition in education: multiple and exclusive representation. Multiple representation does not occur in many school districts because of the problems inherent in two or more organizations or unions representing a specific bargaining unit. In New York City prior to the collective-bargaining elections in 1961, ninety-three organizations were accorded equal-representation rights by the board of education.[3] Although this situation is extreme, there are school districts in which more than one organization claims the right to represent a segment of the employees.

In multiple representation, recognition is usually granted by the board of education on the basis of organizational membership. This recognition is operationalized by one of the following methods: The board's representatives meet separately with representatives of each union, in joint sessions with equal numbers of representatives from each union, or in joint sessions with representatives of the unions proportionally determined. For example, if organization A has 500 members and organization B has 250, A is entitled to twice as many representatives on the negotiating team as B.

Exclusive recognition occurs when a single union represents all the members of a bargaining unit. The technical designation for the union in this role is *bargaining agent.* The bargaining unit consists of all the employees whose salaries, fringe benefits, and working conditions are negotiated by the bargaining agent. The paramount feature of exclusive recognition is that the employer cannot negotiate with anyone in the unit except through the bargaining agent.

Exclusive recognition is the form most widely used in education, for two basic reasons. First, it is mandated for the public sector in many states and widely accepted in most communities, even in the absence of state legislation. Secondly, private business and industry attest to the fact that this is the most effective form of recognition.

Recognition procedures take various forms in education. The three most commonly used are membership lists, authorization cards, and elections. If a union can demonstrate that 51 percent of the employees in a bargaining unit are members of that union, or if 51 percent of the employees in a unit present signatures authorizing a certain union to represent them, the board may recognize this union as the exclusive bargaining agent.

A more common practice is the *representation election,* which is also a necessity in the absence of membership lists or authorization cards signifying majority support. There are a number of reasons why a school board would prefer to hold an election before recognizing a union as the exclusive bargaining agent. Some teachers who join an organization or union may not want that union to represent them in negotiations. Also, teachers join certain unions for social, professional, or other reasons that have nothing to do with negotiations. In some cases, a teacher may be a member of more than one local teachers' union.

The representation election poses several questions that must be addressed by both the school board and the unions seeking recognition:

Who conducts the election?
Who will pay the costs for the election?
What are the ground rules for electioneering?
Who is eligible to vote?
Who will certify the results?
What will be the duration of the certification?

There are no "correct" answers to these questions. Rather, they must be answered within a framework that will take into consideration the variables affecting local situations. A cardinal principle is that the board and unions must maintain credibility; therefore, a third party is often requested to intervene in finding a workable answer to these questions. The Federal Mediation and Conciliation

Service or the League of Women Voters are examples of two independent agencies that can act as the appropriate third party. In many states with collective-bargaining laws, recognition procedures and bargaining-unit determination are mandated. This discussion thus pertains to those states without legislation and where the law allows latitude on these issues. Some states have a Public Employee Relation Board (PERB), which will conduct the election and determine who belongs to the bargaining unit, in addition to investigating charges of unfair labor practices perpetrated either by the management of the school district or the labor union.

It is now necessary to more closely define the term *bargaining unit.* School districts not only employ those who teach many different subjects and on a variety of levels, but also a wide range of specialists: psychologists, nurses, social workers, and attendance officers. In addition, there are a number of classified employees: cooks, custodians, bus drivers, maintenance workers, secretaries, and clerks.

To have collective negotiations, it must be determined what specific category of employees is represented by the bargaining agent that wins the representation election. In practice, this determination must be part of the recognition process, because only those employees in a bargaining unit will be allowed to vote on which union will represent them. The most commonly accepted definition states that the unit is composed of all employees to be covered by the negotiated agreement or master contract.

The fundamental criterion for determining who belongs to the bargaining unit is determined by the "community of interest" principle.[4] Employees have a community of interest if they share skills, functions, educational levels, and working conditions. All elementary and secondary school teachers and guidance counselors clearly have a community of interest and should belong to a particular bargaining unit. Clerks and secretaries, on the other hand, could not be represented effectively by this unit and should constitute a separate one. It is conceivable that a medium-to-large-sized school district might have the following units bargaining separately with the representatives of the school board:

1. Certificated educators, exclusive of supervisors and administrators
2. Building-level administrators
3. Subject-matter coordinators
4. Secretaries and clerks
5. Cooks and cafeteria workers
6. Bus drivers
7. Custodians
8. Maintenance workers

Each of these bargaining units would have a separate agreement or master contract specifying salaries, fringe benefits, and working conditions, which could be quite different from one another. Therefore, a school district may have multiple bargaining units represented by the same bargaining agent, or multiple bargaining agents.

Besides community of interest, there are two additional considerations in determining a bargaining unit. Size is important, because an extremely small unit—of, say, five or ten employees—will have little impact acting alone. In this case, employees would be in a stronger bargaining position if they combined with other categories of employees. In a small school district, for example, there might be two bargaining units: a certificated-employees' unit, including teachers, nurses, psychologists; and a classified-employees' unit, including cooks, custodians, maintenance personnel, and secretaries.

Two categories of employees are traditionally excluded from membership in all bargaining units—"executives" and "confidential employees." In a school district, the assistant, associate, or deputy superintendents are executives. Because they are members of the superintendent's cabinet and share the function and responsibility of the superintendency, they truly constitute the management of the school district. Confidential employees are the secretaries and administrative assistants to the superintendent and other members of the cabinet. Because these employees are privy to confidential information, their membership in a bargaining unit could seriously compromise the negotiating strategies of the school board's team.

A final consideration in determining a bargaining unit is effective school administration. An unreasonably large number of units would be unworkable. If guidance counselors, classroom teachers, speech therapists, music teachers, physical education teachers, and safety education teachers were all covered by different agreements specifying different working conditions, a building principal would have a difficult job supervising the staff.

Two other issues that have surfaced in recent years will have an influence on future negotiations—the agency shop and administrator bargaining units. *Agency shop* is a term borrowed from industry and refers to a question of equity. An employee who is a member of a given bargaining unit may not be a dues-paying member of the union that is the bargaining agent. Under a bargaining agreement with the school board that includes an agency shop clause or if this issue is covered by a state collective-bargaining law, such an employee would be required to pay a fee, usually the equivalent of dues to the union. While such employees could not participate in internal union affairs, they would be allowed to partake in unit activities such as attending meetings called by the negotiating team and voting on ratification of the agreement.

The agency shop is a form of *union security*, which is a term also borrowed from private business and industry. Other forms of union security are also found in master contracts. (1) The *union shop* requires an individual to become a member of the union representing employees within a specific period of time after being hired and to continue such membership as a condition of employment. (2) The *maintenance-of-membership agreement* requires an individual who is a member of the union representing the employees to remain a member until the master contract negotiated by the union is terminated. This also holds true for individuals who become members of the union during a contract period. (3) The *service-fee agreement* mandates that an individual pay his or her share of the cost incurred by a union in executing its function as the exclusive bargaining agent if this individual decides not to become a member of the union. (4) The *irrevocable and exclusive dues check-off agreement* is an authorization by employees to the employer to deduct union dues from their paycheck to be forwarded to the union for a specific period of time. This agreement is afforded only to the exclusive bargaining agent.

A growing number of educational administrators, particularly building principals, are organizing into unions and bargaining with school boards. The reasons administrators are turning to collective bargaining include: decreasing autonomy and power, loss of prestige, economic anxiety, and contagion (teachers are getting theirs; we should too). It appears that this trend will continue during the next decade, and school-board representatives will negotiate with administrator bargaining units.

THE SCOPE OF NEGOTIATIONS

The *scope of negotiations* refers to those matters that are negotiated. In some school districts, negotiations are limited to salaries, while in others, literally hundreds of items are discussed.

Negotiations must not be limited to unimportant matters, or the process will be considered a failure by teachers. What constitutes an important item is, of course, dictated by local circumstances. A school board might be willing to negotiate only on salaries and refuse to consider such items as a grievance procedure or reduction-in-force policy. Yet some of these nonmonetary items are just as vital to teachers as salary. It is, therefore, extremely important to place only mandatory limitations on the scope of negotiations. These limitations refer to items that are illegal because of state and federal constitutions or laws, or are contrary to the policies of the state board of education.

Most state laws stipulate that collective negotiations must be confined to "working conditions." This phrase usually is meant to include salaries and fringe benefits. While the meaning of *salary* is self-evident, there is some confusion over the terms *fringe benefit* and *working conditions.*

A fringe benefit may be defined as a form of compensation that is available to employees as a direct result of a fiscal expenditure by the school district for a specific service. Such services might include: accident benefits, major-medical insurance, hospitalization insurance, pensions, sick pay, dental insurance, and professional-liability insurance.

Working conditions refer to the quality of the employment situation. Teaching in a particular school district might be especially desirable because the district has equitable policies concerning class size, duty-free lunch periods, preparation periods, and sabbatical leave.

A major concern in defining the scope of negotiations for a particular situation is the concept of educational policy. School boards are required by statute to set educational policy. While teachers are deeply interested in educational policy and believe that they should be consulted in formulating it, it is commonly understood that such policy is not subject to negotiation.

The following are examples of policy questions:

1. Should the school district provide a foreign-language program in the elementary grades?
2. Should statistics be offered in the high school mathematics program?
3. Should extracurricular activities be sponsored or supported by district funds?

The obvious problem is that virtually all educational policy decisions have implications for working conditions. For example, funds expended to introduce a foreign-language program in the elementary grades will leave less money to improve fringe benefits for all employees. It is, therefore, often impossible to separate issues pertaining to policy from those pertaining to working conditions.

Finally, it must be remembered that the scope of negotiations is itself negotiated or at least affected by the process of negotiations.

When the parties meet to negotiate, there is no formula that prescribes what is negotiable. Good administration does not eliminate the need for negotiations, but their scope is likely to include those matters that have been administered in an inequitable manner. The relative strength of the parties may affect the scope of negotiations much more than academic versions of what progressive school administrators or organization leaders should negotiate. Legal, personal, political, economic, and organizational factors may have some impact on the scope of negotiations as well as on the resolution of items actually negotiated. In other words, the process of negotiation inevitably affects its scope, and vice versa.[5]

THE BARGAINING PROCESS

The Negotiating Team

The purpose of this section is to analyze those factors that influence the process of negotiation at the bargaining table. The first issue that must be addressed is the composition of the school board's negotiating team.

There is no universally accepted practice in forming a negotiating team; however, the size of a school district appears to have a significant influence on the makeup of the team. In small school districts, a committee of school-board members usually negotiates directly with a team of teachers. In medium-to-large-sized districts, the assistant superintendent for personnel, along with other central-office and/or building-level administrators, might be designated by the superintendent to negotiate with the teachers' union. In some large districts, a chief negotiator is employed on a full-time or ad hoc basis.

The size of the team is relative but should have an odd number of members, to avoid a deadlock in making strategy decisions. Therefore, three, five, or seven members would be appropriate. Generally, a team composed of more than seven members impedes decision making.

Membership on the team may be by job description, appointment, or election. The chairperson and chief negotiator is, of course, the director of employee relations. Additional membership on the team should include building-level principals, because they are the first line supervisors who will be managing the master agreement. Also, many principals have been critical of school boards for "negotiating away" their authority. On a five-member team, one principal from each level (elementary school, junior or middle school, high school), all elected by fellow principals, would give the team high credibility among building administrators. The final member of the team should have some specific expertise in and knowledge of the district's finances. Thus, the assistant superintendent for administrative services or the business manager would be appropriate.

This team must function as an entity over the entire academic year. As will be pointed out later, the bargaining process entails the development of strategies and the construction of proposal packages, which cannot be accomplished only during a few months of the year. While most of the work will fall on the shoulders of the director of employee relations, the committee will need to expend a great deal of time on these issues as well. Consequently, it is advisable to provide those principals who serve on the committee with some compensation, such as a stipend or additional administrative assistance.

The negotiating team for the teachers is, of course, usually composed of teachers. Sometimes the officers of the local organization or union act as the team, while in other situations, a negotiating team is appointed by the union officers or elected by the teachers. If the local is affiliated with a national union, experts in the bargaining process are available to advise union officers.

A final issue concerning the board's negotiating team must be addressed. What if the building administrators organize, form a bargaining unit, and elect a bargaining agent to represent them regarding salaries, fringe benefits, and working conditions? This, of course, is the current trend, especially in large urban school districts. In this case, the same structure for the board's negotiating team may be maintained by substituting assistant superintendents for principals. Because each bargaining unit separately negotiates a master agreement that reflects different working conditions for employees who have different job positions, it is not inconsistent with good administration or governance for principals to negotiate for the board on the one hand and for their membership on the other.

Developing Strategies

The negotiating team is responsible for the entire bargaining process, which must begin with strategy development. This entails two activities, assessing the needs of the school district and establishing goals for negotiations.

Needs assessment may take a variety of forms, but certain tasks must be completed:

1. Review the current master agreement to determine if its provisions meet the goals of the district and allow for effective administration.
2. Study the previous negotiating sessions to determine if the ground rules provide for effective negotiations.
3. Analyze the formal grievances that were filed by both the union and administration.
4. Study the arbitration decisions that were rendered on these grievances.
5. Meet with school district administrators to gather input concerning the provisions of the current master agreement.
6. Meet informally with the union to ascertain their concerns over the current agreement.
7. Confer with the board of education and superintendent to learn their concerns and to establish fiscal parameters.

From this information, the team sets the goals and objectives for negotiations, which are reduced to operational terms in the proposal package. Further, the team is responsible for creating an evaluation criterion that can be applied to the proposals presented by the union's team.

Setting the Ground Rules

With the advice and consent of the negotiating team, the chairperson should meet with the union negotiators to determine the rules under which the at-the-table process will take place. Key points that must be determined include:

The time and place for the sessions
The number of participants
The role of each participant
How each side will present its proposals
Setting a target date for completing negotiations
What kind of school district data will be needed by each side
The conditions governing caucuses
The provisions for recording the sessions
The method to be used in recording counterproposals and agreements
The policy on press releases
What types of impasse procedures will be employed, and when
The format for the written agreement
The procedure for agreement approval by the school board and union membership
What procedures will be used in publishing the ratified agreement

At-the-Table Sessions

There are two reasons for being at the negotiating table. First, by making proposals and counterproposals, the negotiating teams should be able to ascertain what issues are critical to each side. Secondly, each team should be able to assess the other side's bargaining power. This refers to the ability to have the other team agree on an item or the entire proposal package based on your terms.

Political pressure, negotiating skill, and psychology are important sources of bargaining power. Although it is impossible to measure bargaining power exactly, it is apparent that, at some time, the overall advantages of agreement outweigh the overall disadvantages of agreement.

It is very important to keep the board and entire administrative staff informed of the progress at the bargaining sessions. If this is not accomplished effectively, rumors may adversely affect the bargaining power of the board's team.

When an agreement is reached by the negotiating teams, ratification by the respective governing bodies is the final step. The board's team meets with the superintendent and board of education to recommend and explain the agreement. Formal ratification is usually made by signature of the school-board president, president of the union, and attested to by the secretaries of the board and union.

Because negotiating is an art rather than a science, it is extremely difficult to develop a formula for success. Nevertheless, a number of practical hints may be in order. The following are recommendations made to local boards of education by the Ohio School Board Association:

1. *Keep calm. Don't lose control of yourself.* Negotiation sessions can be exasperating. The temptation may come to get angry and fight back when intemperate accusations are made or when "the straw that broke the camel's back" is hurled on the table.

2. *Avoid "off the record" comments.* Actually nothing is "off the record." Innocently made remarks have a way of coming back to haunt their author. Be careful to say only what you are willing to have quoted.

3. *Don't be overcandid.* Inexperienced negotiators may, with the best of intentions, desire to "lay the cards on the table face up." This may be done in the mistaken notion that everybody fully understands the other and utter frankness is desired. Complete candor does not always serve the best interests of productive negotiations. This is not a plea for duplicity; rather, it is a recommendation for prudent and discriminating utterances.

4. *Be long on listening.* Usually a good listener makes a good negotiator. It is wise to let your "adversaries" do the talking—at least in the beginning.

5. *Don't be afraid of a "little heat."* Discussions sometimes generate quite a bit of "heat." Don't be afraid of it. It never hurts to let the "opposition" sound off, even when you may be tempted to hit back.

6. *Watch the voice level.* A wise practice is to keep the pitch of the voice down, even though the temptation may be strong to let it rise under the excitement of emotional stress.

7. *Keep flexible.* One of the skills of good negotiators is the ability to shift position a bit if a positive gain can thus be accomplished. An obstinate adherence to one position or point of view, regardless of the ultimate consequences of that rigidity, may be more of a deterrent than an advantage.

8. *Refrain from a flat "no."* Especially in the earlier stages of a negotiation, it is best to avoid giving a flat "no" answer to a proposition. It does not help to work yourself into a box by being totally negative "too early in the game."

9. *Give to get.* Negotiation is the art of giving and getting. Concede a point to gain a concession. This is the name of the game.

10. *Work on the easier items first.* Settle those things first about which there is the least controversy. Leave the tougher items until later in order to avoid an early deadlock.

11. *Respect your adversary.* Respect those who are seated on the opposite side of the table. Assume that their motives are as sincere as your own, at least until proven otherwise.

12. *Be patient.* If necessary, be willing to sit out tiresome tirades. Time has a way of being on the side of the patient negotiator.

13. *Avoid waving "red flags."* There are some statements that irritate teachers and merely heighten their antipathies. Find out what these are and avoid their use. Needless waving of "red flags" only infuriates.

14. *Let the other side "win some victories."* Each team has to win some victories. A "shutout" may be a hollow gain in negotiation.

15. *Negotiation is a "way of life."* Obvious resentment of the fact that negotiation is here to stay weakens the effectiveness of the negotiator. The better part of wisdom is to adjust to it and become better prepared to use it as a tool of interstaff relations.[6]

Third-Party Negotiations

In recent years, some parents and other school district patrons have been pushing for active involvement in collective negotiations. Proponents of this position have eagerly sought extension of Sunshine laws to require that bargaining sessions be open to the public. Others favor trilateral bargaining, whereby a citizen's group becomes an equal partner in the negotiating process; public response to proposals before an agreement is reached; and even public referendum, by which proposals are voted on by the citizens of the school district. There are many variations on this theme, but the ultimate objective is still the same—citizens' participation in the bargaining process.

Collective negotiating as a process demands refined skills by those sitting at the table. A third party will bring confusion and cloud the basic relationship between labor and management. In addition, school-board members have been elected to represent the interests of parents, students, and district patrons. Third parties seek to usurp this responsibility.

IMPASSE PROCEDURES

It is extremely difficult to define the term *impasse.* Negotiators often have trouble knowing when an impasse has been reached. However, in this discussion, an impasse will be considered a persistent disagreement that continues after normal negotiation procedures have been exhausted. In practice, this situation occurs after one side makes a "best and final" offer that is rejected by the other team. Such an offer is usually taken back by the team to the board or union membership for a vote. This procedure is, of course, a part of the previously agreed-upon ground rules.

Impasse must be expected to occur from time to time, even when both parties are negotiating in good faith. While there are, unfortunately, no procedures that are guaranteed to resolve an impasse, some are more successful than others, and they will be outlined here. It must also be kept in mind that improperly used impasse procedures can aggravate rather than resolve a disagreement. Therefore, a working knowledge of procedures is essential for all participants in the negotiating process.

A number of the states that have passed collective-bargaining laws have also established public-employee relations boards. These boards are charged with implementing the law, which might include making decisions involving recognition, bargaining-unit determination, and deciding on the scope of what is negotiable, in addition to administering impasse procedures, which include mediation, fact-finding, and arbitration.

Mediation

Mediation is the process by which negotiators on both sides of a dispute agree on the need for third-party assistance. The role of the mediator is advisory and, consequently, this individual has no authority to dictate a settlement. Some mediators meet with both parties separately and attempt to ascertain what concessions each might make in order to reach an agreement. This procedure has been most effective when one or both parties consider making concessions to be a sign of weakness.

Meeting jointly with both parties is particularly helpful in assessing the actual status of negotiations and obtaining agreement on the phrasing of the issues. Most mediators will use a combination of separate and joint meetings to facilitate an agreement.

Mediators usually refrain from recommending a settlement until they are sure that their suggestions will be acceptable to both parties. Up until that time, the mediator acts only as a clarifier of issues and thereby attempts to defuse the antagonism between the parties, which is frequently the cause of the impasse.

A mediator may be called into a dispute at any time. In some cases, preventive mediation may even be practiced, by making suggestions useful to the parties early in the negotiations.

Because mediation is a voluntary process, the parties must decide who will mediate and what that person's role will be in the preparatory stages of the actual negotiations. In approximately one-third of the states, this issue is settled by statute and a formal declaration of "impasse" is all that is required to put the process in motion. Often, a master agreement will contain provisions outlining impasse procedures to be followed in renegotiating the agreement. When mediator services are not provided by a governmental agency, the fees for a private mediator are borne equally by both parties to the dispute.

Fact-Finding

This is the procedure by which an individual or a panel holds hearings for the purpose of reviewing evidence and making a recommendation for settling the dispute. Like mediation, fact-finding is a process that is governed by a state statute, provided for in a master agreement, or established by both parties before negotiations begin.

The formal hearing is usually open to the public. Parties that have a vested interest in the dispute are given the opportunity to offer evidence and arguments in their own behalf. It sometimes occurs that fact-finders are requested by both parties to mediate the dispute and avoid further formal proceedings.

The fact-finding report and recommendations are also usually made public. The process is voluntary, and the parties may reject all or part of the report. To a certain extent, the action of the parties will depend upon the public's reactions, which in turn depend partly upon the prestige of the fact-finder.

Arbitration

This is the process by which the parties submit their dispute to an impartial third person or panel that issues a decision that the parties are required to accept. Arbitration can be either mandatory or voluntary. Mandatory arbitration must be established by statute. The voluntary use of arbitration has gained some acceptance in the public sector for handling grievances arising from the interpretation of master agreements.

The Federal Mediation and Conciliation Service

The Federal Mediation and Conciliation Service is an independent agency of the federal government created by Congress in 1947, with a director appointed by the President of the United States. The primary purpose of the FMCS is to promote labor-management peace. To carry out this mission more effectively, the agency has established both regional and field offices staffed by professional mediators.

Federal labor laws do not cover employees of state and local governments. However, if state legislatures fail to establish mediation services for public employees, the FMCS may voluntarily enter a dispute.

The FMCS has the Office of Arbitration Services in Washington, which maintains a roster of arbitrators located in all parts of the country. Upon request, a randomly selected list will be furnished, from which the parties may choose a mutually acceptable arbitrator to hear and decide a dispute.

In summary, it is too difficult to promote one or more impasse procedures as the most effective approaches to handling all persistent disputes that arise at the bargaining table or in grievances over master-contract interpretation. It is more appropriate to think in terms of sequence. Mediation should be the first procedure, followed by fact-finding, and then, where it is permitted by law in negotiations, arbitration. This sequence places the responsibility for resolving the dispute first on the parties themselves. Better and more effective agreements are reached when the parties involved can resolve the issues; and when it is mandated by law, arbitration curtails strikes, which always have a devastating effect on school systems.

WORK-STOPPAGE STRATEGIES

The Scope of Strikes

There is nothing more disruptive to a school district than a strike. As board members, administrators, teachers, and support personnel engage in heated and public argument, schisms occur that often last for years. Community groups also become divided over who is right and who is wrong.

The American Association of School Administrators (AASA) consistently opposes the strike as a weapon when negotiations reach an impasse. The AASA also supports the position that the administrative team has the responsibility to keep the school open, to protect both students who report to school and school property, and to maintain communication between parents, teachers, and the public.

Strikes by public-school employees are illegal or limited by state laws. In the business and industrial community, strikes usually occur when the master contract has expired and a new contract has not successfully been negotiated or when there is a grievance regarding interpretation of the master contract. State laws usually require schools to be in session for a specific number of days, and other statutes address teacher tenure and certification requirements. Thus, a major difference between the private and public sectors when a strike occurs concerns loss of wages and certain working conditions. Teachers usually do not ultimately lose wages when they go on strike because the days on the picket line must be made up in order to comply with state statutes. Further, if they continue to teach as negotiations linger on past the termination date of the master contract, other state laws will protect fundamental working conditions. However, the frequency and intensity of strikes appear to be increasing each year. The news media daily remind us of the magnitude of this issue. There is also no indication that strikes will cease, as school employees, administrators, and teachers become more proficient in the negotiation process.

Ten to fifteen years ago, most teachers felt that a strike was not in keeping with their professional status. They no longer think this way, and the personal fears once associated with a strike also no longer exist. Today, teachers strike over many issues, including: recognition of their unions, salary increases, fringe benefits, working conditions, due process, organizational threats, curriculum control, reduction in force, and community nonsupport. Teachers have also honored strikes by nonteaching personnel and have attempted to get the unions involved in those strikes to support their own.

School-Employee Strike Tactics

A strike by school employees is usually the result of failure at the bargaining table. The objective of any strike is to gain as favorable a settlement as possible from the board of education within the shortest period of time.

A few key issues have been used by teacher unions to rally support for a strike, and these include: pupil-teacher ratio; planning time, particularly for elementary school teachers; and extra pay for extra duty, particularly for secondary school teachers. With decreasing enrollments and inflation, the focus has been on issues related to job security, such as evaluation procedures and policies regarding reduction in force.

In a strike, school-employee unions, especially teacher unions, have almost unlimited resources at their disposal from their state and national affiliates. In very sensitive strikes, as many as 100 field staff members may be available to help the local union.

A careful examination of several strikes shows the following tactics to be some of the most commonly used by teachers' unions:

1. Making the community highly aware of the reasons for the strike, mostly via handbills, advertisements in the local press, and news coverage.
2. Placing the blame on a specific person, such as the superintendent or school-board president. This tactic will channel the pressure exerted by parents and the community.
3. Encouraging local and state politicians to become involved in the dispute. School-employee groups represent a sizable number of votes.
4. Working diligently to gain support from other unions in the community.
5. Staging a strike in the late spring, because this will interfere not only with graduation but also with state aid, which is usually calculated on a certain number of days' attendance before the end of the school year.

Although some strikes do occur spontaneously because of unexpected developments, most teacher strikes are well orchestrated. Generally, teachers' unions are aware weeks or even months in advance that certain negotiable demands may produce a strike.

Administrative Strategies

If a school system finds itself in the middle of a strike without an adequate plan of action, it indicates that the board of education has not been paying attention to current developments or the situation in its own school district. In fact, the superintendent and his or her cabinet should have a carefully developed strike plan even in the most tranquil of school settings. This plan should operate at both the district and building levels. The American Association of School Administrators has developed a series of steps in a plan that can serve as a guide for administrators and school boards in establishing their own district plans.

BEFORE A STRIKE

District-Level

1. Develop the overall district plan as well as a board policy statement well in advance of an anticipated strike (preferably, when there is absolutely no indication of a strike).
2. Provide as early as possible for the notification of news media, parents, staff, of the likelihood or possibility of a strike.
3. Notify staff members of the applicable state law and school board policy concerning a work stoppage and the legal ramifications of such action.
4. Establish provisions for a Decision-Making Center to have the overall direction of a strike and assign specific responsibilities to those key people in the Center.
5. Make contacts with police, fire, health, telephone, and other community/state agencies likely to be needed or contacted during a strike.
6. Prepare a list of names and telephone numbers for the specific individuals in each agency who can be contacted day or night in emergency situations.
7. Provide for "hot line" telephones for citizens and staff members so they may receive strike information.
8. Install a bank of unlisted telephones in the Decision-Making Center to facilitate ongoing and continual communications.
9. Obtain, or make provisions to obtain, two-way radio systems for strategic points in the district (or mobile car radios, beeper systems).
10. Develop building strike plans and reporting systems for daily status reports from each building.
11. Notify the news media of the media area and provide the time(s) and place of daily (or more often) briefings concerning the strike.
12. Have the board of education pass the necessary legal resolutions required to deal with the strike (restraining orders, injunctions, picket line restrictions, formal notification to personnel on strike, etc.).
13. Continue to seek a solution to the strike and keep such initiative on the side of the administration and board.

Building-Level

1. Develop with each building principal a building Strike Plan in conformance with the overall district plan.
2. Secure back-up personnel for each building principal to act in his or her stead during the work stoppage.
3. Make provision within the building Strike Plan for a daily, early-morning report to the Decision-Making Center.
4. Make provision for a daily written report listing the names of staff who reported for duty and the numbers of pupils in attendance at the building.
5. Make provision for continuity of communications in the event that telephone lines are unusable.

6. Make provision for each building principal to have specific guidelines and authority to close the building when the safety and health of the pupils are threatened, or when it is impossible to carry on an educational program.
7. Make provision for adequate building security (leaving lights on at night, security guards, etc.).

AFTER A STRIKE

District-Level

1. Notify all groups.
2. Hold briefing session for all administrators and board members.
3. Prepare building principals for the return of teachers.
4. Issue public statement detailing strike settlement to news media.
5. Begin making plans to defuse "anti-climactic" emotions.

Building-Level

1. Do not allow striking teachers to return to the classrooms until all substitute teachers are out of the building.
2. Make plans to focus major attention on the educational program and learning environment for students.[7]

When the Decision-Making Center mentioned in the plan is established at the central office, duties are assigned by the superintendent of schools, with the advice of his or her cabinet. Central-office administrators are assigned specific tasks to be performed during the strike that correspond to the provisions of the AASA plan. The director of labor relations could be given the task of notifying staff members of the state law and of board policy concerning strikes and the legal ramifications of such actions, while the director of public relations notifies the news media of the time and place for daily briefings concerning the strike. Likewise, the building principal and, if it is a large school, the administrative team are responsible for implementing the building-level provisions.

ADMINISTRATION OF THE MASTER AGREEMENT

The process of collective negotiation is usually ineffective unless the agreements reached are put into writing. Therefore, written master agreements are essential, because they formalize the basic rights governing the parties in terms of their relationship and reduce controversy over the content of the agreement.

Provisions of the Agreement

Most master agreements are extremely detailed and replace board of education policies covering working conditions. There are certain common items that are included in most agreements and are deemed essential:

1. Recognition of the union as the exclusive bargaining agent
2. A statement of purpose
3. The duration of the agreement and method for renegotiating the agreement before the expiration date
4. Incorporation of a grievance procedure
5. Incorporation of impasse procedures
6. Description of who is a member of the bargaining unit
7. A statement concerning dues check-off
8. A fair practice statement
9. Salary schedules and guidelines for the duration of the agreement[8]

Figure 10-1, Table of Contents from the Dade County master agreement, is an example of the types of articles and appendices that operationalize these provisions.

The style and format of the master agreement will sometimes be dictated by state statutes, but in the absence of legislation, school boards and unions must look elsewhere for help. In many cases, teacher associations affiliated with national unions have access to model master agreements, which can be adapted to local situations. In fact, some models are complete in every detail, and only specific data must be filled in.

Implementing the Master Agreement

It is the responsibility of the administration to implement and interpret the provisions of the agreement. Furthermore, the administration is limited only by the specifics of the master agreement. This lack of limitations is commonly referred to as *management prerogative.*

In the day-to-day interpretation of the agreement, it is certainly possible for violations to occur. Most written agreements, therefore, provide for a grievance procedure by which individuals, the union, or the administration alleges that the master agreement is being violated or misinterpreted.

Most grievance procedures contain the following common elements:

1. A careful definition of the term *grievance*
2. The purpose of the grievance procedure
3. A clause stating that a person making or testifying in a grievance will not face prejudicial treatment

**FIGURE 10-1: TABLE OF CONTENTS FOR A CONTRACT
BETWEEN THE DADE COUNTY PUBLIC SCHOOLS
AND THE UNITED TEACHERS OF DADE FEA/UNITED,
AFT, LOCAL 1974, AFL-CIO**

Article

Appendix

4. A clear outline of the appropriate steps to be taken in a grievance and the time allotments between each step
5. In the case of arbitration, who will bear the costs and the qualifications required of an arbiter

SUMMARY

Collective negotiation has become a way of life in American education; over half the states have enacted collective-bargaining laws affecting teachers. The underlying reason for collective negotiation is participation in the decision-making process, which is a natural extension of our democratic government. Teachers and administrators want to have some control over the priorities established by school boards when these affect their salaries, fringe benefits, and working conditions.

Collective negotiations may be defined as the process by which representatives of the school board meet with those of the district employees to make proposals and counterproposals in order to reach agreement on salaries, fringe benefits, and working conditions for a specific period of time. The board of education must adopt a policy that will give the administration authority to implement negotiations.

Collective actions by employees have a long history in the private sector, going as far back as the medieval guilds. These actions are directly affected by economic, political, and social conditions. There are four major congressional acts that provide legal guidelines for collective bargaining in the private sector: The Norris-LaGuardia Act of 1932, The National Labor Relations Act of 1935, The Labor-Management Relations Act of 1947, and The Labor-Management Reporting and Disclosure Act of 1959.

Collective negotiations in the federal government are affirmed by Executive Orders 10988 and 11491. Federal employees have the right to organize and bargain collectively but cannot strike.

Public-school teachers are state employees working in a local unit, the school district. As such, they are not covered by federal legislation, but by the acts of state legislatures. There are substantial differences in state statutes granting collective-bargaining rights to teachers.

There are six aspects to the collective-negotiation process: recognition and bargaining-unit determination, the scope of negotiations, the bargaining process, impasse procedures, work stoppages, and master-agreement administration.

Recognition and bargaining-unit determination answers the question: "Who represents whom?" Recognition is the acceptance by an employer of a bargaining agent as the authorized representative of a bargaining unit. There are two types of recognition, multiple and exclusive; the latter has been the most effective. The three most commonly used recognition procedures are membership lists, authorization cards, and elections. In an election, a third party such as the Federal Mediation and Conciliation Service should be engaged to handle the mechanics of the election process.

The bargaining unit is composed of all employees to be covered by the negotiated master agreement. The criteria for deciding who belongs to the unit includes a community of interest among the members, effective bargaining power, and effective school administration.

The scope of what is negotiable usually includes salaries, fringe benefits, and working conditions. A major problem in defining "scope" is the fine line between educational policy, which is the prerogative of the school board, and conditions of employment, which are negotiable.

The at-the-table bargaining process must begin with the formation of a negotiating team. Ann odd-numbered team composed of the director of employee relations, building principals, and a central-office fiscal administrator has the greatest potential for being effective. This team is responsible for developing strategies, formulating goals, setting the ground rules, proposal preparation, and participating in negotiating sessions. Once an agreement is reached, the team makes a recommendation to the school board, which formally ratifies the agreement.

If disagreement at the table persists after normal negotiating procedures have been exhausted, an impasse has been reached. The three usual procedures for resolving an impasse are mediation, fact-finding, and, where permitted by law, arbitration. Mediation is the voluntary process by which a third party intervenes for the purpose of ending the disagreement. In fact-finding, an individual or panel holds hearings for the purpose of reviewing evidence and making a recommendation for settling the dispute. Arbitration occurs when both sides submit the dispute to an impartial third person or panel that issues a decision which the parties are required to accept.

There is nothing more disruptive to a school district than a strike, which is sometimes used by unions when negotiations reach an impasse. Although strikes by teachers are illegal in most states, the number of strikes appears to be on the increase. It is extremely important, therefore, for the administration to develop a strike plan, even in the most tranquil of school settings.

The process of collective negotiation is usually ineffective unless the agreements are put into writing, which formalizes the basic rights governing the parties and reduces controversy. It is the responsibility of the administration to implement and interpret the master agreement. Furthermore, the administration is limited only by the specifics of the agreement. This lack of limitations is commonly referred to as *management prerogative.*

In the day-to-day interpretation of the master agreement, violations may occur. Most written agreements, therefore, provide for a grievance procedure by which individuals, the union, or the administration may allege that the agreement is being violated.

IMPLICATIONS FOR EDUCATIONAL ADMINISTRATORS

The foregoing discussion of collective bargaining for public-school employees has three implications for educational administrators.

First, many teachers and administrators shun the use of the terms *labor* and *management.* They see themselves as professionals and believe these designations alter their status and do not truly reflect their attitudes. The terms are functional, and only refer to the relationship of employee categories as they interact in an organization. For example, attorneys who work in the legal department of a large corporation and are supervised by a department head constitute the labor force in that department. Their department head represents management. These designations have nothing to do with the quality of their performance or the professional nature of their responsibilities. Management carries out planning and supervisory functions. Labor performs the tasks that meet the objectives of the organization. School districts have the mission to teach; administrators (management) supervise the teachers (labor) in fulfilling this objective.

Second, collective bargaining is here to stay; therefore, it must be utilized as a method of bringing about good labor-management relations. Some states are still dealing with the conflicts between various segments of their populations as they attempt to draft and pass a collective-bargaining law for public-school employees. In those states, it is imperative for administrator organizations to engage in lobbying activities that will influence the passage of a collective-bargaining law that will support, rather than hinder, the effective management of school districts. In those states with collective-bargaining laws, administrators must content themselves with monitoring the implementation of the legislation. When the law interferes with effective management, they might choose to test the law in the judicial arena, the courts.

Third, educational administrators must make a quantum leap from collective bargaining to the concept of employee relations. Those in private business and industry have understood for many years the importance of demonstrating that the company cares about the welfare of its employees and appreciates their ideas and opinions. The establishment of employee-supervisor committees charged with monitoring the implementation of the master contract and discussing ways and means of increasing productivity has created an atmosphere of cooperation in some companies, the advantages of which extend far beyond the negotiating process. This can also be accomplished in education. Faculty meetings generally do not achieve this goal, nor do they include classified personnel, who also have a wealth of talent that can help to improve the educational environment of a school district. Employee-supervisor committees can carry on what was begun as a consequence of collective bargaining and may even make future negotiations more productive.

SELECTED BIBLIOGRAPHY

AMERICAN ASSOCIATION OF SCHOOL ADMINISTRATORS, *Helping Administrators Negotiate, Volume I: AASA Executive Handbook Series.* Washington, D.C.: The Association, 1974.
——— , *Work Stoppage Strategies, Volume VI: AASA Executive Handbook Series.* Washington, D.C.: The Association, 1975.

ANDREE, R. G., *Collective Negotiations.* Lexington, Mass.: D. C. Heath & Co., 1970.

COFFIN, ROYCE A., *The Negotiator: A Manual for Winners.* New York: American Management Association, 1973.

CRESSWELL, ANTHONY, *Education and Collective Bargaining.* New York: McCutchan Publishing Corporation, 1976.

DAVEY, HAROLD W., *Contemporary Collective Bargaining* (3rd ed.). Englewood Cliffs, N.J.: Prentice-Hall, Inc., 1972.

DEMPSEY, RICHARD A., and LLOYD C. HARTMAN, *Collective Bargaining in Public Education: A Manual for School Administrators.* Swarthmore, Pa.: A. C. Croft, Inc., 1970.

EDUCATION COMMISSION OF THE STATES, *Cuebook II: State Education Collective Bargaining Laws.* Denver: The Commission, 1980.

KARRASS, CHESTER L., *Give and Take: The Complete Guide to Negotiating Strategies and Tactics.* New York: Thomas Y. Crowell Company, 1974.

LIEBERMAN, M., and M. H. MOSKOW, *Collective Negotiations for Teachers.* Chicago: Rand McNally & Company, 1966.

MOSKOW, MICHAEL, JOSEPH J. LOEWENBERG, and EDWARD C. KOZIARA, *Collective Bargaining in Public Employment.* New York: Random House, 1970.

NATIONAL EDUCATION ASSOCIATION, *Negotiations for Improvement of the Profession: A Handbook for Local Teacher Association Negotiators.* Washington, D.C.: The Association, 1971.

WEITZMAN, JOAN, *The Scope of Bargaining in Public Employment.* New York: Praeger Publishers, 1975.

NOTES

1. Education Commission of the States, *Cuebook II: State Education Collective Bargaining Laws* (Denver: The Commission, 1980), p. v.

2. Modeled on the job description for the director of employee relations in American Association of School Administrators, *Helping Administrators Negotiate* (Arlington, Va.: The Association, 1974), pp. 22-24.

3. Myron Lieberman and Michael H. Moskow, *Collective Negotiations for Teachers* (Chicago: Rand McNally & Co., 1966), p. 92.

4. Ibid., p. 129.

5. Ibid., p. 247.

6. Ohio School Boards Association, *Practical Hints on Collective Negotiations* (Westerville, Ohio: The Association, 1980).

7. American Association of School Administrators, *Work Stoppage Strategies* (Arlington, Va.: The Association, 1975), pp. 48, 49, 58.

8. Lloyd W. Ashby, James E. McGinnis, and Thomas E. Pering, *Common Sense in Negotiations in Public Education* (Danville, Ill.: The Interstate Printer and Publisher, Inc., 1972), pp. 59-60.

APPENDIX A: AN EXAMPLE OF THE SCOPE OF COLLECTIVE-BARGAINING LAWS

STATE	NUMBER OF STATUTES[1]	TYPE OF LAWS — LOCAL[2]	STATE[3]	OMNIBUS[4]	PROFESSIONAL COVERAGE[5] K-12 CC[8]	PROFESSIONAL COVERAGE[5] PS	CLASSIFIED COVERAGE[6] K-12 CC[8]	CLASSIFIED COVERAGE[6] PS	SUPERVISOR COVERAGE[7] K-12 CC[8]	SUPERVISOR COVERAGE[7] PS	UNION SECURITY PROVISIONS[9]	
Alabama												AL
Alaska	2	X		X	X	X		X	X		X	AK
Arizona												AZ
Arkansas												AR
California	3	X	PS		X	X	X	X	X		X	CA
Colorado					X		X	X				CO
Connecticut	3	X	X		X	X	X	X	X	X	X	CT
Delaware	2	X			X	X	X	X			X	DE
Florida	1			X	X	X	X	X			X	FL
Georgia												GA
Hawaii	1			X	X	X	X	X	X	X	X	HI
Idaho	1	X		X	X				X			ID
Illinois												IL
Indiana	1	X			X						X	IN
Iowa	1			X	X	X	X	X			X	IA
Kansas	2	X		X	X	X	X	X			X	KS
Kentucky							X					KY
Louisiana			PS,CC									LA
Maine	2	X			X	X	X	X	X		X	ME
Maryland	2	X			X	X	X	X	X		X	MD
Massachusetts	1			X	X	X	X	X	X	X	X	MA

		MI	MN	MS	MO	MT	NE	NV	NH	NJ	NM	NY	NC	ND	OH	OK	OR	PA	RI	SC	SD	TN	TX	UT	VT	VA	WA	WV	WI
Michigan	1				X				X		X	X			X		X	X	X		X				X		X		X
Minnesota	1				X				X		X	X			X		X	X	X		X				X		X		X
Mississippi						X					X				X														
Missouri	1				X				X		X	X			X		X	X	X		X				X		X	X	X
Montana	1				X				X		X	X			X		X	X	X		X				X		X	X	X
Nebraska	2	X	X		X				X		X	X			X		X	X	X		X				X		X	X	X
Nevada	1				X				X		X	X			X		X	X	X		X				X		X	X	X
New Hampshire	1				X				X		X	X			X		X	X	X		X				X		X	X	X
New Jersey	1				X		X		X		X	X			X		X	X	X		X				X		X	X	X
New Mexico						X				X		X			X			X			X								
New York	1				X				X		X	X			X		X	X	X		X				X		X	X	X
North Carolina																													
North Dakota	1	X			X				X		X	X			X		X	X	X		X				X		X	X	X
Ohio						X									X			X											
Oklahoma	1	X			X				X		X	X			X		X	X	X		X				X		X	X	X
Oregon	1	X			X				X		X	X			X		X	X	X		X				X		X	X	X
Pennsylvania	1	X			X				X		X	X			X		X	X	X		X				X		X	X	X
Rhode Island	3	X			X				X		X	X			X		X	X	X		X				X		X	X	X
South Carolina																													
South Dakota	1	X			X				X		X	X			X		X	X	X		X				X		X	X	X
Tennessee	1				X				X		X	X			X		X	X	X		X				X		X	X	X
Texas																													
Utah																													
Vermont	3	X			X				X		X	X			X		X	X	X		X				X		X	X	X
Virginia																													
Washington	4	CC			X				X		X	X			X		X	X	X		X				X		X	X	X
West Virginia																													
Wisconsin	2	X			X				X		X	X			X		X	X	X		X				X		X	X	X

227

APPENDIX A *(Continued)*

STATE	NUMBER OF STATUTES[1]	TYPE OF LAWS LOCAL[2]	TYPE OF LAWS STATE[3]	TYPE OF LAWS OMNIBUS[4]	PROFESSIONAL COVERAGE[5] K-12	PROFESSIONAL COVERAGE[5] CC[8]	PROFESSIONAL COVERAGE[5] PS	CLASSIFIED COVERAGE[6] K-12	CLASSIFIED COVERAGE[6] CC[8]	CLASSIFIED COVERAGE[6] PS	SUPERVISOR COVERAGE[7] K-12	SUPERVISOR COVERAGE[7] CC[8]	SUPERVISOR COVERAGE[7] PS	UNION SECURITY PROVISIONS[9]	
Wyoming	1	X													WY
District of Columbia	1	X			X		X	X			X		X	X	DC
TOTALS		19	7	17	32	12[8]	24	27	12[8]	24	20[8]	5	13	26	

[1] Represents the number of separate statutes summarized on the table for each state.

[2] Coverage for local-level employees only.

[3] Coverage for state-level employees only. California, Maine, and Washington laws are specific for postsecondary and/or community colleges.

[4] Coverage for employees of more than one governmental level.

[5] Teachers or personnel with similar or higher status.

[6] Below the rank of teacher; nonadministrative support personnel.

[7] Any or all levels of supervisors and administrators, in one or more laws in the state.

[8] This column is checked only if community colleges are noted specifically in law. State structures vary, and community colleges may be included in the K-12 system, in the postsecondary system, or may be a separate system.

[9] This column is checked if union security provisions are present in one or more of the state laws.

APPENDIX B: GLOSSARY
OF SELECTED COLLECTIVE-BARGAINING TERMS

Agency Shop. This term is used when employees who are not members of an employee organization, but who are represented by it during the bargaining process and in the administration of a bargained agreement, are required to pay a service fee to the organization.

Arbitration. A procedure whereby parties unable to agree on a solution to a problem (i.e., at impasse in a contract negotiation or a grievance procedure) will be bound by the decision of a third party.

Bargaining Unit. A group of employees organized as a single unit and having the right to bargain, through their designated representative(s), with the employer.

Certification. As the term applies in the recognition process: designation, by an authorized person or agency, of the employee organization representing a bargaining unit as an "exclusive representative" for bargaining purposes.

Community of Interest. As used in determining an appropriate bargaining unit: similar work, interests, salaries, concerns, etc.

Contract. A written agreement on the terms and conditions of employment arrived at through the bargaining process.

Court Review. The means through which a court of appropriate jurisdiction may consider and rule upon actions or findings of a labor relations board or other involved agency or individual.

Decertification. The withdrawal of authorization as an exclusive representative from an employee organization. May occur when another employee organization successfully challenges the qualifications of the first organization, or as a penalty for violation of law, rule or regulation.

Dues Checkoff. Deduction of employee organization dues from members' paychecks for remission to the organization treasury. Some states laws do not permit this practice; others do. When permitted, the dues deduction procedure often is negotiated as part of the contract between employer and employee bargaining unit.

Employee Organization. A group of similar employees organized for the purpose of bargaining their salaries, wages, and terms and conditions of employment with their employer. Most teacher organizations are affiliated with the National Education Association or the American Federation of Teachers. Often used interchangeably with *union* in the area of labor relations.

Exclusive Representation. An employee organization has exclusive representation when it is recognized by the employer, for bargaining purposes, as the sole representative of the kinds of employees who are members of the bargaining unit.

Fact-Finding. The process of gathering and analyzing accurate facts, information, and testimony to be used as a basis for recommendations for the resolution of a bargaining impasse or grievance charge.

Fair Share Fee. An amount proportionate to members' dues in an employee organization that is paid to the organization by nonmembers who are, nevertheless, represented by the organization in a bargaining relationship. Such nonmembers are a part of the bargaining unit, but not of the employee organization that represents them. A form of service fee, based on the proportion of dues that is directly related to the services the nonmember employee receives from the organization. Often negotiated.

Grievance. An allegation by an employee or by the employee organization that the employer or one of its agents, often in the process of implementing a contract, is guilty of misapplication, misinterpretation, or violation of one or more specific provisions of the existent contract.

Impasse. That stage in negotiations at which two parties are, or appear to be, unable to achieve agreement on the issues still on the bargaining table. There is an apparent lack of agreement among state laws and among state labor relations personnel as to the point at which impasse occurs: when mediation has failed, or when fact-finding has failed.

Impasse Resolution. A process aimed at resolving disagreements that occur during the bargaining of a contract. Three steps may be, but are not necessarily, involved: mediation, fact-finding, and arbitration. Also known as *interest resolution.*

Injunctive Relief. An order by a court to perform or cease to perform a specific activity.

Intervention/Intervenor. A challenge to an employee organization's right to be an exclusive representative for a bargaining unit. May be issued by a competing organization or one or more employees. Most state laws limit the times for such intervention to specific points in the establishment of a bargaining relationship, during or after the term of a contract.

Legislative Body. A policy-making body that has the authority to levy taxes and/or make appropriations.

Maintenance of Membership. A requirement that employees who are members of an employee organization that has been certified as an exclusive representative remain members during the term of a bargained contract.

Management Rights. Certain rights, privileges, responsibilities and authority requisite to the conduct of an enterprise by its management.

Mediation. That form of impasse resolution (usually implemented first) in which a third party meets with the two parties involved in the dispute, together and/or separately, in order to perform a catalytic function in an effort to help the parties reach an agreement.

Recognition. The accomplishment of the status, by the employee organization with the employer, of collective bargaining agent for a unit of defined extent.

Representation Election. An election held to identify an appropriate employee organization as the exclusive representative of employees in a defined bargaining unit. The employee organization receiving a majority of votes is the winner.

Scope of Bargaining. Bargainable items—the limits, if any, of the appropriate subject matter for bargaining. If such are not set by law, they are determined by the interaction at the bargaining table. If there is not agreement on the scope of bargaining, decisions may be made by a public employment relations board, other administering agency, individual, or by an appropriate court.

Service Fees. A sum of money paid to the bargaining unit by nonmember employees who are, nevertheless, represented by the bargaining unit. Some state laws permit these fees; others do not. Service fees may be equal to a unit member's regular dues; they may be a certain percentage of these dues; they may be equal to that portion of membership dues that is used to cover the expense of negotiating and administering a contract. In some states, non-members represented by a negotiating unit who have valid religious objections to the payment of service fees to an organized bargaining unit may be granted an exemption from the requirement; or their service fee may be remitted to an appropriate charity.

Showing of Support/Interest. Submission of evidence by an employee organization wishing to represent a bargaining unit that it has adequate support/interest/membership from personnel in the bargaining unit. This may be in the form of signature cards, petition signatures, etc.

Strike. A concerted work stoppage, usually used as an effort at the time of impasse to accomplish a contract on terms acceptable to the union.

Union. An employee organization having as one of its purposes the bargaining of terms and conditions of employment with an employer.

Union Security. A blanket term for rights, granted to a union by law or agreement, that reinforce its position as exclusive representative. Dues deduction and service fees are forms of union security, as are specified periods of time during which the union's standing as exclusive representative may not be challenged.

Union Shop. This term applies when an employee is required under the terms of a bargained agreement to become a member of the bargaining unit within a short time after initial employment in order to retain the job. Membership must be maintained during the term of the bargained agreement. In rare cases, union shops are permitted under state law.

Unit Determination. The process of deciding which employees will be in a proposed bargaining unit. Criteria for determination include community of interest, practicality. In some states, units are specifically defined by law.

Unit Modification. A change in the composition (kinds of employees) of a bargaining unit.

Reproduced, with modifications, from Education Commission of the States, *Cuebook II: State Education Collective Bargaining Laws* (Denver: The Commission, 1980), pp. 74–78.

11

Students learn more effectively if they are presented with a well-planned course of studies and if they are held accountable for their education.

The Role and Function of the Curriculum and Pupil-Personnel Administrators

This chapter deals more directly than the other chapters with pupil-related issues. The first section, on the instructional program, presupposes an acquaintance with the learning-instructional process and provides teachers and administrators with a frame of reference for analyzing how responsibilities are delegated in relation to program development. The steps for program development as presented are applicable not only to the regular instructional program but also to remedial programs and those for the gifted, as well as extracurricular ones.

The second part of this chapter deals specifically with the rights and responsibilities of students, and provides information that the director of pupil-personnel services can use in developing administrative procedures and guidelines for the management of student behavior.

JOB DESCRIPTION FOR THE ASSISTANT SUPERINTENDENT FOR CURRICULUM DEVELOPMENT

Job Summary

The assistant superintendent for curriculum development is responsible for the administration of the school district's curriculum-design program. This includes the establishment and maintenance of effective two-way communication between the various organizational levels and the formulation, recommendation, and implementation of curriculum policies.

Organizational Relationship

The assistant superintendent for curriculum development has a line relationship with the superintendent of schools and reports directly to him or her, serving as the chief adviser to the superintendent on the curriculum. The assistant superintendent has a staff relationship with other administrators; a cooperative-professional one with nonadministrative personnel with whom he or she works; and a line relationship with the director of federal programs, director of community and adult education, director of special education, director of pupil-personnel services, and subject-matter coordinators, all of whom report directly to him or her.

Organizational Tasks (see Figure 11-1)

The assistant superintendent for curriculum development is responsible for the evaluation and supervision of the administrators who report to him or her.

This individual is responsible for developing and spending budgets for federal instructional and support programs, adult and community education, special education, and the district's pupil-personnel program.

The assistant superintendent carries out the school district's needs-assessment and standardized pupil-achievement testing programs. These data are used to analyze the effectiveness of the instructional program.

FIGURE 11-1: ORGANIZATIONAL CHART FOR A CURRICULUM DEPARTMENT

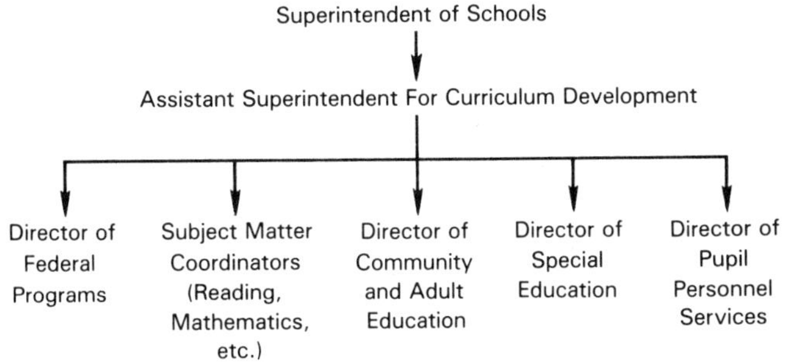

With the assistance of curriculum coordinators, teachers, building principals, and other administrators, the assistant superintendent is responsible for designing the curriculum and instructional units to meet the district's educational goals and objectives. In addition, he or she is responsible for the selection of textbooks and instructional supplies and materials, with the assistance of curriculum coordinators, teachers, and building principals.

Job Requirements

In terms of educational requirements, the assistant superintendent for curriculum development should possess:

Appropriate state administrator certification
A doctorate in curriculum development
Formal course work in curriculum, instruction, and research methodology
At a minimum, classroom teaching and building-level administrative experience

THE INSTRUCTIONAL PROGRAM

The instructional program is, of course, the central concern of every school district, because it is through it that students are educated. The instructional program is also rather elusive. In order to more thoroughly understand it, it is necessary to define and clarify a set of concepts.

Human beings have always sought to gain a greater knowledge and understanding of the world. History, in fact, can be viewed from the perspective of humans' taming the elements and harnessing them in such a manner as to enhance the quality of life. Countless scientists and explorers have attempted to quantify and categorize the physical world. Others have sought to explore the human condition as expressed through communication and socialization. In developing the process for quantifying and studying reality, there have emerged bodies of organized knowledge commonly referred to as subject-matter *disciplines.* Physics, mathematics, biology, and all other related physical sciences are attempts to isolate a segment of reality and quantify and categorize it. Those interested in languages and the fine arts attempt to interpret another aspect of reality, creative expression and communication. The social and historical sciences isolate human events and interpret their meaning in relation to socialization. Physical health and skills enhance an individual's perception of reality.

While this is an oversimplification of the development of subject-matter disciplines, it does explain the existence of organized bodies of knowledge that have been developed into a curriculum by educators interested in transmitting this knowledge to others. Of course, the facts, concepts, formulas, and processes that constitute a discipline can never be completely transmitted to anyone, at any level, because all disciplines are constantly expanding, and no one is capable of assimilating so much knowledge.

Therefore, educators must select what will be taught to students, at what level, and in what sequence. Teaching is the process of deciding on and implementing the most effective method for transmitting the facts, concepts, formulas, and processes that are to be learned by a specific group of students. The psychology of human development has taught us that learning occurs in a "building-block" configuration. New skills, concepts, and ideas are assimilated by the learner in sequence with those previously learned skills, concepts, processes, and ideas going as far back as early childhood. Learning is defined as a change in human capability that is retained and is not simply ascribable to the process of growth.[1] That which is taught is the *curriculum.*

This curriculum is organized by teachers into *instructional units,* each composed of lesson plans constituting how the curriculum is taught. For example, a high school economics curriculum could be organized into and offered in two one-semester courses. Instructional units for the first semester might deal with: (1) defining land, labor, and capital; (2) describing the type and quantity of those resources that are necessary for production in the U.S. economy; and (3) understanding how such production generates income for spending, saving, and investing. Lesson plans set forth the instructional methods that the teacher will employ to transmit the concepts in an instructional unit. Articles from *The Wall Street Journal* about the American auto industry and its relationship to foreign oil prices could be used when discussing the types and quantity of resources necessary to the health of the U.S. economy. Learning to analyze our economy becomes a primary objective of this lesson plan.

Thus, the instructional program consists of the curriculum derived from subject-matter disciplines organized into instructional units and presented to students through lesson plans.

Developing the Instructional Program

The instructional program should reflect the desires and values of the school community. Educators in some school districts believe that the instructional program and its development are the prerogative of the professional staff. While the professional staff plays a significant role here, its expertise essentially consists of constructing the instructional units and lesson plans and instructing the students. The following should clarify not only the steps involved in developing the instructional program, but also identify who is responsible for each one.

First, schools belong to the people, and as such must reflect their values and beliefs under the parameters established by the federal and state constitutions, federal and state laws, and court decisions. Members of the board of education, as the elected representatives of those living within a school district's boundaries, are, therefore, directly responsible for translating the values and beliefs of the community into educational goals and objectives. Ongoing input from students, parents, teachers, administrators, and other citizens is essential if the school board is going to truly understand the needs and desires of the district's constituents. The director for community relations can help gather much of the needed input through surveys. In addition, state departments of education and the U.S. Office of Education have a great deal of material that will assist school boards as they attempt to formulate local goals that are in harmony with national and state educational objectives. Educational goals usually fall into the following developmental categories: (1) intellectual, (2) physical, (3) social, (4) emotional, and (5) career. The board of education should formally promulgate educational goals for the school district, review their relevance on a continual basis, and, when necessary, revise them. It is necessary to have formal educational goals to give direction to those on the professional staff, in order for them to carry out their responsibilities (see Figure 11-2).

Second, the assistant superintendent for curriculum development, curriculum coordinators, other administrators, and teachers under the direction of the superintendent are responsible for translating the educational goals established by the school board into a curriculum that constitutes the body of knowledge, skills, and values that are to be taught. Curriculum in this sense, therefore, not only includes the concepts, formulas, facts, and processes of a discipline such as geography, but also societal values, such as freedom, respect for individual rights, and the free-enterprise system. Furthermore, the curriculum provides opportunities for students to develop their potential such that, after completing high school, they are able to choose whether to continue their education or enter the work force. Thus, vocational as well as college-preparatory programs are necessary for an effective instructional program. Extracurricular and athletic programs enhance and actualize certain values and skills acquired in the instructional program.

Third, curriculum coordinators, teachers, and building-level principals are responsible for organizing the curriculum into instructional units and lesson plans.

FIGURE 11-2: FACTORS INFLUENCING CURRICULUM DESIGN

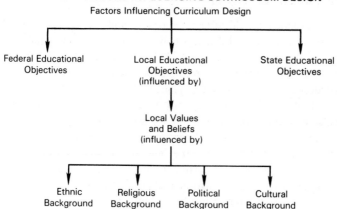

FIGURE 11-3: DEVELOPING THE INSTRUCTIONAL PROGRAM

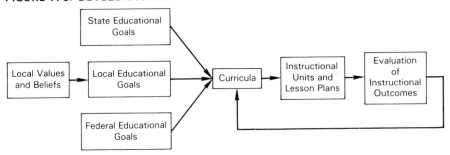

Site-specific curriculum is a term that is often used by educators to designate the adaptation of the curriculum to the specific needs of the students who live in a given area.

Fourth, measuring the effectiveness of the instructional program is essential if modifications are to be made in organizing and presenting the curriculum through instructional units and lesson plans. Minimum competency testing and standardized achievement testing are two instruments that will provide the board of education, administration, and instructional staff with a great deal of information and insight.

"A minimum competency test is designed to determine whether an examinee has reached a prespecified level of performance relative to each competency being tested."[2] Many states have developed and require students to pass a minimum competency test in order to demonstrate that they have acquired certain basic skills.

Standardized achievement tests measure the skills and knowledge acquired by students, by comparing their performance with national and regional standards.[3]

Nonobjective methods may also be used to determine if the instructional program is meeting the needs of students and the desires of parents. Parents and students can be surveyed concerning their perceptions about the quality of education. Further, alumni can be contacted and asked to comment about how well the instructional program prepared them to meet the challenges of their posthigh-school life (see Figure 11-3).

Supervising the Instructional Program

The instructional program is implemented by teachers and other professionals through the learning-instructional process, which takes place in and outside the classroom. It is obvious that the success of the instructional program depends upon the quality of both the instruction provided by teachers and the support services provided by other professionals such as guidance counselors.

Monitoring the quality of teaching and services is the responsibility of the building principal. This usually includes the formal evaluation of employee performance.

Special-Education Programs

In the 1970s, two laws were passed by Congress that have had a direct effect upon the instructional program as it relates to handicapped children. The thrust of all civil-rights legislation is equal treatment under the law; minority groups and females are included. The difference between such laws and the two dealing with the handicapped lies in their implementation. In order for the handicapped to be treated on an equal basis with other students, they must receive special treatment. For example, access to educational programs for the handicapped might require modifying existing school facilities.

Section 504 of the Rehabilitation Act, 1973, specifically addresses the accessibility requirements of educational facilities to handicapped students, teachers, and other employees. Chapter 7 deals to a great extent with the implementation of Section 504.[4]

Public Law 94-142, the Education of All Handicapped Children Act of 1975, stipulates that public schools must educate handicapped students in the "least restrictive environment." Further, an "individual educational program" must be developed and implemented for each handicapped student.

In order for students to be designated handicapped, they must be tested to determine the specific nature of the handicap. Before being placed in a special class, the school officials must—

1. Notify the parents or guardians of the child, in their primary language if it is not English, that the school intends to change the student's educational placement, including a full explanation of the reasons for the change.
2. Provide an opportunity for the parents or guardians to receive an impartial due-process hearing, examine all relevant records, and obtain an independent evaluation of the student.
3. Provide an individual who is not a school employee to act as a surrogate parent when the natural parents or legal guardians are unavailable.
4. Make provisions that will insure that the decision rendered in the due-process hearing is binding, and subject only to judicial review.
5. Proceed to develop an individual educational program for the handicapped student, which should include mainstreaming the child, whenever possible, into programs and activities with nonhandicapped children.

The director of special education should be responsible for insuring that test materials and other vehicles for identifying, classifying, and placing students in special-education programs are selected and administered in a nondiscriminatory manner in terms of race, sex, and national origin.

The second part of this chapter deals with the rights and responsibilities of students and the role and function of the director of pupil-personnel services. As indicated in Figure 11-1, a number of other administrators function within a curriculum department. However, only the pupil-personnel administrator will be discussed here, because of the importance of appropriate pupil behavior to the successful implementation of a school district's curriculum. Further, only if the rights and responsibilities of students are respected, can administrators expect students to conduct themselves well.

In the following pages, the rights and responsibilities of students as a consequence of court decisions are elaborated; these should constitute the basis for student-conduct codes.

JOB DESCRIPTION FOR THE DIRECTOR OF PUPIL-PERSONNEL SERVICES

Job Summary

The director of pupil-personnel services manages the school district's pupil-personnel policies and is responsible to the assistant superintendent for curriculum development as well as for maintaining effective two-way communication between the various levels of the school district's organization.

Organizational Relationship

The director of pupil-personnel services has a line relationship with the assistant superintendent for curriculum development, acting as chief adviser about pupil services, and reports directly to him or her. The director has a staff relationship with other administrators, a cooperative-professional one with nonadministrative personnel, and a line relationship with district-wide psychometrists, psychologists, social workers, and guidance counselors. These professional and nonadministrative staff members report directly to him or her.

Organizational Tasks

The director of pupil-personnel services is responsible for the evaluation and supervision of pupil-personnel specialists, who report to him or her. He or she develops and spends the budget for the pupil-personnel services division. The psychological assessment of individual students, counseling and guidance services, pupil-referral services, and social work services are also the responsibility of the director.

With the assistance of teachers, building principals, and other administrators, the director is responsible for developing pupil-personnel policies, rules, and regulations, along with conduct codes.

Job Requirements

In terms of educational requirements, the director of pupil-personnel services should possess:

Appropriate state certification as a pupil-personnel specialist.
A master's degree in counseling and guidance, social work, psychology, or a related academic discipline.

Formal course work in administration, and preferably a master's degree in educational administration, as well as course work in school law, supervision, personnel administration, and central-office administration.

Experience as a practicing pupil-personnel specialist and preferably some experience as a department chairperson in a school setting.

THE RIGHTS AND RESPONSIBILITIES OF STUDENTS

The children and youth of our nation are of vital concern to those in every level of government and have received considerable attention, particularly in terms of legislation and court cases. As a school district addresses pupil behavior, the underlying principle guiding its policy making must be that children are citizens, and, therefore, have all the rights and privileges of citizens. The legal difference between adults and children is that the latter are not required to exhibit the same level of responsibility as the former. This does not mean that children are free from responsibility for their actions, but that their responsibility is limited. The intent of the following discussion is to clarify the level of rights and responsibilities of students as defined by legislation and case law, although this may change in the future. It is most unlikely that these rights and responsibilities will be diminished through the legislative or judicial process.[5]

Religion

All students have the right to observe or not observe a religion. The school cannot interfere with the right by requiring, establishing, or conducting religious services. Further, the school board and administration are forbidden to create policies or administrative procedures that favor one religion over another or religion over nonreligion.

In enjoying this right, students have the responsibility not to interfere with the rights of others as they observe their religious beliefs.

This right to religious noninterference is clearly outlined in the following court cases: *Engle* v. *Vitale*, 370 U.S. 421, 431 (1962); *Abington School District* v. *Schempp*, 374 U.S. 203 (1963); *Epperson* v. *Arkansas*, 393 U.S. 97, 107-108 (1968).

Speech and Expression

Four areas must be considered here. First, students have a right to express a viewpoint through the spoken word or other forms of expression, such as wearing an armband decorated with a symbol of a cause or belief. In exercising this right, students have the responsibility not to *materially or substantially* disrupt school operations and interfere with the rights of others. Further, students are responsible under the law for the legal consequences of slanderous speech. This right is set forth in *Tinker* v. *Des Moines Independent Community School District,* 393 U.S. 503, 514 (1969).

Second, students have the right to publish and distribute literature that was written independently of school-related courses and activities. However, students are responsible for following the rules established by school officials as to the time, place, and manner for distributing such literature. Further, students are responsible under the law for the legal consequences of libel. *Riseman* v. *School Committee of Quincy,* 439 F. 2d 11-8 (1st Cir. 1971) applied the disruptive test of the Tinker case to the distribution of literature in establishing this right.

Third, students have a right to dress and groom themselves in accordance with their own taste or that of their parents. School district officials may restrict this right only for a legitimate health or safety reason and if less drastic measures are inadequate to protect the health or safety of the student and/or others. Further, school officials must be cautious not to discriminate on the basis of sex in applying the health and safety restrictions, and cannot require a more restrictive code for participation in extracurricular activities.

Students are responsible for dressing and grooming themselves in such a manner that they are not immodest or provocative, which, in turn, would cause material or substantial disruption to school operations.

In addition to the Tinker case, another significant decision was rendered, in *Breen* v. *Kahl,* 296 F. Supp. 702 (W.D. Wis.), aff'd, 419 F. 2d 1034 (7th Cir. 1969), which helped to establish this right.

Fourth, students have the right not to participate in saluting the American flag or in saying the Pledge of Allegiance, if so doing violates their beliefs. It is not necessary for students to leave the classroom when such activities occur, and they may be required to be seated quietly during the ceremony. Such students are not permitted to disrupt those who wish to participate. The right of nonparticipation was set forth in *West Virginia State Board of Education* v. *Barnette,* 319 U.S. 624, 634 (1943) and further refined in *Goetz* v. *Ansell,* 477 F. 2d 636 (2nd Cir. 1973) and *Banks* v. *Board of Public Instruction,* 314 F. Supp. 285 (S.D. Fla.), aff'd 450 F. 2d 1103 (5th Cir. 1973).

Press

Students have the right to gather, write, and editorialize on the news and to distribute official and/or unofficial school newspapers. This right should be exercised without prior censorship and without fearing reprisal for the content of the published material. Faculty advisers may intervene only when material may be libelous or legally prohibited on the grounds of obscenity. In such a situation, the principal or his or her designee should consult with the district's attorney, who, within five school days of the suppression of the material, should render a legal opinion as to whether the material is in violation of contemporary legal standards. The decision is immediately binding but subject to an appeal and grievance procedure.

Students are responsible not only to conform to the law in regard to libel and slander, but also to adhere to sound journalistic ethics. In addition, student newspapers should allow the expression of opinions contrary to editorials, through letters to the editor and guest columns.

There is some ambiguity on the legal issues surrounding student journalism. However, there have been lower federal-court decisions upholding students' rights to publish an official newspaper without prior censorship, as in *Zucker* v. *Panitz,* 299 F. Supp. 102 (S.D.N.Y. 1969).

Assembly

Students have the right to assemble peacefully in order to express their views on issues that may or may not be related to school affairs. As with rights previously discussed, such students are not permitted to materially and substantially disrupt school operations. When determining if an assembly interferes with school operations, only the conduct of the demonstrators must be taken into consideration, not that of the audience, which, if disruptive, is subject to disciplinary action. Further, students must adhere to those administrative rules governing the time, place, and manner of assembly.

In exercising this right, the test of disruptiveness established in the Tinker case is applicable with the refinements of *Gebert* v. *Hoffman,* 336 F. Supp. 694 (E.D. Pa. 1972).

Grievance and Appeal Procedures

Students have the right to a grievance procedure and the right of appeal when a question arises concerning the scope of their rights. A grievance procedure should follow the line of authority of the school district. For example, a grievance involving a teacher should be made to the building principal, one involving a principal should be made to the superintendent of schools, and one involving the superintendent should be made to the board of education. The appeal process should also follow the same line of authority. Thus, a decision concerning a grievance involving a teacher and rendered by the building principal could be appealed to the superintendent and then to the school board, if the superintendent's decision is unacceptable.

The grievance and appeal procedure should be outlined in writing and perhaps incorporated into a student handbook. Time constraints should also be indicated, to ensure a speedy resolution of the grievance. For example, a student should file a grievance with the building principal within ten days of a problem's occurrence. The principal should have at least five days to investigate the grievance and render a decision, whereupon the student might have five days to appeal the decision of the principal to the superintendent of schools, and so on.

It is the responsibility of the students to know and follow the grievance and appeal procedure. The following constitutes the major legal sources of authority for establishing such procedures: 42 U.S.C. 1983 (1970) (Codification of the Civil Rights Act of 1971); *Strickland* v. *Inlow,* 348 F. Supp. 244 (W.D. Ark. 1972); *Strickland* v. *Inlow,* 485 F.2d 186, 191 (8th Cir. 1973); *Wood* v. *Strickland,* 420 U.S. 308, 322 (1975).

The Right to an Education

Students have a right to receive an education that will allow them the opportunity to develop their intellectual, social, emotional, and physical potential to the extent that they are able to become productive citizens of their community, state, and nation. Furthermore, no student shall be denied access to educational programs or extracurricular activities or discriminated against in any manner on the basis of race, color, national origin, sex, handicap, marital status, or because of pregnancy.

Students are responsible for attending school punctually and regularly, for adhering to all school rules and procedures, and for respecting the rights of others by not engaging in behavior disruptive to the educational process.

There has been considerable legislative and judicial activity directly related to equal access of educational opportunities. What follows is a partial listing of those sources that should be consulted for a thorough understanding of students' rights to an education: Title VI, Civil Rights Act, 1964, 42 U.S.C. 2000d. (1970); HEW Reg. 45 C.F.R. 80.3 (1976); 35 Fed. Reg. 11595 (1970); Title IX of the Educational Amendments of 1972, 20 U.S.C. 1681 (1970) as amended 20 U.S.C. 1681 (a) (6) (Supp. V. 1975); P.L. 94-482, 412 (October 12, 1976); 20 U.S.C. 1681 (a) (1970); 45 C.F.R. 86 (1976); HEW Press Release, Statement by Casper W. Weinberger, Secretary of Health, Education and Welfare, June 3, 1975; 45 C.F.R. 86.3 (1976); 45 C.F.R. 86.34 (a) (1976); HEW Press Release, supra note 51 at 3; *Brown* v. *Board of Education,* 349 U.S. 294, 301 (1955); *Griffin* v. *County School Board,* 377 U.S. 218 (1964); *Green* v. *County School Board,* 391 U.S. 430 (1968); *Runyon* v. *McCrary,* 427 U.S. 160 (1976); *Lau* v. *Nichols* 414 U.S. 563 (1974).

Student Records

Students aged eighteen and the parents of younger students have a right to review their own or their children's official school records and the right to a hearing for the purpose of challenging the appropriateness and validity of such records. Students and parents are responsible for following the administrative rules regarding time and place for reviewing such records and participating in a hearing. In addition, students should exercise discretion in discussing their records with other students.

The Family Educational Rights and Privacy Act of 1974 and the accompanying regulations (HEW Reg. 45 C.F.R. 99, 1976) present a detailed explanation of this right and outline certain exceptions to the law.

Search, Seizure, and Police Interrogation

Students have the right to be free from unreasonable searches of their person, school locker, and personal property. The following constitute the minimal requirements of a reasonable search: (1) a designated school official shall be the only individual authorized to search a student, his or her locker, or personal property; (2) the search must be based on probable cause, which is defined as facts leading a prudent person to believe that some item subject to seizure is in the student's possession; (3) a reasonable attempt must be made to allow the student to be present when searching the locker or personal property. The concept of probable cause has created some concern on the part of school officials. Certain factors, however, should be considered when applying the probable-cause criterion, including the student's age, record in school, seriousness of the problem, and urgency of making the search. Further, when a law-enforcement official desires to interrogate a student, that student has a right to have his or her parents or a guardian present at the interrogation. If a parent or guardian is unavailable, a teacher or some other school official should be present and the student should be advised of the right to legal counsel and to remain silent.

It is the responsibility of all students to adhere to the law and not have illegal items in a locker or on their person. The legality of search and seizure and its limitation have been tested in the following cases: In re W. 29 Cal. App. 3d 777, 105 Cal. Rptr. 775 (1973); *People* v. *D.*, 34 N.Y. 2d 483, 358 N.Y.S. 2d 403, 407 (1974); *Katz* v. *United States*, 389 U.S. 347, 351 (1967); *Mapp* v. *Ohio*, 367 U.S. 643, 651-657 (1961).

Discipline

Students have rights in two areas that involve discipline, suspension/expulsion, and corporal punishment. To deprive a student of an educational opportunity even for a short period of time is very serious. Suspension and/or expulsion should be invoked only as a last resort for a serious infraction after other means of handling the problem have proven ineffective. Students should be provided with a written disciplinary code that outlines those offenses that may result in suspension and/or expulsion.

Students have procedural rights where a short suspension is involved. In an informal conference, the building principal or his or her designee should (1) provide students with oral or written notice of charges, (2) provide an explanation of the charges to students if they are denied, and (3) allow students to relate their version of the events that may result in suspension. Of course, the principal may suspend a student without due process if there is a clear and present danger of physical injury to school personnel or students. Due process should be afforded the student as soon as practicable in such a case. Time constraints should be placed upon the use of suspension. For example, the building principals might be given the authority to suspend a student for up to five school days. When a student returns to school, he or she should be given the opportunity to make up any classwork and examinations that were missed.

Students involved in long-term suspension and expulsion from school by the superintendent or school board have certain procedural rights. First, they are entitled to a hearing on the charges, during which they may be represented by an attorney. Second, students have the right to call witnesses, present documentary evidence, and cross-examine witnesses. Upon appeal to the courts, students should be provided, at no expense, with a copy of the proceedings. Of course, the superintendent or school board must render a decision within a specified period of time. For example, a decision based on the facts presented at the hearing could be required within five days of the hearing. If the superintendent conducted the hearing, the student must appeal the decision to the board of education before going to the courts for review.

Students also have the right to be free from physical violence. However, corporal punishment has always been a legitimate disciplinary procedure in American education if used for corrective rather than punitive reasons and if administered in such a way as not to embarrass or injure the student.

Physical force may be used against a student in certain circumstances, as when that person is threatening physical injury to others, in self-defense, or for the protection of property. The amount of force used must be reasonable and necessary to prevent the injury or destruction.

Students are responsible for following the disciplinary code of their school and observing all administrative rules and procedures. Students must also respect one another and the adults who interact with them if there is going to be a positive and caring atmosphere in the school.

Two significant court cases dealing with discipline, which provided a basis for this discussion, are: *Lopez* v. *Williams,* 372 F. Supp. 1249 (S.D. Ohio 1973) and *Goss* v. *Lopez,* 419 U.S. 565 (1975).

Developing a Code of Student Rights and Responsibilities

No code of conduct will be effective unless it is developed with input from all members of the school community. Teachers, parents, administrators, and students must be actively involved in the research and formulation process. If a code is created solely by the administration and passed on to the student body, the ingredients necessary for effective school discipline—understanding and cooperation—will be lacking. Five major steps can be taken to ensure that an effective code will be established.

First, a committee of students (at the middle, junior high, and high school levels), parents, teachers, and administrators should be commissioned by the superintendent, through the director of pupil-personnel services, to study the need to develop or update a code of student rights and responsibilities. Each segment of the school could be allowed to choose its own representative on the committee. For example, the student council could appoint the student representatives, the PTA could select the parents, and the faculty, the teachers. Very large committees have been found ineffective, and a committee of five, seven, or nine members very functional. To avoid deadlocks, an uneven number is appropriate. A survey of the students, parents, teachers, and administrators would be very helpful in analyzing the needs in a given school.

Second, the committee should conduct a review of the literature dealing with student rights and responsibilities. Other schools should be contacted about their codes, and, if possible, copies of those codes reviewed by the committee. Local, state, and federal agencies, along with educational associations and civil-liberties organizations, can also provide valuable information about the content of such a code.

Third, the committee can then proceed to draft a code using the data researched and the suggestions provided by members of the school community. Certain critical questions should be addressed by the committee as the members work through the task of codification. The following can serve as a checklist that focuses attention on essential aspects of an effective disciplinary code: (1) Are the provisions of the new code precise and easily understood by parents, students, and all members of the school community? (2) Are the format and construction of the manual convenient and serviceable? (3) Does the code contain rules that are necessary to the effective operation of the school?

Fourth, a public hearing could be held on the code to receive comments and suggestions on how to improve its provisions. Having local newspapers publish the time and place of the hearing along with an outline of the draft code and information on where to receive the complete draft would help to generate public awareness and interest in attending the hearing.

Finally, because the superintendent of schools commissioned the committee to review and write the code on student rights and responsibilities, it is necessary for the superintendent to approve the final document and to make it public, probably in the form of a student handbook.

One additional comment should be made. Because new legislation will be passed, case law may modify previous decisions, and society and the student-body composition will change, the code should be reviewed and possibly updated at least every five years.

SUMMARY

The instructional program is the central concern of every school district, because through it, the school system can educate students. Throughout history, we have sought to learn and understand more about the world. In developing the process for quantifying and studying reality, bodies of organized knowledge commonly referred to as subject-matter disciplines have emerged. The facts, concepts, formulas, and processes that constitute a discipline can never be completely transmitted to anyone, at any level, because it is constantly expanding. Therefore, educators must select what will be taught to students at what level and in what sequence. This is termed the curriculum.

The curriculum is organized by teachers into instructional units and lesson plans. Thus, the instructional program is composed of the curriculum derived from subject-matter disciplines organized into instructional units and presented to students through lesson plans.

There are four steps involved in developing the instructional program: (1) The school board must translate the values and beliefs of the community into educational goals and objectives. (2) The administrative and instructional staff are responsible for translating these educational goals into a curriculum that constitutes the body of knowledge, skills, and values to be taught. (3) The instructional staff and building-level administrators should organize the curriculum into instructional units and lesson plans. (4) The effectiveness of the instructional program must be measured if modifications are to be made in organizing and presenting the curriculum.

The instructional program is implemented by teachers and other professionals through the learning-instructional process, which takes place inside and outside the classroom. Monitoring the quality of teaching and support services offered to students is the responsibility of the building principal. This process usually includes the evaluation of employee performance, using an evaluation instrument.

The 1970s saw the passage of two laws, The Rehabilitation Act of 1973 and The Education for All Handicapped Children Act of 1975, that have had a direct effect upon the instructional program as it relates to handicapped children. Section 504 of the Rehabilitation Act specifically addresses the accessibility requirements of educational facilities. The Education for All Handicapped Children Act stipulates that public schools must develop an individual education program for each handicapped student.

The U.S. Congress and the federal judiciary have addressed the rights and responsibilities of students. They involve the following areas: (1) freedom to observe or not observe a religion, (2) freedom of speech and expression, (3) freedom of the press, (4) freedom of assembly, (5) the right to a grievance and appeal process, (6) the right to an education, (7) the right to inspect school records, and (8) freedom from search, seizure, and interrogation.

In creating an effective code of conduct regarding student rights and responsibilities, the board of education must actively involve teachers, parents, administrators, and students.

IMPLICATIONS FOR EDUCATIONAL ADMINISTRATORS

This presentation on the instructional program and pupil relations has three implications for educational administrators.

First, for some time, confusion has existed about the role of the curriculum administrator in relation to supervising the instructional process. The contention in this chapter is that the design of curriculum requires the leadership and expertise of administrators who have specialized education and experience in needs assessment and curriculum design. Supervising teachers is the responsibility of the building principal, not the curriculum administrator. However, a building principal can certainly devise a process for involving curriculum specialists, by providing them with input concerning teachers' grasp of the subject matter taught and the appropriateness of the teachers' instructional methodology and use of instructional materials.

Second, all building-level and central-office administrators should have a rudimentary knowledge and understanding of curricular concepts, because the curriculum is the core of the instructional process.

Third, recent court decisions and legislation have more clearly defined the rights and responsibilities of students. Lack of knowledge and understanding about student rights is no excuse for violating them. Therefore, building-level administrators must make a concerted effort to remain informed about legal and judicial developments involving student rights and responsibilities, and to develop administrative rules and regulations that protect these rights.

SELECTED BIBLIOGRAPHY

DEPARTMENT OF HEALTH, EDUCATION AND WELFARE, *The Rights and Responsibilities of Students: A Handbook for the School Community.* Washington, D.C.: U.S. Government Printing Office, 1979.

ENGLISH, FENWICK W., and ROGER A. KAUFMAN, *Needs Assessment: A Focus For Curriculum Development.* Washington, D.C.: Association for Supervision and Curriculum Development, 1975.

FOSHAY, ARTHUR W., ed., *Considered Action for Curriculum Improvement.* Alexandria, Va.: Association for Supervision and Curriculum Development, 1980.

FRYMIER, JACK and others, *Annehurst Curriculum Classification System: A Practical Way to Individualize Instruction.* West Lafayette, Ind.: Kappa Delta Pi Press, 1977.

JOYCE, BRUCE R., *Selecting Learning Experiences: Linking Theory and Practice.* Alexandria, Va.: Association for Supervision and Curriculum Development, 1978.

POSNER, GEORGE J., and ALAN N. RUDNITSKY, *Course Design: A Guide to Curriculum Development for Teachers.* New York: Longman, 1978.

TURNBULL, H. RUTHERFORD, and ANN TURNBULL, *Free Appropriate Public Education: Law and Implementation.* Denver: Love Publishing Co., 1978.

WATERMAN, FLOYD T., and others, *Designing Short Term Instructional Programs.* Washington, D.C.: Association of Teacher Educators, 1979.

YARD, GEORGE J., *Exceptionalities of Children and Adults.* St. Louis: Midwest Regional Resource Center, 1978.

NOTES

1. Robert M. Gagne, *The Conditions of Learning* (New York: Holt, Rinehart and Winston, Inc., 1964), p. 5.
2. Ronald K. Hambleton and Daniel R. Eignor, "Competency Test Development, Validation, and Standard Setting," in *Minimum Competency Achievement Testing: Motives, Models, Measures, and Consequences,* ed. Richard M. Jaeger and Carol Hehr Tittle (Berkeley: McCutchan Publishing Corporation, 1980), p. 369.
3. Bela H. Banathy, *Instructional Systems* (Palo Alto: Fearon Publishers, 1968), p. 62.
4. Ronald Clelland, *Section 504: Civil Rights for the Handicapped* (Arlington, Va.: American Association of School Administrators, 1978), p. 4.
5. U.S. Department of Health, Education and Welfare, *The Rights and Responsibilities of Students: A Handbook for the School Community* (Washington, D.C.: U.S. Government Printing Office, 1979), p. 1.

12

The Role and Function of the Building Principal

The role and function of building principals will vary in application because of the unique characteristics of the particular communities in which they practice. Students from various cultural backgrounds will exhibit a variety of needs, and their parents will have expectations that reflect their cultures.

Elementary school principals' tasks are different from those performed by middle/junior high school and senior high school principals. Of course, the converse is also true. At the same time, building principals have much in common at all levels in terms of role and function, as will be seen in this chapter. All principals have leadership responsibilities. Their functions are divided into the following components: managing the professional staff, the instructional program, pupil-personnel services, support services, and the school's community-relations program.

Before elaborating on these management functions, certain preliminary concepts must be clarified in order to fully understand the discussion that follows. First, the principalship is not simply a position, but a professional career. Historically, the principalship evolved from the duties that were performed by the headmaster in the mid-to-late 1800s. These duties centered around being the chief disciplinarian, ordering textbooks and supplies, and generally supervising the schoolhouse, in addition to teaching. Released time from teaching to perform these duties was a significant step forward in delineating the principalship as a distinct career within the educational profession.

There is very little resemblance between the headmaster and the contemporary building principal, who is more concerned with improving the instructional program through curriculum development and teacher supervision, as well as with establishing high expectations for students in terms of behavior and achievement. Certain individuals perceive the principalship as a stepping stone to the central-office positions of assistant superintendent and superintendent of schools. This mentality has been addressed in the various publications of the National Association of Secondary School Principals and the National Association of Elementary School Principals as detrimental to the role and function of the building principal. Today's principal should command the respect of the entire educational community.

Second, building principals must exhibit certain leadership characteristics if they are to educate students successfully. How they exercise this leadership must also be consistent with those models that have been identified as most successful.

Third, building principals are first and foremost executives.[1] As such, they are responsible for managing functions through developing processes and procedures. For example, one aspect of managing personnel entails developing a process for orienting newly hired teachers that includes providing them with information about the community, students, the school building, curriculum, classroom procedures, and so forth.

As executives, principals should delegate different aspects of the orientation program to their assistants or other staff members who have expertise in a particular area. For instance, the guidance counselor can orient newly hired teachers to the school's standardized achievement-testing program. The team-management approach to building-level administration, as presented in Chapter 3, therefore, should be used to fulfill executive responsibilities.

In summary, the essence of building-level leadership is the ability of the principal to create the environment within which the expertise of other professionals can be exploited. Through goal-setting techniques supported by supervising personnel, the principal directs this professional expertise toward the fulfillment of the school's mission.

JOB DESCRIPTION FOR THE BUILDING PRINCIPAL

Job Summary

Building principals are responsible for supervising the professional and support-services staffs assigned to their buildings. They also must manage the school's instructional program, pupil-personnel services, support services, and community relations. This includes establishing and maintaining effective two-way communication between the various organizational levels within the school.[2]

Organizational Relationship

Building principals have a line relationship with the appropriate assistant superintendent in charge of secondary or elementary education, to whom they report directly. The building principal serves as the chief executive administrator of a school and has a line relationship with the assistant principals, teachers, staff members, and classified employees assigned to that building. He or she has a cooperative relationship with other administrators in the school district.

Organizational Tasks

The building principal is directly responsible for establishing administrative processes, procedures, and techniques for managing the pupil-personnel, instructional, support-services, and community-relations programs. He or she is also responsible for implementing the school district's evaluation and supervisory processes for professional and classified personnel assigned to his or her building.

Job Requirements

In terms of education and experience, the building principal should possess:

Appropriate state administrator certification
A master's degree in educational administration (minimum)
Formal course work in the areas of curriculum, supervision, administration, school law, and finance
Classroom teaching or professional staff experience in a school

MANAGING PROFESSIONAL PERSONNEL

Education is a service-rendering profession. The service provided will be directly affected by the caliber of the professional staff. While all aspects of building-level administration are important, managing the professional staff is the foundation upon which all other functions will rest. If a school has microcomputers in every classroom, videotape recorders, and unlimited instructional materials but mediocre teachers, the quality of instruction will be inferior to that provided in another school with superior teachers and little technological equipment. While schools must keep abreast of the latest advances in technology and should provide teachers with appropriate equipment and supplies, the quality of the teachers and staff is, and always will be, the critical element in a meaningful educational experience.

The Administrative Staff

The administrative staff directly influences the morale in a building and the effectiveness and efficiency of its programs. In small schools, the administration may consist of only the principal. Medium-to-large schools will probably have assistant principals. In departmentalized secondary schools, certain teachers may be designated in each instructional discipline as the department chairpersons. Consequently, the administrative team in a school may consist of the principal, assistant principals, and department chairpersons.

The principal is the chief executive officer of the school and is responsible for the overall management of all functions. Assistant principals share the responsibility of the principalship and should be delegated to manage certain functions. For example, in a large senior high school with a pupil enrollment of 2,500 or more, one assistant principal could manage the pupil-personnel function, with other assistant principals managing support services and the instructional program. Usually, the principal and all assistant principals will share teacher evaluations, because of their difficulty and the time involved. In most states, assistant principals are required to have the same certification or license as principals and, therefore, may perform or share duties reserved for the latter. Likewise, most state departments of education have guidelines regarding when assistant principals should be added to the administrative staff. A rule of thumb is to have one administrator for every 700 students in a building, with an assistant principal for every additional 700 students.

Department chairpersons are usually not licensed and/or professionally educated administrators. They have expertise in their individual disciplines and are utilized by the principal in developing the curriculum and instructional materials and selecting textbooks, interviewing candidates for teaching positions in their departments, orienting newly hired teachers about departmental procedures and programs, and providing the principal or assistant principals with input concerning teacher performance. Chairpersons perform a valuable service but do not share the responsibilities of the principalship.

Selection of Staff

The selection process is a central-office-personnel function whereby the assistant superintendent for personnel ensures that the school district has the right number of people with the appropriate skills. However, this process cannot be effectively implemented without the cooperation of building principals and their staffs.

Yearly, principals should be asked to make a projection of the number of teachers and other professional staff members they will need, along with the types of skills these individuals should possess. The personnel department should then recruit personnel and develop a selection process to meet these needs. In hiring staff members and teachers, candidates should be interviewed by the principal, an assistant principal, the chairperson of the department in which the employee will be placed, and other teachers. Establishing interviewing procedures and developing the selection criteria are also the responsibility of central-office personnel. The major reason for involving building principals is that they (or assistant principals) will be the immediate supervisors of the new employees.

Department chairpersons and teachers should be part of the selection process because they can provide significant insight into candidates' academic and experiential qualifications.

Orientation of New Staff

Like the selection process, the orientation of newly hired employees is first a function of central-office personnel. Some districts have a very elaborate orientation, which may include a luncheon during the week before the opening of school, at which the school board president and superintendent, along with other central-office administrators, address the new employees about various aspects of the community and highlight the benefits of working for the school district. In addition, the new staff member will be required to fill out appropriate payroll forms and make decisions about fringe benefits.

At the building level, it is usually the responsibility of the principal and his or her staff to orient the new teacher or staff member to the building, instructional program, student body, community, building and classroom procedures, and other staff members. Various techniques can be used to accomplish this task, which might include assigning an "old pro" to help the new employee who will help answer the inevitable questions that the new position brings. The guidance department, media-center staff, and department chairperson are valuable resources too. In other words, the principal is directly responsible for building-level orientation and should call upon other staff members for help.

Placement and Utilization of Staff

The placement and effective utilization of staff members and teachers is, after the evaluation process, the most difficult task facing the building principal. Certain aspects of placement are givens. For example, in most states, teachers are permitted to teach only the grade level or subject matter for which they are licensed; and it is better to give teachers assignments they desire and are qualified for by virtue of academic preparation and/or experience.

However, to do so may cause some difficulties. First, there are sometimes positions that must be filled by staff members who possess only minimal qualifications. Secondly, on occasion, qualified employees may not like their assignments. In either case, the building principal must make the decision about staff assignments based on (1) the needs of the students, (2) the effective implementation of programs, and (3) the best use of available human resources.

There is no way to be infallible in effectively placing and utilizing the staff. In the final analysis, such decisions must be made by the principal in collaboration with assistant principals and department chairpersons. Clearly, the principal's experience and professional judgment will be involved.

Supervision and Evaluation of Staff

The primary responsibility of the principal is to supervise teachers and staff members. This is usually formalized by performance evaluation. The purpose of supervising teachers and staff members is to improve instruction and services to students.

It is commonplace for individuals to become complacent about themselves and their work. Performance evaluation is the method by which the administration observes, analyzes, interprets, and makes suggestions for improvement to teachers and other staff members such as guidance counselors and librarians.

Many different methods and evaluation instruments can be used by the principal to carry out this responsibility. Appendix A presents an evaluation instrument with a stated philosophy and procedure that represents a traditional approach to teacher evaluation. The instrument identifies three major areas (teaching performance, professional qualities, and personal qualities) that are to be measured based upon the teacher's behavior. Appendix B lists a number of indicators in each category and subcategory of the evaluation instrument that can be used to determine the quality of this behavior.

Different faculties in different communities have special needs that may not be met by the evaluation procedures and instrument presented here. The principal is responsible for devising a method and instrument that will produce two-way communication between the staff members and teachers with him or her, such that performance will be improved. In many school districts, the evaluation process and instrument are developed by the central-office personnel department. In this case, it is essential that the principals and representatives of the teachers and staff are allowed to give input into the evaluation process. Also, it is critical to incorporate into this process a grievance procedure by which successive levels of management are called upon to review an evaluation that an employee believes to be a misrepresentation of performance.

Two major issues will be discussed over the next decade or so concerning the evaluation process. These must be considered by the building principal. The first is how performance evaluation can be interfaced with a merit-pay system. The second concerns peer and staff evaluation of the principal in addition to the traditional approach, in which an assistant superintendent or the superintendent of schools evaluates the principal's performance.

Staff Development

Directly related to the improvement of performance by teachers and staff members via the evaluation process is the responsibility for staff development. At times, an individual may need specialized help in order to improve performance. This can be accomplished through staff development, by which individuals can attend seminars, workshops, and even graduate courses to improve their professional skills and, thereby, their performance. Individual counseling by staff members with particular expertise or through counseling provided by outside agencies can help a teacher or staff member improve personal skills.

Some form of staff development is needed in every school, thanks to advances in technology and because of educational research. While such activities are usually the responsibility of those in the central office, the principal can conduct a needs assessment of his or her staff and present suggested models and methods by which they can be met.

A recent phenomenon is the individually tailored staff-development program.

All principals submit a proposal to the central office setting forth workshops, courses, and the like, that would be useful in improving their administrative skills.

Termination of Staff

If the performance of a teacher or staff member does not improve to an acceptable level after the individual has been given an opportunity to change and even, through the staff-development program, to acquire professional and/or personal skills that would improve it, employment with the school district must be terminated. The principal is critical to the termination process, because it is his or her performance evaluation that will become the basis for terminating an individual's employment. Thus, it is vital that the principal document and scrupulously follow the school district's policies and state statutes. The principal must allow every employee his or her due-process rights and a chance to improve performance, but the principal must also see to it that students receive the best possible instruction and level of service.

Staff Morale

We know that morale is good in an organization when the majority of individuals within it believe the fulfillment of their professional and personal desires, hopes, and ambitions is directly related to their employment.

In practical terms, this means that other administrators, teachers, and staff members are treated fairly and respectfully by the principal. In addition, they are given the opportunity to participate in decisions concerning issues that affect the school, such as textbook selection and curricular innovations. This can be accomplished through various techniques, including the use of committees to make recommendations to the principal. It also means that individuals have an opportunity to improve their life-style through salary increases and fringe-benefit programs that are comparable with others in public-sector employment. Finally, morale is good when teachers and other employees are given an opportunity to improve their professional skills through staff-development activities.

MANAGING THE INSTRUCTIONAL PROGRAM

The heart of building-level administration is managing the instructional program, because this constitutes the *raison d'être* of every school and school district.[3] Chapter 11 contains a detailed presentation of significant definitions and concepts of curriculum and learning, and examines the process of developing what is to be taught. Here, the role and function of the building principal as complementary to that of the assistant superintendent for curriculum and supervision in managing the instructional program will be considered.

At the building level, managing the instructional program means implementing a centralized curriculum, creating procedures for the selection of instructional materials and textbooks, and managing a learning-resource center.

Because learning is sequential, a school district should develop a kindergarten through grade twelve curriculum that meets the needs of every student, including the developmentally handicapped as well as the gifted. Curriculum guides must be developed by central-office administrators with input from teachers and building principals if students are to be instructed in areas that meet both their individual needs and the expectations of the entire community and board of education. A *site-specific* curriculum allows the principal and his or her staff to adapt it to the specific requirements of a certain geographical attendance area. The principal and staff must select the instructional materials that coincide best with the cultural and environmental background of the school's student body in order to teach the district's approved curriculum.

Classroom instruction is augmented by a learning-resource center, which can provide teachers and students with materials and equipment for studying a particular aspect of the curriculum. Learning-resource specialists can also give instruction both on the proper use of a learning-resource center and on esoteric topics.

MANAGING PUPIL-PERSONNEL SERVICES

Pupil-personnel services are important because they help to meet students' needs and protect their rights so that they can take full advantage of the instructional program.

While the admission and orientation of new students is a rather informal process in the elementary school and becomes increasingly specific in middle/junior high and high school, the considerations are the same at every level. Students must be informed about the policies and rules governing their behavior, know where to go and how to get assistance when they need it, have information about the school building, and be encouraged to participate in extracurricular activities. In short, they must feel that they are an integral part of the school community and that its staff cares about them.

In secondary schools, students must be enrolled in courses that meet their own and their parents' expectations and are suited to their abilities. Thus, the testing and guidance provided by qualified counselors are an important aspect of pupil services. When students have adjustment problems or need professional psychological help, the guidance counselor can assist not only the student, but also the parents and teachers.

To help students become active members of the school community, the principal should develop appropriate student activities, such as student government, intramural sports, and student clubs, in addition to interscholastic athletics.

The student-health program is another important pupil-personnel service. School nurses and health specialists should be considered by the principal as more than care-givers to those who are ill. They can help to teach hygiene and nutrition and to counsel students who have health or physical problems.

Finally, it is imperative that the principal establish procedures for keeping student records such that the rights of students and parents are assured and security is maintained. Chapter 11 covers student rights and responsibilities in detail.

In managing pupil-personnel services, the principal should establish programs and monitor the performance of the specialists involved. An evaluation of the pupil-personnel-services program should be performed by the principal at regular intervals, such as every two years.

MANAGING THE SCHOOL'S SUPPORT SERVICES

As the services rendered by school districts have increased, along with the intricacies of programs and the number of students, the building-level principal has been given a new responsibility: managing the school's support services.

Some of the services most commonly found in the contemporary school are as follows:

1. While budgeting and purchasing are usually central-office functions, planning and spending the budget should be initiated at the building level.[4] Most school districts have developed a decentralized approach to budgeting, in which the building principal submits a proposed budget for supplies, instructional materials and textbooks, equipment, capital improvements to the building, and certain purchased services such as equipment-maintenance agreements. This budget is then incorporated into that of the school district and presented to the board of education for approval. Once it is approved, the principal is required to implement it by submitting purchase requisitions for specific items to the central-office business department. The budget consists of line items that are categorical designations, such as textbooks for the Science Department; the purchase requisition specifies which textbooks, how many, and from what company they should be ordered. In effective budgeting and purchasing, the principal involves the department chairpersons, teachers, and staff members in constructing and implementing the budget. Without their involvement, the principal may be criticized for not meeting the material needs of the programs. In larger schools, an assistant principal is usually assigned to the overall management of budgeting and purchasing.
2. Once supplies, materials, textbooks, and equipment have been delivered to the school, the principal must maintain an inventory of who has what. Educators are notorious for lending items to fellow teachers or staff members. This is usually not a problem unless equipment is involved. If there is a fire, vandalism, or some other disaster that destroys equipment and materials or textbooks, the cost of replacing materials and equipment cannot be recovered from the district's insurance company without a demonstrated and effective inventory system. Also, it will be difficult to construct a budget if information is not available about the use and consumption of supplies, materials, and so on. Finally, an inventory process identifies what teacher/staff members abuse the supply-and-materials budget.

3. Supervising the classified staff is a most important responsibility of the principal, because secretaries, custodians, cooks, and bus drivers have direct contact with students and other constituents of the school. Therefore, the quality of their performance can have a positive or detrimental effect upon the school's image in addition to affecting the quality of services rendered to students. Thus, it is important for the principal to initiate a performance-evaluation process for classified personnel whose objectives are the same as those involving the professional staff.

4. Food service and transportation are critical adjuncts of the instructional program. You can't teach children unless you get them safely to school; and children cannot learn as well when they are hungry. The principal generally must monitor the quality of these services and report on them to the central-office administrators responsible for the overall management of the food-service and transportation programs. Developing a working relationship with bus drivers and cafeteria workers is also important in order to be able to handle those problems that occur with students as they ride the school bus and dine in the cafeteria.

5. All the mechanical, electrical, plumbing, and other systems in a building will need maintenance and repair from time to time. The principal and, perhaps, the assistant principal charged with managing the facility must identify quickly where repairs and maintenance are needed and initiate the process for getting these taken care of by custodians or the district's maintenance personnel. Without continuous vigilance, buildings can deteriorate so badly that the instructional program is affected and the safety of students and employees jeopardized.

MANAGING THE COMMUNITY-RELATIONS PROGRAM

In any newspaper, on any day of the week, in any city, at least one article about education can be found. Over the last twenty-five years, taxpayers, parents, and students have become increasingly vocal about school policies, procedures, and programs. Their perceptions have not always been complimentary; indeed, at times, they have been scathing indictments.

A major responsibility of the building principal involves the ability to manage communications effectively between the school and its constituencies, who can be divided into two groups: internal and external publics. The internal publics are other administrators, teachers, staff members, and students. The external publics consist of parents, taxpayers in the school district, news-media personnel, and others interested in the school.

It is very important that the principal have a clear concept of what constitutes a community-relations program, which is not a public-relations program as viewed from the perspective of a corporation. Rather than "selling" the school and its programs, the principal should be "communicating" its mission and its goals, and the progress that is being made to reach them. Further, there must be two-way communication, so that these publics can express their concerns and ideas about the objectives of the school.

The community-relations program will be effective only if it is continuous, rather than opportunistic. The purposes of an effective program are as follows: (1) to develop an awareness of and understanding about the objectives of public education in general and the individual programs of the school in particular, (2) to keep the publics informed about the work of the school, and (3) to gain support from the various publics for public education and the school's programs.

The American Association of School Administrators has developed a list of principles that can be used by the principal in developing a community-relations program for his or her school:

1. School public relations must be honest in intent and execution.
2. School public relations must be intrinsic.
3. School public relations must be continuous.
4. School public relations must be positive in approach.
5. School public relations should be comprehensive.
6. School public relations should be sensitive to its publics.
7. The ideas communicated must be simple.[5]

Effective community relations must be multifaceted. Therefore, such a program should incorporate a number of aspects, including:

1. How visitors to the school are greeted.
2. How relations with the press and other news-media agents are handled.
3. How the students can act as community-relations agents.
4. How teachers and staff members interact with external and internal publics.
5. How classified personnel interact with all publics.
6. How parent-teacher associations/organizations can help the school communicate with its constituents.
7. How student and staff publications can communicate with the various publics.
8. How volunteers and community-resource people can be used in school programs.

Finally, the principal must evaluate the effectiveness of the school's community-relations program. There are many ways of doing so. Perhaps the most common is to make up a survey form that can be given to a sample of the school's constituents, asking them to rate its community-relations program.

SUMMARY

The role and function of the building principal will vary depending upon the characteristics of the particular community. Elementary school principals' tasks differ from those performed by their middle/junior high school and senior high school equivalents. At the same time, they share a great deal in terms of role and function, as was emphasized in this chapter.

The principalship is not simply a position, but a professional career. The building principal is first and foremost an executive who is responsible for managing functions that are actualized by establishing processes and procedures. The principal must exhibit leadership in order to educate students successfully.

A job description of the building-level principalship should include the following: The principal is responsible for supervising the professional and support-services staffs assigned to his or her building. He or she is also responsible for managing the school's instructional, pupil-personnel-services, support-services, and community-relations programs. This includes establishing and maintaining effective two-way communication between the various organizational levels within the school.

In managing the professional staff and (in larger schools) assistant principals, it is important that the principal utilize team management and share the responsibility of the principalship with assistants, by delegating certain functions to them. Those related to the management of the professional staff include: selecting the staff, orienting newly hired members, placing and utilizing them, the all important staff evaluation, staff development, and, when necessary, termination.

A final consideration related to the management of the professional staff is the responsibility of the building principal to create an atmosphere within which good staff morale can be fostered and maintained.

At the building level, the instructional program must be managed, by implementing a centralized curriculum, creating procedures for the selection of instructional materials and textbooks, and managing a learning-resource center.

Managing pupil-personnel services is a very important responsibility because students must have their needs met and rights accorded if they are to take full advantage of the instructional program. Pupil-personnel services include: the admission and orientation of new students; in secondary schools, the scheduling of students in appropriate courses; providing counseling for students who are having adjustment problems and referring students to other professionals when necessary; maintaining a student health program; and establishing procedures for maintaining student records so that the rights of students and parents and security are all assured.

The principal is responsible for managing the support services in the building, which include: constructing a building-level budget and initiating the purchase of supplies, materials, textbooks, and equipment from the approved budget; maintaining an inventory of these items; supervising the classified staff assigned to the building; monitoring food services and transportation; monitoring repairs and maintenance in the school.

Over the last twenty-five years, taxpayers, parents, and students have become increasingly vocal about school policies, procedures, and programs. Thus, the building principal is now responsible for developing and maintaining a community-relations program. It should be concerned with initiating two-way communication between the school's internal and external publics. Internal publics are the administrators, teachers, staff members, and students. Parents, taxpayers of the school district, news-media personnel, and others interested in the school constitute the external publics.

IMPLICATIONS FOR EDUCATIONAL ADMINISTRATORS

This discussion of the role and function of the building principal has three implications for educational administrators.

First, the principalship is a professional career, which must be recognized as such by boards of education and central-office administrators as well as building principals. The expertise required to be an effective principal is different from that required of central-office administrators; thus, the principalship should not be viewed as a stepping stone to a central-office position.

Second, the building principal is an executive responsible for the overall management of the school's staff and programs, rather than being the lead teacher or headmaster. Today's school requires a principal who not only understands the instructional process but also has a solid foundation in management techniques, so that he or she has the skills necessary to efficiently and effectively manage such functions as budgeting, transportation, and the physical plant.

Third, the building principal is a public-relations agent for the school district and the school. He or she must attend school functions and be visible in the community, which makes the principalship a more than full-time occupation.

SELECTED BIBLIOGRAPHY

ERICKSON, DONALD A., and THEODORE L. RELLER, *The Principal in Metropolitan Schools.* Berkeley: McCutchan Publishing Corporation, 1979.

GORTON, RICHARD A., and KENNETH E. McINTYRE, *The Senior High School Principal, Volume II: The Effective Principal.* Reston, Va.: National Association of Secondary School Principals, 1978.

OVARD, GLEN F., *Administration of the Changing Secondary School.* New York: Macmillan Company, 1971.

PARIS, WILLIAM L., and SALLY BANKS ZAKARIYA, *The Elementary School Principalship in 1978: A Research Study.* Washington, D.C.: National Association of Elementary School Principals, 1979.

SERGIOVANNI, THOMAS J., and FRED D. CARVER, *The New School Executive: A Theory of Administration* (2nd ed.). New York: Harper & Row, Publishers, Inc., 1980.

STOOPS, EMORY, and RUSSELL E. JOHNSON, *Elementary School Administration.* New York: McGraw-Hill Book Company, 1967.

NOTES

1. Thomas J. Sergiovanni, Martin Burlingame, Fred D. Coombs, and Paul W. Thurston, *Educational Governance and Administration* (Englewood Cliffs, N.J.: Prentice-Hall, Inc., 1980), p. 29.

2. "A Principal's Job Description," *The Executive Educator,* 3, no. 6 (June 1981), 25.

3. Edgar L. Morphet, Roe L. Johns, and Theodore L. Reller, *Educational Organization and Administration: Concepts, Practices, and Issues,* 4th ed. (Englewood Cliffs, N.J.: Prentice-Hall, Inc., 1982), p. 300.

4. Roe L. Johns, Edgar L. Morphet, and Kern Alexander, *The Economics and Financing of Education,* 4th ed. (Englewood Cliffs, N.J.: Prentice-Hall, Inc., 1983), p. 356.

5. American Association of School Administrators, *Public Relations for America's Schools, 28th Yearbook* (Washington, D.C.: The Association, 1950), pp. 17-33.

APPENDIX A

TEACHER EVALUATION REPORT

LINDBERGH SCHOOL DISTRICT
4900 So. Lindbergh Blvd.
St. Louis, MO 63126

TEACHER _____ SCHOOL _____ YEAR _____

SUBJECT OR GRADE _____ YEARS IN SYSTEM _____

STATUS OF TEACHER   ( ) PROBATIONARY   ( ) TENURED

PHILOSOPHY: Evaluation is a means of improving the quality of instruction.

PURPOSES: 1. To improve the quality of teaching and services to the
                   students.
                2. To enable the teacher to recognize her/his role in the total
                   school program.
                3. To assist the teacher in achieving the established goals of the
                   curriculum.
                4. To help the teacher identify her/his strengths and weaknesses
                   as a personal guide for her/his improvement.
                5. To provide assistance to the teacher to help correct
                   weaknesses.
                6. To recognize the teacher's special talents and to encourage
                   and facilitate their utilization.
                7. To serve as a guide for renewed employment, termination of
                   employment, promotion, assignment, and unrequested leave
                   for tenured teachers.
                8. To protect the teacher from dismissal without just cause.
                9. To protect the teaching profession from unethical and incom-
                   petent personnel.

IMPLEMENTATION: The evaluation is to be made by the building principal, grade
                principal, assistant principal, or acting principal.
                   If a teacher does not agree with an evaluation, she/he may re-
                quest an additional evaluation to be made by another administra-
                tor of her/his choice.
                   Evaluation of a probationary (non-tenured) teacher's services
                will be made semi-annually during the probationary period with
                one of the evaluations completed during the first semester, and
                both completed before March 15. Each evaluation must be pre-
                ceded by at least one classroom visit.
                   Evaluation of a permanent (tenured) teacher's services will be
                made every year with the evaluation completed before March 15.
                Each evaluation must be preceded by at least one classroom visit.

DEFINITION OF TERMS:

1. Superior: consistently exceptional.
2. Strong: usually surpasses the standards of Lindbergh School District.
3. Average: generally meets standards of Lindbergh School District.
4. Improvement needed: occasionally does not meet standards of Lindbergh School District.
5. Unsatisfactory: does not measure up to standards of Lindbergh School District.

Rating of Unsatisfactory or Improvement Needed must include a written comment describing the cause for the rating.

NOTE: The space at the end of this form marked "Principal's Comments" may be utilized to record the observations of the teacher's exceptional performances and/or to record the principal's recommendations for improvement.

The space at the end of this form marked "Teacher's Comments" may be utilized by the teacher to record any comment or comments which she/he wishes to make.

I. TEACHING PERFORMANCE	Superior	Strong	Average	I-N	Unsatis-factory
	1	2	3	4	5
A. Plans and organizes carefully					
1. Lesson is well planned					
2. Sets definite goals including student participation					
3. Makes clear, specific assignments					
4. Is familiar with appropriate guide and adapts to the recommendations therein . . .					
5. Provides for individual and group instruction					
B. Is skillful in questioning and explaining					
1. Asks thought provoking questions					
2. Gives clear explanation of subject matter . .					
.3. Exposes students to varying points of view					
4. Is aware of both verbal and non-verbal acceptance or rejection of students ideas, and uses this skill positively					

C. Stimulates learning through innovative activities and resources

	Superior	Strong	Average I-N	Unsatis-factory
	1	2	3	4	5

1. Encourages class discussion, pupil questions and pupil demonstrations . . . .

2. Uses a variety of teaching aids and resources . . . .

D. Displays knowledge of and enthusiasm for subject matter taught

E. Provides a classroom atmosphere conducive to good learning

   1. Maintains a healthy and flexible environment . . . .

   2. Observes the care of instructional material and equipment . . . .

F. Keeps adequate and accurate records

   1. Records sufficient quantitative and qualitative data on which to base pupil progress reports . . . .

G. Has wholesome relationship with pupils

   1. Knows and works with pupils as individuals

   2. Encourages relationships that are mutually respectful and friendly . . . .

   3. Uses positive language with students which is devoid of sarcasm . . . .

H. Initiates and preserves classroom and general school management and discipline

   1. Rules of pupil conduct have been developed and teacher requires observance of these rules . . . .

   2. Rules of safety have been developed and teacher requires observance of these rules

   3. Emphasizes importance of both developing and maintaining self-respect and respect for others . . . .

II. PROFESSIONAL QUALITIES

   A. Recognition and acceptance of out-of-class responsibilities

	Superior	Strong	Average	I-N	Unsatis-factory
	1	2	3	4	5
1. Participates in the general and necessary school activities					
2. Sometimes volunteers for the "extra" duties					
3. Serves on school committees					
B. Intra-school relationship					
1. Cooperates effectively and pleasantly with colleagues, administration and non-professional personnel					
C. Public relations					
1. Cooperates effectively and pleasantly with parents					
2. Practices good relationships between school and community					
D. Professional growth and vision					
1. Accepts constructive criticism					
2. Participates in conferences, workshops and studies					
3. Tries new methods and materials					
E. Utilization of staff services					
1. Makes proper use of available special services					
F. Understands the growth patterns and behaviors of students at various stages of development and copes satisfactorily with situations as they occur.					
G. Ethical behavior					
1. Protects professional use of confidental data					
2. Supports the teaching profession					

DEFINITION OF TERMS FOR PERSONAL QUALITIES

S—**Satisfactory:** meets or surpasses standards for Lindbergh School District teachers.

I—**Improvement needed:** does not measure up to standards Lindbergh School District teachers meet.

III. PERSONAL QUALITIES

	Superior	Strong	Average	I-N	Unsatisfactory
	1	2	3	4	5

A. Health and Vigor

    1. Has a good and reasonable attendance record

    2. Is cheerful . . . .

    3. Displays a sense of humor . . . .

B. Speech

    1. Is articulate . . . .

    2. Can be heard and understood
       by all pupils in the room . . . .

    3. Speaks on the level of pupils' understanding

C. Grooming and appropriateness of dress

    1. Practices habits of good grooming . . . . . .

D. Promptness in meeting obligations

    1. Reports to classes on time . . . .

    2. Performs assigned tasks properly . . . .

    3. Completes reports on time . . . .

A copy of the written evaluation will be submitted to the teacher at the time of the conference following the observation(s). The final evaluation report form is to be signed and retained by the principal, and a copy is to be retained by the teacher. In the event the teacher feels the evaluation was incomplete, inaccurate, or unjust, she/he may put the objections in writing on the back of this form. Teacher's signature acknowledges that the conference has taken place.

DATE OF OBSERVATION(S) ⎯⎯⎯⎯⎯⎯⎯⎯⎯⎯⎯⎯⎯⎯⎯⎯⎯⎯⎯

TIME OF OBSERVATION(S) ⎯⎯⎯⎯⎯⎯⎯⎯⎯⎯⎯⎯⎯⎯⎯⎯⎯⎯⎯

LENGTH OF OBSERVATION(S) ⎯⎯⎯⎯⎯⎯⎯⎯⎯⎯⎯⎯⎯⎯⎯⎯⎯⎯

DATE EVALUATION MADE ⎯⎯⎯⎯⎯⎯⎯⎯⎯⎯⎯⎯⎯⎯⎯⎯⎯⎯⎯⎯

PRINCIPAL'S COMMENTS

OVERALL EVALUATION _____

PRINCIPAL'S SIGNATURE _____ DATE _____

TEACHER'S COMMENTS

TEACHER'S SIGNATURE _____ DATE _____

APPENDIX B:
LINDBERGH SCHOOL DISTRICT
INDICATORS FOR THE TEACHER EVALUATION INSTRUMENT

Indicators for the evaluation items in the Teacher Evaluation Instrument were developed by the administrators in the Lindbergh School District. The indicators are representative of the kind of teaching-learning techniques the evaluator will be looking for when observing a teacher in a classroom situation. It was expected that each teacher would perform the skill as listed but that the final evaluation would be based on the degree of performance.

I. *TEACHING PERFORMANCE*
    A. *Plans and organizes carefully*
        1. *Lesson is well planned*
           a. Written plans are available and followed by classroom teacher.
           b. Lesson includes preview, statement of objective and review.
           c. Lesson fits within an allotted time frame.
           d. Lesson follows a logical sequence.
           e. Lesson meets the needs of the student group.
           f. Long and short range goals are clearly defined.
           g. Lesson indicates the teacher has used the concept of diagnosis and prescription.
           h. Lesson is flexible to permit spontaneous teaching.
           i. Plans and procedures are provided.
           j. Materials and equipment are readily available.
        2. *Sets definite goals including student participation.*
           a. Long and short range goals are clearly defined.
           b. Students are involved in the goal setting process when appropriate.
        3. *Makes clear, specific assignment*
           a. Reasonable and clear assignments are given in written form.
           b. Adequate time is given for clarification and discussion of assignment.
        4. *Is familiar with appropriate guide and adapts to the recommendation therein*
           a. Lesson reflects thorough knowledge of curriculum guide.
           b. Long range planning for coverage of objectives in curriculum guide is indicated.
        5. *Provides for individual and group instruction*
           a. Lesson provides for individual instruction.
           b. Lesson provides for group instruction.
           c. Type of instruction is suited to lesson presented.
    B. *Is Skillful in Questioning and Explaining*
        1. *Asks thought provoking questions*
           a. Asks questions requiring more than a one word answer.
           b. Questions stimulate critical and divergent thinking.

      c. Written questions are thought provoking.

      d. Questions asked stimulate a response from students.

  2. *Gives clear explanation of subject matter*

      a. Obtains response indicating understanding before continuing further explanation.

      b. Presents ideas in a logical sequence.

      c. Consistently uses correct grammar and vocabulary suited to the student.

      d. Presents accurate and complete content information.

  3. *Exposes students to varying points of view*

      a. Establishes a background of general information on the topic before presenting varying points of view.

      b. Presents varying points of view consistent with curriculum.

      c. Elicits from students their points of view.

  4. *Is aware of both verbal and non-verbal acceptance or rejection of students' ideas, and uses this skill positively*

      a. Does not show rejection through verbal or physical expression.

      b. Does not allow peer-rejection.

      c. Praises, elicits and responds to student questions and answers before proceeding.

C. *Stimulates learning through innovative activities and resources*

  1. *Encourages class discussion, pupil questions and pupil demonstration*

      a. Listens patiently to students' comments, questions and answers.

      b. Questions are asked according to students' ability to answer correctly.

      c. Gives each student an opportunity to participate.

  2. *Uses a variety of teaching aids and resources*

      a. Looks for and uses models, manipulative materials, films, outside speeches, worksheets, records, etc.

      b. Materials and resources are appropriate for the lesson.

      c. Displays materials that are coordinated with the lesson.

D. *Displays knowledge of and enthusiasm for subject matter taught*

  1. *Displays knowledge of subject matter taught*

      a. Displays knowledge of content of textbook(s).

      b. Demonstrates competence and familiarity with subject matter.

      c. Has comprehensive knowledge of related disciplines and uses it when appropriate.

      d. Answers students questions readily and thoroughly.

      e. Probes for knowledge of content presented (encourages questions and activities that are designed to stimulate critical thinking).

      f. Goes beyond the textbook to enhance the content (may be observed by use of films, resource persons, reference materials, charts, etc.).

  2. *Enthusiasm*

      a. Students respond positively to the teacher. (Do the students appear interested? Are they listening to the teacher? Are they

awake? Are they talking to other students? Do they appear bored?)
   b. Interest and enthusiasm is evidenced from the teacher's presentation.
   c. Responds positively to the students, both verbally and visually.
   d. Elicits enthusiastic response from the students, to the questions and answers.
   e. Uses techniques which engender enthusiasm in students (a change of pace, voice inflections, body movement).

E. *Provides a classroom atmosphere conducive to good learning*
 1. *Maintains a healthy and flexible environment*
   a. Sets the tone for students to feel free to ask and to respond to questions (students are not intimidated).
   b. Classroom atmosphere is controlled but not dominated by the teacher (students interact with the environment).
   c. Differing views and values are allowed to be discussed.
   d. Positive interpersonal relationships are easily observed.
   e. Uses humor in proper perspective.
   f. Room reflects students' work.
 2. *Observes the care of instructional material and equipment*
   a. Equipment in use is carefully supervised.
   b. Equipment or material not in use is properly stored.
   c. Equipment is properly maintained and/or reported to the office for repair.
   d. Desks are devoid of writing and graffiti.
   e. Promotes respect for instructional materials and equipment.

F. *Keeps adequate and accurate records*
 1. *Records sufficient quantitative and qualitative data on which to base pupil progress reports*
   a. Records a number of written assignments, test scores, daily grades, and exam grades in the grade book (indicators of each student's performance).
   b. Quality of data recorded shows relationship between the objectives and grades.
   c. Daily attendance is correctly recorded.

G. *Has wholesome relationship with pupils*
 1. *Knows and works with pupils as individuals*
   a. Individual strengths and weaknesses of each student have been identified.
   b. Knows and calls each student by name.
   c. Listens carefully and politely to each student.
   d. Encourages student ideas and concentrates on their response.
   e. Student does not hesitate to ask for clarification.
   f. Students appear to be an active part of the class.
   g. Creative responses are encouraged.
 2. *Encourages relationships that are mutually respectful and friendly*
   a. Encourages positive behavior by maintaining complete control of self.

      b. Words and actions are positive.

      c. Exhibits qualities of warmth toward students.

      d. Elicits student responses.

      e. Sets an example of respect.

      f. Is sensitive to students' moods.

      g. Behavior is consistent with all students and situations.

      h. Handling of misconduct centers on the conduct or behavior, not the student.

      i. Requires student attention and gives attention in return.

  3. *Uses positive language with students which is devoid of sarcasm*

      a. Praises and elicits responses from students.

      b. Sarcasm is not used.

      c. Is positive in actions, voice tones, and movements.

      d. Tone of voice is moderate and even.

H. *Initiates and preserves classroom and general school management and discipline*

  1. *Rules of pupil conduct have been developed and teacher requires observance of these rules*

      a. Classroom incidents handled so as not to interrupt entire class.

      b. Pupils are aware of rules and regulations.

      c. Students understand and follow room routine readily without teacher's direction.

      d. Demonstrates behavior which is achievement oriented or businesslike.

      e. Is consistent and fair in expectations of behavior.

      f. Students enter room quietly and take seats.

      g. Students ask and receive permission to change patterns.

  2. *Rules of safety have been developed and teacher requires observance of these rules*

      a. Classroom behavior shows a concern for safety.

      b. Safety procedures are properly posted and followed.

      c. Horseplay is not tolerated.

      d. Plays an active and positive role in the supervision of hall, restrooms, lunchrooms, and pre and post class times of students as well as at assemblies.

      e. Classroom is free of hazards.

  3. *Emphasizes importance of both developing and maintaining self-respect and respect for others*

      a. Encourages positive behavior by maintaining own self-control.

      b. Uses words and actions which are positive.

      c. Exhibits qualities of warmth.

      d. Elicits positive student responses.

      e. Sets an example of respect.

      f. Is sensitive to student moods.

      g. Behavior is consistent with all students.

      h. Handling of misconduct centers on the conduct and not the student.

      i. Requires student attention and gives attention in return.

j. Consistently maintains self-control.

II. *PROFESSIONAL QUALITIES*

   A. *Recognition and acceptance of out-of-class responsibilities*

      1. *Participates in the general and necessary school activities*

         a. Performs assigned duties consistently.

         b. Follows the school time schedule.

         c. Attends and participates in school related activities.

         d. Participates in assigned meetings.

         e. Plays an active and positive role in the supervision of hall, restrooms, lunchrooms, and pre and post class times of students as well as at assemblies.

      2. *Sometimes volunteers for the "extra" duties*

         a. Accepts responsibilities other than those considered general or necessary.

         b. Initiates volunteer services to the over-all school program.

      3. *Serves on school committees*

         a. Serves on district and/or school committees.

         b. Attends school and district committee meetings.

         c. Participates in school or district level committees.

   B. *Intra-school relationship*

      1. *Cooperates effectively and pleasantly with colleagues, administration and non-professional personnel*

         a. Relationships with other professionals indicate acceptance of differing views or values.

         b. Practices relationships that are mutually respectful and friendly.

         c. Shares ideas, materials and methods.

         d. Informs appropriate personnel of school related matters.

         e. Cooperates fairly and works well with all school personnel.

         f. Is effective in providing a climate which encourages communication between themselves and professional colleagues.

   C. *Public Relations*

      1. *Cooperates effectively and pleasantly with parents*

         a. Maintains good communication with parents.

         b. Keeps best interest of student in mind.

         c. Provides a climate which opens up communication between the teacher and parent.

      2. *Practices good relationship between school and community*

         a. Enhances school involvement with communities.

         b. Encourages community involvement and attendance in school situations.

   D. *Professional Growth and Vision*

      1. *Accepts constructive criticism*

         a. Asks positive questions.

         b. Responds pleasantly to criticism.

      2. *Participates in conferences, workshops and studies*

         a. Is engaged in activities which promote professional growth.

         b. Engages in professional activities which are not required.

      3. *Tries new methods and materials*
        a. Uses new methods and materials at appropriate times.
        b. Modifies materials when needed.
        c. Understands new techniques before using.
   E. *Utilization of Staff Services*
      1. *Makes proper use of available special services*
        a. Makes use of and cooperates with district service personnel (guidance, library, supervisory, specialists and classified staff members).
        b. Utilizes Special School District services as appropriate.
        c. Makes student recommendations and referrals to appropriate staff members as needed.
   F. *Understands the growth patterns and behaviors of students at various stages of development and copes satisfactorily with situations as they occur*
        a. Uses a variety of techniques to achieve desired work and skills, and adjusts the techniques to the age and maturity of the student.
        b. Does not expect identical behavior from all students, but allows for individual differences.
        c. Is understanding and sympathetic to students with special learning and behavior problems.
   G. *Ethical Behavior*
      1. *Protects professional use of confidential data*
        a. Confidential information concerning students and their parents and staff members are not discussed in the lounge, cafeteria or in the classroom.
        b. Respects confidential information.
      2. *Supports the teaching profession*
        a. Positive attitude toward teaching.
        b. Uses positive statements regarding teaching, students, school, and profession.

III. *PERSONAL QUALITIES*
   A. *Health and Vigor*
      1. *Has a good and reasonable attendance record*
        a. Absences are infrequent and justifiable.
        b. Places emphasis on assigned duties.
        c. Except in cases of extreme illness, is present at school and is prepared.
      2. *Is cheerful*
        a. Allows occasional humorous interruptions.
        b. Can relax and joke with students.
        c. Laughs with, not at, others.
      3. *Displays a sense of humor*
        a. Smiles easily.
        b. Has a friendly attitude.
   B. *Speech*

1. *Is articulate*
   a. Consistently uses appropriate grammar.
   b. Communicates clearly.
2. *Can be heard and understood by all pupils in the room*
   a. Consistently uses appropriate tone of voice.
   b. Is easy to hear and understand.
3. *Speaks on the level of pupils' understanding*
   a. Uses appropriate vocabulary and examples according to students' level of understanding.

C. *Grooming and appropriateness of dress*
   1. *Practices habits of good grooming*
      a. Is clean and neat.
      b. Clothes are appropriate for job task.
      c. Dress adds to rather than detracts from classroom performance.

D. *Promptness in meeting obligations*
   1. *Reports to classes on time*
      a. Arrives at classroom before students.
      b. Classroom is open and in readiness prior to student arrival.
      c. Classroom preparations do not interfere with obligations.
      d. Arrives in the building at the required time.
   2. *Performs assigned tasks properly*
      a. Tasks are completed on time.
      b. Tasks are completed to letter and in spirit of the assignment.
   3. *Completes reports on time*
      a. Does not have to be reminded of reports which are due.
      b. Completes reports according to expectations of administrator.
   4. *Arrives in the building at the required time*

Epilogue

This book has covered a lot of territory in relatively few pages, describing the role and function of familiar central-office and building-level administrators in addition to those rather obscure but very important administrators such as the director of buildings and grounds. The reader who has just finished this book might miss a significant point because of the many details presented here. That point, simply stated, is that there is unity among diversity in all administrative positions. This is true, of course, in every organization that has a well-defined mission. Chapter 3 was devoted to explaining how its mission molds an organization into a managerial structure that becomes the delivery system for that mission. Because administrators manage diverse functions, they must have a common set of values in order to develop strategies necessary to reach the goals established by the board of education.

Thus, it is important for practicing and would-be administrators to have an indication of what will be expected of them in the future as far as personal characteristics are concerned.

Watergate kindled an intense interest in what constitutes ethical behavior not only in government but also in private business and industry. The *Wall Street*

Journal published a series of articles in October 1983 specifically targeting the private sector that exemplifies this interest. The first article was entitled, "Executives and General Public Say Ethical Behavior Is Declining In U.S." Likewise, the scope of ethical considerations has broadened in educational institutions over the last few years because issues have become more specific. While professional educational administrators have always recognized the necessity of being aboveboard, the climate in contemporary society is such that administrators must be able to show that their work is based on a system of ethics. The American Association of School Administrators and many other such organizations have developed codes of ethical conduct that can serve as a guide to administrators. What is vital is for administrators to learn to carry out their professional responsibilities in such a manner that their integrity cannot be questioned. Short-term solutions and arbitrary decisions, therefore, must be judiciously avoided.

In addition, administrators must become "joiners," and should give of their time and talents to lobby for education, seeking support from the general public and from legislators. For example, increased funding for education will not simply happen. Professional educators must join with concerned citizens in demonstrating to legislators the need to increase funds. The best way to exert such influence is to become involved in educational-administrator organizations.

Technological advances in the last five years have presented educational administrators with unique opportunities and significant challenges. Administrators must become competent in the use of technology, or our schools will slip even further behind the private sector. Not only must administrators learn how to utilize microcomputers to perform administrative tasks such as pupil scheduling, attendance reporting, grade reporting, and inventory control, but they also must introduce them into the curriculum. Children and young people must be exposed to the microcomputer in a sequential program that begins with computer awareness and goes on to use the machine as an instructional aid and, finally, culminates in learning how to program computers. Leadership will be required of educational administrators to develop strategies for preparing teachers, staff members, students, and parents to utilize this new technology and understand other future advances. The excitement of these new developments makes educational administration an extremely desirable career.

On the other hand, in order to balance involvement in the new technology, administrators must become more humanistic. Technological advances tend to isolate individuals from one another and emphasize solitary activities. What happens, in essence, is that information collection, storage, and use increase, while human interaction decreases. Finally, we will know more but understand less, with an accompanying decrease in human-relations skills.

The educational administrator must, therefore, see the necessity of developing innovative ways to interact with teachers, staff members, students, and parents. The quality-circle approach to problem solving initiated by the Japanese is, of course, one of the most obvious ways to tap the human resources available in addressing issues of common concern.

Perhaps equally important is the need for educational administrators to recognize that the technological society of the future will require people to have a deeper appreciation for the fine arts. Art, music, drama, and so on demonstrate and communicate feelings, attitudes, and beliefs in an information-oriented society.

Educational administrators of the future, therefore, must be scrupulously ethical, and active in promoting the goals of education. At the same time, they must understand and make use of technological advances, as well as appreciate the necessity of creating ways to improve human interaction.

Index